SLAVERY ON THE PERIPHERY

Slavery on the Periphery

The Kansas-Missouri Border in the
Antebellum and Civil War Eras

KRISTEN EPPS

The University of Georgia Press

ATHENS

Parts of chapters 1 and 2 are based on "Before the Border War: Slavery and the Settlement of the Western Frontier, 1825–1845," in Bleeding Kansas, Bleeding Missouri: The Long Civil War on the Border, edited by Jonathan Earle and Diane Mutti Burke (Lawrence: University Press of Kansas, 2013), 29–46. Copyright © 2013 by the University Press of Kansas. Reprinted courtesy of the University Press of Kansas.

Paperback edition, 2018
Published by the University of Georgia Press
Athens, Georgia 30602
www.ugapress.org
© 2016 by Kristen Epps
All rights reserved

Printed digitally

Most University of Georgia Press titles are
available from popular e-book vendors.

Library of Congress has cataloged the
hardcover edition of this book as follows:
Names: Epps, Kristen.
Title: Slavery on the periphery : the kansas-missouri border in the antebellum
and civil war eras / Kristen Epps.
Description: Athens : The University of Georgia Press, [2016]
Identification: LCCN 2016951034 | ISBN 9780820350509 (hardback : alk. paper) |
ISBN 9780820350516 (ebook)

LC record available at https://lccn.loc.gov/2016951034

Paperback ISBN 978-0-8203-5471-8

For Grandma Carol

Contents

Illustrations

Figures

Tables

ACKNOWLEDGMENTS

Although I did not know it at the time, an internship at the Kansas Historical Society in the summer between my sophomore and junior year of college would inspire a steadfast interest in the Bleeding Kansas era. I first questioned why we knew so little about the African American presence on this border while working in the storage bay, at a desk nestled between filing cabinets and stacks of musty newspapers. For this reason, my first thanks must naturally extend to my colleagues and friends at the Kansas Historical Society, who welcomed me into the archives with open arms and who have been a great joy to work with in the years since. Each of them has helped me locate missing or misfiled sources, obtain photo permissions, or just commiserate about the challenges of research during breaks behind the circulation desk. I would like to personally thank Teresa Coble, Craig Dannenberg, Lin Fredericksen, Bob Knecht, Nancy Sherbert, Virgil Dean, Matt Veatch, and Pat Michaelis for their assistance and encouragement. I would be remiss if I did not also thank the many other archivists and librarians who assisted me in this work, including the staff of the Western Historical Manuscript Collection in Columbia, who faithfully shipped their collections to the reading room at the University of Missouri—Kansas City so I could avoid lengthy research trips, and those at the Spencer Research Library, including Deborah Dandridge, Letha Johnson, and Sherry Williams. Librarians and archivists at the Huntington Library, State Historical Society of Missouri, Midwest Genealogy Center, Missouri History Museum Library and Research Center (especially Dennis Northcott), both the Central Plains and

Washington, D.C. branches of the National Archives, and the Jackson County Historical Society (particularly David Jackson) have done much to aid the development of this manuscript. I am also deeply grateful to the interlibrary loan staff at both Colorado State University—Pueblo and the University of Central Arkansas for the many hours they spent ordering and processing books.

This project was made possible through a number of research grants and fellowships, including an Alfred Landon Historical Research Grant (Kansas Historical Society), a Richard Brownlee Fund Grant (State Historical Society of Missouri), travel awards from the Department of History at the University of Kansas, faculty development grants at Colorado State University—Pueblo, a Summer Research Award through the Hall Center for the Humanities in Lawrence, and a Mellon Fellowship at the Huntington Library in California. This financial assistance was crucial to my progress as a scholar. I extend special thanks to everyone, including my department chairs, Matt Harris and Colette Carter, who supported these applications and saw something valuable in my work.

I have been unusually blessed in finding outstanding mentors and delightful colleagues at my doctoral institution, at the universities where I have served as faculty, and in other venues, like the Southern Historical Association. At the University of Kansas, I won the advisor lottery when Jonathan Earle agreed to supervise my dissertation, and his unfailing enthusiasm and sage advice have remained a constant in the years since my graduation. I lucked out again when I found other outstanding mentors in Leslie Tuttle, Kim Warren, Jennifer Weber, and Ann Schofield. KU also brought me lifelong friends who lent a sympathetic ear, especially Jeremy Prichard, Sally Utech, John Schneiderwind, Nicole Anslover, Kim Schutte, Kyle Anthony, Becca Slaton Anthony, Karen Beth Zacharias, Jason Roe, Christine Anderson, and many others. Tai Edwards, who was my sounding board during the dissertation process, has continued to be a good friend and provided helpful feedback on the current manuscript. Friends and colleagues at Colorado State University—Pueblo from various departments and disciplines provided invaluable support in my first years on the tenure track, especially Audrey Dehdouh-Berg, Paul Conrad, Brigid Vance, Judy Gaughan, Joel Johnson, Dorothy Heedt-Moosman, Alegría Ribadeneira, Scott Gage, Juan Morales, Barbara Brett, Katie Devine, Iver Arnegard, and Steve Liebel. Here at the University of Central Arkansas, I found kindred spirits in Kelly Houston Jones, Story Matkin-Rawn, Mike Rosenow, Taine Duncan, Heather Yates, Sonia Toudji, and Michael Kithinji. I am grateful to my department chair, Wendy Lucas, and Dean

Maurice Lee, and to everyone else in my department for their encouragement. I extend my deepest gratitude toward Kelly Kennington (my compatriot in the Early American Places series), Chris Childers, Rachel Shelden, Diane Mutti Burke, Jeremy Neely, Nicole Etcheson, Aaron Astor, Hilary Green, Paul Quigley, Matt Mason, Kristen Oertel, and others who provided advice and insightful feedback on conference papers or chapter drafts, all of which helped direct my project into new and interesting avenues. Thanks also to the two anonymous readers and the editorial staff of the Early American Places series and University of Georgia Press (especially Walter Biggins). Last, my thanks to all the #twitterstorians and those on the #GraftonLine who built a truly special scholarly community that connects likeminded academics even over great distances.

Finally, I am extraordinarily indebted to my family for their love and support. I have never been good at heartfelt expressions in written form, so just trust me when I say I would not have succeeded in academia or in life without my parents, David and Kim; my sister, Bethany; my grandpa, Vern; or the other loved ones who believed in me even when I did not believe in myself. You mean the world to me. Thank you.

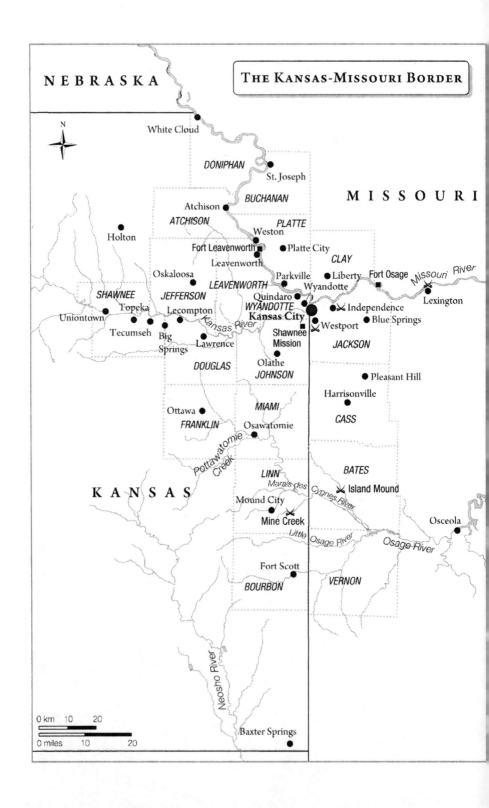

THE KANSAS-MISSOURI BORDER

SLAVERY ON THE PERIPHERY

Introduction

In the later years of the nineteenth century, as Kansas "old timers" who had experienced Bleeding Kansas began to pass away, a dedicated librarian at the Kansas Historical Society undertook a letter-writing campaign to collect information about slaves who lived here in those tumultuous days before Kansas statehood and the Civil War. Abzuga Adams, known simply as Zu, was the daughter of Franklin G. Adams, the first secretary of the society, which had been founded in 1875. This woman, who at one time described herself as a "cataloguing machine," meticulously collected the responses she received and kept careful records of slaves and slaveholders whose names appeared within these letters, in preparation for a brief speech on slavery in Kansas.[1] She concluded her speech with these words: "Altho the information obtained is in most instances meager, it will serve as a nucleus around which may be gathered by further effort, the whole number."[2] While her intent was not to present the African American perspective, and her stories harbored racist undertones, thanks to her dedication these reminiscences of "slavery days" have been preserved for future generations.

However, both in popular culture and among academic historians who study the peculiar institution, knowledge of slavery's existence in territorial Kansas largely passed away with the demise of Kansas's charter generation. No one would deny that Kansas and Missouri played a central role in the political dialogue over slavery's expansion during the 1850s, but for the most part slavery—as an institution already present on the

Kansas-Missouri border—has received little attention from scholars. This book will resume the work that Zu Adams began by chronicling the rise and fall of slavery in this region from the earliest years of white settlement in the 1820s into the post–Civil War period. More specifically, this work analyzes nineteen counties on the border—a site of intense turmoil over the extension of slavery—to understand the lived experience of slaves and slaveholders and how slaves negotiated the social terrain of this frontier society (see map frontispiece).[3] Many of the slaves and white settlers in this region came from the South, particularly the Upper South states of Tennessee, Maryland, and Kentucky. These emigrants (whether slaves, slaveholders, or nonslaveholders) brought their Upper South culture with them as they settled the West.[4] Instead of focusing on the clashing ideologies that shaped this political and social fault line, my analysis highlights how slavery shaped the region economically, politically, and socially.

There were many characters in this drama. By necessity, understanding slavery mandates that we come to terms with the complexities of the owner-slave relationship, but whenever possible I reinforce that enslaved people were at the center of this narrative. Slavery *as a labor system* (not merely as an abstract ideological and political concept) was part of life in these frontier communities, and consequently, African Americans are a visible presence in this story. None of these black men, women, and children are well known today, and most lived a life of obscurity in their own time. Yet, their stories show that slavery in the nineteenth century was not confined to the South. The border region offers an excellent window into how regional differences, including the Western influence, affected the contours of slavery.

In *Slavery on the Periphery*, I contend that the Kansas-Missouri border and its slave system demonstrate that slavery could flourish in a region on the outskirts of white American society, that slaves were central to the story of Bleeding Kansas and the Civil War in the West, and that mobility was a core feature of slaves' experiences in the region. Unlike slavery in the Deep South, but not unlike the Upper South, this was a small-scale system characterized by slaves' diverse forms of employment, close contact between slaves and slaveholders, a robust hiring market, and the prevalence of abroad marriages (marriages where spouses lived in different households). In the 1850 census, the first federal census to collect data on the size of slaveholdings, a high proportion of slaveholders in the Upper South, particularly Missouri, owned fewer than twenty slaves, the common definitional threshold for a plantation.[5] Slave mobility was a key factor in shaping the contours of border communities, as slaves and slaveholders grappled for control over geographic spaces. Tracing the functioning of these contested spaces provides the most direct, provocative access to African Americans' experiences.

In this book I explain how these contested spaces functioned, particularly how slaves and slaveholders built separate visions for African American mobility.[6] For the enslaved, mobility could be a force for independence. Slaves regularly tested social and geographic boundaries, and taking control of their movements was often proactive, not merely reactive. Resistance often required some autonomy and access to locales outside the farm or plantation. Slaves might flee their owners, or travel in secret to visit loved ones, as just a few examples. Mobility mattered for their day-to-day survival, although mobility could also be a force for disruption and upheaval. Slaves also accessed the landscape at the behest of whites, who sold them away from family, hired them out on distant farms, or forced them to emigrate west.

For slaveowners, slave mobility had to be limited, controlled, and manipulated. Slaveholders' visions for slave mobility were both inward looking and outward looking. They envisioned ways to confine slaves' movements within designated areas, dictate the workings of their interior lives, determine their roles in the household, and question who controlled or had access to local spaces. But, they also looked outward and exploited slaves' mobility in order to conduct daily business, help build the local infrastructure, and encourage the development of a robust economy. Analyzing such movement highlights one component of a larger social geography of labor, which can be defined as the study of how humans and social systems use space, including the patterns and processes by which they influence labor relationships, settlement patterns, transportation, urban development, and other social and political functions. Slaveholders strove to reproduce the "social and cultural forms" of slavery, even as slaves struggled to resist those strictures.[7] We must reevaluate how place and space functioned within these border communities.

The particulars of slavery's expansion into this region also demonstrate how borderlands were, as Pekka Hämäläinen and Samuel Truett have noted, "ambiguous and often-unstable realms."[8] Borders, whatever their configuration, instilled a sense of belonging in local residents even as that local identity was sometimes in flux.[9] The region that became Kansas and Missouri constituted a borderland in two ways. Conceived as a single unit, the region was a border between the United States and "unsettled," little-understood lands out west (although this American perception changed as settlement increased in California and Oregon).

In the early nineteenth century, this was a place where native, white, and African American cultures converged and people of differing lifeways (including Northerners and Southerners) struggled to adapt to the hardships of life on the periphery of American settlement. This story, like that of other North American borderlands, cannot be divorced from Euro-American expansion. Kansas and Missouri had indigenous populations of Kansa, Osage, Wichita, and Pawnee, and later emigrant tribes from the East settled on the border, survivors of the U.S. government's removal policies. Some of these emigrant tribes owned slaves themselves, and their presence contributed to slavery's place here. Unlike other borderlands, however, for much of its modern history this was not a transnational border between colonial empires. In this sense, the entire region was a boundary between "civilization" (as white Americans would describe it) and indigenous Indian populations.

But this was also a borderland in another sense: there was a constantly evolving internal border *within* the region—the line between Kansas and Missouri—which is the borderland that forms the heart of this study. It began as the border between Missouri and "Indian country," then became the border between Missouri and Indian Territory, Missouri and Kansas Territory, and, finally, between Missouri and the state of Kansas. Aside from a few counties along the Missouri River, there are no geological or topographical features to distinguish one side from the other, and from the early 1800s until the present, this was a border confined within the United States. This internal borderland saw a dramatic revisioning in only a few decades, evolving from a liminal, hybrid space where Southern culture and unfree labor slowly consumed other influences, to a boundary between states where individuals on either side maintained many social and economic ties, even as the two populations became increasingly divided in their political sentiments. By the late 1850s, there was a clear demarcation between Kansas and Missouri, freedom and slavery, North and South, at least in theory. The political violence of Bleeding Kansas exemplifies this border's instability and ambiguity, and the Civil War finally saw it to fruition. Of course, although historians often accentuate the political and social divisions, situating these two states on different trajectories, it is important to also consider this an intact region with as many similarities as differences. Placing Missouri and Kansas within the same narrative explains the ties that bound people together, as well as the inevitable conflicts and adaptations that came with the settlement process.[10] The history of the Kansas-Missouri line must be framed as a shared history.

While this book might be best categorized as a social history of the African American and slaveholding communities, it also has a place within the scholarly discussion about the sectional conflict that preceded the Civil War. This conflict over slavery's expansion, here known as Bleeding Kansas, captured the imagination of the nineteenth-century public. A brief perusal of editorials and articles in national newspapers like *Harper's Weekly* and the *New York Tribune* quickly demonstrates the country's awareness of Western politics. Conversations that were central to American identity formation in the early and mid-nineteenth century all had their place in the West: Manifest Destiny, slavery's expansion, the rise of democracy, and paternalistic government policies that displaced Native Americans. Since nineteenth-century contemporaries elsewhere in the United States appropriately recognized the significance of affairs in Missouri and Kansas, a thorough knowledge of slavery's development in this region is central to understanding American discourse on the slavery question.[11] In fact, analyzing this slave system reinforces the importance of political debates over its expansion, because Bleeding Kansas exposed the fundamental disparities between Northern and Southern worldviews. As Nicole Etcheson writes, "free staters envisioned a republic of white men; proslavery men, a republic of slaveowners."[12] African Americans themselves also shaped the future of the republic, despite attempts to limit their economic, political, and social power. The driving point behind this book is simply this: enslaved African Americans were not marginal to the story of Bleeding Kansas and the Civil War on this border. Understanding these individuals' experiences helps us better understand the high stakes of the sectional conflict, since rhetorical strife over slavery's expansion ran parallel to slavery's actual (not merely theoretical) establishment in the West. The victor in the sectional struggle of the 1850s would help determine bondspeople's future, either by touting their continued enslavement or by promoting emancipation and civil rights.

For the purposes of assessment, at times I will reference other Upper South states—Kentucky and Tennessee in particular—and locations elsewhere in Missouri. A significant number of emigrants into the border region hailed from these states. In most respects, the slaveholding communities that existed along this line shared striking similarities with slavery elsewhere in the Upper South.[13] These were all states where small-scale slaveholding took root early in their respective territorial (or colonial) periods, and where it was common for slaveholders to cultivate cash crops such as hemp and tobacco alongside staple crops like corn and

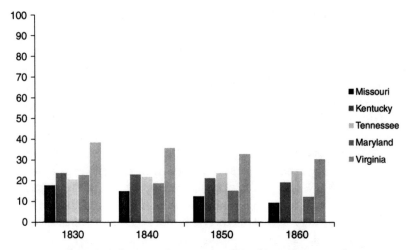

FIGURE 1. Slave Population as Percentage of Total Population in the Upper South, 1830–1860. United States Bureau of the Census, *Fifth, Sixth, Seventh, and Eighth Censuses of the United States*, 1830–1860, Population Schedules and Slave Schedules (Washington, D.C.: Government Printing Office, 1831–1864).

wheat. Slave hiring and abroad marriages were also significant in shaping the African American experience in small slaveholding households, and while enslaved blacks worked to resist white control, slaveholders and their nonslaveholding white allies struggled to maintain a racial hierarchy. Slavery's continued existence was predicated on whites' use of political, legal, and social channels to strengthen the system and maintain control over the black population. Of course, the nature of small-scale slaveholding itself dictated that slaveholders imposed their ideals onto a much smaller institution. Ultimately, slavery on this border functioned in much the same way that slavery functioned in the Upper South, at least during the early decades. As sectional tensions grew heated, particularly during Bleeding Kansas, slavery saw its first significant challenge. Then, when Kansas became a state in 1861 and the Civil War began, African Americans and their allies participated in a multiracial, full-scale offensive that would bring down the peculiar institution once and for all.

Despite the prevailing belief that there is little surviving evidence of slaves' perspectives, given the small scale of the institution here, it is possible to partially re-create the day-to-day lives of enslaved people, even if their thoughts, feelings, and worldviews often remain hidden in shadow. As Jill Lepore has so aptly stated, microhistorians "tend to betray people who have left abundant records in order to resurrect those who did not."[14] In this case, there were no abundant records to abandon, but the intent remains the same, as these enslaved men and women can indeed be "resurrected" through intense analysis of extant documents. African American history remains a ripe field for microhistorical techniques.[15] Sources from this region that directly provide the enslaved perspective are an especially rare but immensely valuable find. Most sources that former slaves directly created or dictated—such as reminiscences, pension file affidavits, and WPA interviews recorded during the 1930s—have been filtered through a white lens.[16] Unfortunately, in many cases, information about the black experience must be gleaned from sources created by white slaveholders or other whites who witnessed slavery in action. This has posed a challenge. In all cases I have approached these white-authored sources with a cautious, critical eye and examined them within the context of the secondary literature and slave reminiscences from those who were enslaved outside the border region (of which there are many). These sources include correspondence, maps, journals, newspapers, advertisements, scrapbooks, military records, and public records such as wills, tax lists, court records (civil, criminal, and probate), statutes, land deeds, and bills of sale. Whenever possible, I have verified the information found therein and cross-referenced it with public records such as census data. White rhetoric may have shaped the available source material, and consequently our interpretations of slavery, but slaves' voices can still be heard through these fragile ties to the antebellum period.

Given its significance, why then have slaveholding and the slave experience on the border received so little attention from historians? Based on a cursory glance, aggregate census data describing the slave population on the border implies that the slave system was a minor element of the frontier settlement process and that slaves and slaveowners comprised an insignificant and unimportant segment of border society. The total slave population in these Missouri border counties in 1850— four years before the formation of Kansas Territory—was approximately 10,030, or 16 percent of the total population.[17] Kansas Territory's first official census, taken in February 1855, stated that there were 193 slaves in the territory and 151 free blacks (with slaves alone making up 2 percent of the population), although Kansas old timers later recalled that the correct number was higher, as slaves and slaveholders came into the territory after this census was taken.[18] These territorial censuses, though useful for limited statistical analysis, are also riddled with inaccuracies.[19] While the slave system remained small in terms of numbers, and it was unevenly distributed across the region, social and political influence cannot be measured merely through statistics.

Contrary to what one may assume based on these census figures, in key ways the slave system was central to the establishment of these border counties and their evolution into a mature society. Although they did not articulate their intentions in such precise terms, these slaveowners worked to transform a *society with slaves* into a *slave society* (with varying success). According to Ira Berlin, in a society with slaves, "slaves were marginal to the central productive processes . . . slavery was just one form of labor among many. . . . In slave societies, by contrast, slavery stood at the center of economic production." Slaveholdings in societies with slaves were generally small scale, and although they lacked some of the strictures of large-scale operations, they were no less violent or coercive.[20] Like the charter generations that fall under the scope of Berlin's study, slaveholders here were persistent and tenacious in their commitment to instituting a system that reinforced white superiority and established hegemonic rule over the enslaved population (which slaves constantly frustrated in the continued struggle for power).

For many historians, the fact that slavery in Kansas and Missouri existed on the far reaches of Southern influence has meant that this story is tangential, an assumption readily seen in the secondary literature. My work builds upon this literature but also remedies significant lapses in the historical narratives of Bleeding Kansas, slavery, and race relations in the American West. Indeed, as historian Gunja SenGupta has noted, "the invisibility of African Americans as anything other than objects of white discourse represents perhaps the most serious weakness in the existing state of Bleeding Kansas historiography."[21] Unsurprisingly, classic monographs that discuss slavery on the national level—books by esteemed historians like Eugene Genovese, James Oakes, Ira Berlin, and Jacqueline Jones—are virtually silent on the matter of Western slavery, focusing instead on Southern states more frequently associated with slave labor. In recent years, some historians, like Dylan Penningroth, Keith Griffler, Stephanie Camp, Daina Ramey Berry, and Anthony Kaye, have begun to approach slavery's history as a story of active African American communities that served as sites of both resistance and acculturation, of negotiation and not of hegemony. These new works have challenged the traditional framework that privileges large plantations, but they do not address the slave system in Kansas or Missouri, where small-scale slaveholding dominated. Those historians who research the African American experience in the trans-Mississippi West do little better when it comes to addressing slavery on the Kansas-Missouri line. Quintard Taylor's *In Search of the Racial Frontier* and William Loren Katz's *The Black West* agree that African Americans shaped the West, but neither work addresses how African American slavery manifested itself on this frontier.

Because this border was a site of cultural exchange among Southerners, Northerners, foreign nationals, and native peoples, this work also fits within the broader historiography of the earliest white settlements in the Missouri River basin and outlying areas. For instance, Stephen Aron's *American Confluence* argues that in the Mississippi River valley, as with other confluence regions like the Missouri River basin, the "creative adaptations and constructive accommodations" of the settlement process profoundly influenced developing conflicts but also encouraged cooperation.[22] Aron's work in particular inspired me to think more creatively about the various groups moving into the border region and their ability to shape new identities based on various cultural influences. It is important, in my mind, to recast the narrative of expansion to include people of African descent.

As for Kansas Territory and western Missouri specifically, the trend in recent decades has centered on the political contexts and ideological origins of the Bleeding Kansas crisis. Perhaps the most well-known recent monograph on Kansas Territory comes from Nicole Etcheson, whose excellent book *Bleeding Kansas: Contested Liberty in the Civil War Era* examines territorial politics, arguing that both proslavery and free-state forces were motivated by concern for their own white liberties. Kristen Tegtmeier Oertel's *Bleeding Borders: Race, Gender, and Violence in Pre-Civil War Kansas* incorporates race into the Bleeding Kansas narrative by asserting that "Indians, blacks, and women shaped the political and cultural terrain in ways that discouraged the extension of slavery but failed to challenge a racial hierarchy that relegated all people of color to inferior social status."[23] Likewise, Jeremy Neely's *The Border Between Them: Violence and Reconciliation on the Kansas-Missouri Line* stretches into the post–Civil War period to examine how Missourians and Kansans overcame border rivalries and developed similar views on the defining movements of the late nineteenth century, such as industrialization and railroad expansion. His conclusion regarding slaveholding, however, insists "the ownership of African American slaves held only a marginal presence in this frontier society."[24] R. Douglas Hurt's book *Agriculture and Slavery in Missouri's Little Dixie* locates Missouri slavery within the history of slavery more generally, comparing its agricultural and labor systems to other Upper South states, including Virginia, Kentucky, and Tennessee. An excellent study of Missouri slavery by Diane Mutti Burke, *On Slavery's Borders: Missouri's Small-Slaveholding Households, 1815–1865*, argues that small-scale slaveholding, in contrast to the large plantation systems of the Deep South, took root in Missouri and fostered a different relationship between slaves and slaveowners based on close physical proximity. These works all provide valuable glimpses of the black experience in Kansas and western Missouri, building the foundation for further analyses of slavery on this border.

Although the historiography of the Civil War and Reconstruction is far too vast to detail here, the discourse that shapes our understanding of this conflict often ignores or trivializes the story of the trans-Mississippi theater, doing little better when it comes to analyzing the African American experience in border states such as Missouri. Three works that consider the importance of this border-state narrative—Michael Fellman's *Inside War: The Guerrilla Conflict in Missouri during the American Civil War,* Christopher Phillips's *Missouri's Confederate,* and Aaron Astor's *Rebels on the Border: Civil War, Emancipation, and the Reconstruction of Kentucky and Missouri*—pay special attention to the unique position of Missouri, a slave state that did not secede from the Union. While each of these is immensely useful for seeing how disunionists clashed verbally and physically with loyal citizens, the voices of African Americans are not central to any of these monographs, although Astor's work comes closest to a full-scale analysis of slavery in these two border states. I believe that understanding slavery on the border is crucial to historians' analysis of emancipation during the intense guerrilla conflict that consumed Missouri in the war years.

The chapters that follow portray how slavery functioned at this cultural crossroads and scrutinize historians' previously held assumptions about the African American experience on the Kansas-Missouri line. Chapter 1, "Westward Ho!: Southern Settlement on the Frontier, 1820–1840," sets the stage for this story by tracing American and French settlement on the border and the founding of early counties in western Missouri. In addition to slaveholding whites and enslaved blacks who emigrated, some native tribes who relocated to northern Indian Territory (what is now Kansas) had a history of slaveholding that extended into their postremoval period. The fledgling communities here found their footing due to slaveholders who brought their Southern slaveholding culture with them to the frontier.

The second chapter, "Becoming Little Dixie: The Creation of a Western Slave Society, 1840–1854," covers slavery's centrality to both government and society, beginning in the 1840s when this region saw a sharp increase in emigration. During this period, slaveholders sought to perpetuate the slave system, even as slaves resisted slaveholders' control and carved out a limited degree of independence. This was a period where sectional strife was not yet a defining feature of life, a fact that allowed slaveholders to maintain their political power and social status.

The third chapter, "Contested Ground: The Enslaved Experience during Bleeding Kansas, 1854–1857," describes Southern settlement in the newly created Kansas Territory and begins the story of how slavery functioned during the heated crisis that eventually spawned the Civil War. Popular sovereignty, which gave local residents the power to accept or reject slavery in the territory, turned Kansas into a battleground over slavery's extension. While the rhetoric of free-soil proponents and proslavery supporters dominated the country's perceptions of this contest, the conflict cannot be understood without examining how slavery functioned at the ground level.

Chapter 4, "The Tide Turns: The Demise of Slavery on the Border, 1857–1861," continues the story of Bleeding Kansas by examining the period after roughly 1857, at which point Southern settlement and proslavery ideology in Kansas decreased, and antislavery settlers began to form a critical mass of the territory's population. It also discusses how slaveholders in Missouri regulated slaves' movements, while slaves continued to escape, seeing Kansas (rightly or wrongly) as a safe haven for fugitives.

The fifth chapter, "Entering the Promised Land: The Black Experience in the Civil War Years, 1861–1865," brings this story to a head by examining the mass self-liberation that shaped African American life on the border during the Civil War. Former slaves made their way to Kansas independently or hurried to safety behind Union lines, and some men enlisted in the military hoping to bring about the ultimate freedom for their people. National attention to the formation of black military units primarily focused on the eastern theater, so in the West, former slaves and white locals (especially those who were abolitionists) drove recruitment.

The epilogue briefly outlines slavery's legacy on this border, examining African American emigration in the postwar years (known as "The Exodus") while also investigating the challenges that black Kansans and Missourians faced in their transition to freedom.

Each of these chapters reconsiders historians' present understanding of slavery by offering new insights into how the peculiar institution took shape on the Kansas-Missouri line. Here a diverse blend of native, black, and white cultures converged to create a world based on elements of the old and the promise of the new. Zu Adams began charting this tale over one hundred years ago, but it is only by seeking out African American voices that we can truly understand slavery on this geographic periphery.

1 / Westward Ho! Southern Settlement on the Frontier, 1820–1840

In the fall of 1827, George Sibley, factor at Fort Osage on the Missouri River and an authority on the West, penned a letter to his acquaintance Archibald Dorsey. From his "cottage" in what is now the outskirts of Kansas City, Missouri, Sibley touted the great advantages of life there, detailing, among other things, the price of land in newly opened Jackson County and the pleasant prospects for a healthy hemp and tobacco crop. He noted with some foresight that "Tobacco and Hemp will no doubt be our Staple commodities." To produce such crops, slave labor would be readily available. "The usual prices for common labourers by the month, white or black, is $13 a month, or 50 cents a day," he wrote. "The best slaves hire for about $120 a year—common ones for about $80. Slaves who are mechanics, or carpenters, smiths, masons hire for about $20 a month but are not much in demand—at present slaves are high in prices—first rate men are worth from 400 to 500 dollars, Lads 3 to 400—Women and Girls from 2 to 300 dollars." There were, by his estimation, "strong inducements for people to settle in it from the old States, especially such as have large families and are not wealthy."[1] Sibley had a distinct vision for this region, situated at the confluence of white, native, and black cultures: he foresaw the establishment of a yeomanry whose few slaves would "provide substantial comforts, make domestic improvements & render life easy, comfortable, and happy."[2] Although Sibley's own experience as an explorer, government factor, and surveyor made him exemplary, the Sibley household's attitude toward slavery fit just such a model, with Sibley owning at least two slaves by 1813, including one woman who likely worked in the home and a man named George who was Sibley's cook and manservant. This household was one of many to settle in western Missouri, establishing small-scale slavery in the region and shaping the social and political identity of this American crossroads.[3]

Slaveholders' westward emigration, like that of their nonslaveholding Southern and Northern counterparts, was motivated in large part by their desire for greater economic opportunities and upward mobility, two concepts that went hand in hand with the availability of cheap, fertile land out west. Slaveholders in the early nineteenth century looked toward land that held the promise of a bountiful harvest, booming business, or other professional and personal accomplishment. Kinship ties also loomed large for enterprising Southerners, as mobility was no barrier to continued community. Chain migration, as David Hackett Fischer and James Kelly observed in their study of Virginia, "was common in this great hegira."[4] Families and friends used those relationships to determine where to emigrate, and often this meant settling near those of comparable social standing and with similar worldviews. In what is now eastern Kansas and western Missouri, these newcomers generally hailed from Upper South states like Tennessee, Virginia, Kentucky, and Maryland. With such demographic dominance, as Diane Mutti Burke has concluded, these Southerners "ultimately had the greatest influence on the development of the new land."[5] Contemporaries noted such emigration with enthusiasm. John Mason Peck, a Baptist minister who traveled throughout the Missouri River valley, remarked that "it seemed as though Kentucky and Tennessee were breaking up and moving to the 'Far West.'"[6] Slaveholding emigrants and the enslaved members of their households dramatically reshaped the West's political and social landscape, building a foundation of slaveholding the impact of which would remain for decades.

While many of the aforementioned impulses also applied to Northern emigrants, unlike Northerners, white Southern emigrants insisted in word and deed that the future of slavery lay in the West. As historian James Oakes observed, this was the binding that brought white Southerners of disparate classes together, since "what united small slaveholders with the sons of planters was the goal of purchasing land and slaves and moving west in pursuit of that goal."[7] Moreover, what united nonslaveholding Southerners with their slaveholding neighbors—despite some deep-seated class antagonisms—was a common cultural insistence on slavery's necessity not only for economic reasons but also to maintain the South's strict racial order. The West's potential as a "safety valve" for slavery—an outlet for maintaining the Southern way of life and thus promoting its superiority—made it powerfully attractive to white Southerners of all stations. While most historians conceive of this expansion in terms of the cotton revolution and plantation culture in the Deep South, these impulses also saw fulfillment in the Upper South. Most slaveholders did not give a second (or even first) thought to whether or not they would import slave labor, since in their minds black and white were inextricably linked, and human property was essential to the success of their new ventures. Simply put, this "gigantic growth machine" of slavery could no longer be contained in the East.[8] Expansion, then, would have profound individual benefits for a slaveholding household, as well as systemic implications for the peculiar institution writ large.

This emigration of Southern slaveholding culture also reflects the mobility within the enslaved population. Enslaved emigrants found themselves participating in a westward movement designed to ensure their continued enslavement on a structural level as well as a personal one. The men, women, and children who relocated during the Second Middle Passage, as Ira Berlin terms it, would have profoundly different experiences than those they left behind.[9] While their desires, thoughts, and fears have been lost to us, there can be no doubt that they had apprehensions about their new lives. For those who traveled forcibly at the hands of slave traders, the trauma they experienced in slave pens and en route further colored those same worries. As Berlin notes, kinship bonds often suffered in this forced migration, as did slaves' sense of identity, whether this relocation came through sale or traveling alongside white owners heading westward.[10] Bondspeople carried their own cultural mores and expectations, hoping to re-create some semblance of order and stability in their new homes, even as forces outside their control delineated their movements.

These involuntary migrants to the border region found themselves in distant communities on the outskirts of American settlement, far removed from major spheres of influence, but guided nonetheless by the cultural expectations and value systems that slaveholders transplanted out West. Slaves worked alongside whites to build homes, improve the land, cultivate gardens, and construct outbuildings with few resources and much labor, all while navigating the racial borders of these communities and scouting out opportunities for resistance. African Americans shaped the region's social geography, though they lacked the ability to fundamentally influence local government and legal institutions. If the story of the West considers whites' mobility, that should be no less true for the enslaved. Chattel slavery was becoming both a Western and a Southern phenomenon.

Enslaved people living on the border prior to Missouri statehood also encountered a syncretic world exhibiting a remarkable degree of demographic diversity, a world in which their struggles to adapt were accompanied by a relative ease of mobility. In the early 1800s, the Kansas-Missouri line did not yet exist on any European or American map, but the region enjoyed a convergence of waterways that made it a crossroads of native, European, and American cultures. As historian William Foley has noted, "not clearly situated in any of the four national geographic sections, and yet a part of all, Missouri and its people personify American pluralism."[11] However, western Missouri and northern Indian Territory (which would become Kansas Territory in 1854) was a zone of transition in the 1820s and 1830s, where longtime denizens witnessed the demise of French cultural authority, a crumbling fur trade on the Missouri River, the exclusion of indigenous tribes like the Osage, the challenges of statehood and slavery's expansion, the repercussions of the Indian Removal Act, and increased American emigration, all over the course of mere decades.

Meanwhile, the border region was becoming an extension of the small-scale slaveholding culture that existed elsewhere in the Upper South. As Diane Mutti Burke has observed, Missouri had the highest number of small-scale slaveholdings anywhere in the United States, aside from Delaware.[12] Small-scale enterprises held several advantages for slaveholders. Owning a few slaves was a relatively small investment that could garner impressive returns without requiring significant capital. Additionally, it allowed owners to address diverse and fluctuating labor needs promptly by simplifying the process of allocating labor; slaves often acquired diverse skill sets, which was not always the case on large plantations that relied on specialized tasks. Slaves in a small-scale system might find themselves working in agricultural, business, or domestic spaces all within a short timeframe. Small-scale slaveholding also required less infrastructure. Overseers, detailed schedules, and complicated management techniques were uncommon, due to a smaller labor force, which meant slaveholders could invest more time in other pursuits. Or, in very small households, owners might then be free to work alongside their slaves and thus commit their own labor to their business or agricultural enterprises. Some of these elements might also be possible on large plantations, but small-scale slaveholding granted a flexibility that was enticing to many whites in the Upper South.

Many founding fathers of western Missouri counties, and the leading governmental, cultural, and religious figures in neighboring Indian Territory, were small slaveholders who enjoyed significant cultural and political capital. This was a trend borne out across the South as slaveowners' formidable political and social connections gave them unprecedented authority.[13] Here slaveholders occupied an elite status (though not the only elite status) because their ability to own and care for slaves illustrated wealth in a society where deprivation was the norm for many migrants scraping by as they established farms and businesses. There were also nonslaveholding emigrants from Northern states, but the region's character came thanks to Southerners (whether slaveholding or nonslaveholding) who supported slavery. This was, to borrow the words of Ira Berlin, a "society of slaves" on its way to becoming a "slave society," at least if the hopes and prayers of slaveholders—and the deepest fear of slaves—were to come true.[14] Though Western and Southern (and to some extent Northern) society was being refigured and reconstituted on this border, many of the same markers of elite status continued to dominate the social landscape.

African Americans' enslavement in the region began only after scattered European and American settlements spread along the Missouri River, since tribes indigenous to eastern Kansas and western Missouri—the Osage, Kansa, Wichita, and Pawnee—did not embrace African slavery. It first took root in the 1810s and 1820s, at roughly the same time as Missouri's statehood, but slavery's existence elsewhere in Missouri predated American settlement in the region, extending back to French Louisiana. French miners digging for silver and lead in southeastern Missouri first used black slaves as early as 1719 or 1720. The scarcity of labor in this region made some French settlers contemplate using native slaves, but by the 1750s, French settlements along the Mississippi River were generally committed to African slavery.[15] To regulate this growing labor force, the French government instituted the "Black Code," or *Code Noir*, in 1724. This codified France's philosophical and legal conception of chattel slavery. Like the model found in the British West Indies and the Old South, the French model aimed to restrict black mobility and enforce white authority through violence, but it included key provisions recognizing that "although slaves were property, they were also human beings with souls to be saved."[16] It differed from American slave labor practices by condemning rape and the selling of small children apart from their parents, forbidding labor on Sundays and holidays, and condemning the torture or murder of a slave by their owner. Slaves must also be baptized into the Catholic faith. There were serious punishments in place, however, for slaves who assaulted or stole from their master or mistress. Like other slave codes, the *Code Noir* may have been the legitimate authority on such matters, but in day-to-day life, slaveholders likely developed their own idiosyncratic practices and implemented the *Code Noir* as they saw fit.[17]

Likewise, the Spanish, who gained nominal control of the region in 1763, continued to use slave labor, although the Spanish slave code differed in some respects from the *Code Noir*. For instance, slaves subject to Spanish law could testify before the court in certain civil cases, own property, and purchase their freedom. The most significant event during Spanish rule, regarding slavery, occurred on December 6, 1769, when the territorial governor abolished Indian slavery once and for all. By the 1772 census, almost 38 percent of non-Indian residents were of African descent. Unlike French miners who used slave labor, slaves under Spanish control primarily worked in agriculture. This Spanish phase came to an end, however, with the turn of the nineteenth century. Overwhelmed by debt and the administrative red tape that accompanied any large-scale colonial effort, the Spanish quietly transferred Louisiana back into French hands in 1801. After the French lost control of their colony in Saint Domingue during the Haitian Revolution, Napoleon offered to sell Louisiana to the United States at a discount. With this Louisiana Purchase of 1803, one of the crowning achievements of President Jefferson's tenure in office, the border region settled into American hands.[18]

Americans who had already put down roots along the Missouri and Mississippi Rivers grew concerned over the transfer of power, not only because the United States might refuse to recognize their land grants (acquired under Spanish colonization) but also because slaveholders in Upper Louisiana (the area north of the thirty-third parallel) feared slavery might be outlawed. While Congress allowed slavery in the Territory of Orleans to the south, the U.S. government had not dictated whether or not the peculiar institution would be sanctioned throughout the rest of the Louisiana Purchase.[19] Eventually the United States assuaged these doubts by instituting a slave code that was stricter than the laws that existed under French or Spanish rule. Thus, by 1805, when Upper Louisiana established its own territorial government, slaveholders in what would become Missouri and Kansas had only grown more confident in their right to hold human property.[20]

American settlements in these early years, however, were congregated along the Mississippi River with only a smattering of homesteads adjacent to the Missouri River. Areas to the west remained under native control throughout the political reshuffling that occurred during the early 1800s. Tensions between American settlers and native tribes who inhabited the border region—particularly the Osage—existed at various points on the Missouri frontier, thanks to increased American emigration and ensuing pressures on the area's natural resources. Osage lands stretched throughout western Missouri and eastern Kansas, and their displeasure with the United States encouraged depredations against white settlements. Meriwether Lewis, who was elected territorial governor in 1807, attempted to regain control by giving the Osage an ultimatum: they would stop their attacks on white neighbors or lose the U.S. government's protection and access to trade goods.[21]

In order to maintain peaceful relations and reinforce American dominance, the U.S. government built Fort Osage, which stands fewer than fifteen miles from modern-day Independence in Jackson County, Missouri. This fort, erected in 1808, was the second American fort built within the Louisiana Purchase. General William Clark, whose leadership during the Corps of Discovery expedition received widespread acclaim, chose the site. To keep local tribes in check, secure the frontier, and help assimilate native tribes, federal officials established a government trading factory within the fort. Clark oversaw the construction of a log palisade, barracks to house a company of soldiers, four blockhouses, a store made of two connected cabins, and other outbuildings. A trading post was an incentive for native tribes to resume a congenial relationship with the white leadership of Upper Louisiana. To facilitate this peaceful accord, General Clark sent Nathan Boone (Daniel Boone's son) and an interpreter to the Osage villages to arrange for a conference at the new fort.[22] This rapport would also be crucial in engineering the process of eastern removal in later years, a central component of American expansion. By the early 1820s, the countryside circling Fort Osage—known as Six Mile country—was home to the Osage and pioneer families of both American and French descent.[23]

During these conversations, Clark discovered that Osage leaders were eager to demonstrate allegiance to the United States. He capitalized on their agreeable outlook and brokered a treaty where the Osage would relinquish their claim to the land between the Missouri and Arkansas Rivers, which included much of the border region. Some Osage later followed Clark to Saint Louis in protest of the treaty's terms, prompting some revisions, but the revised treaty of August 31, 1809, remained similar to Clark's original text. In return for ceding their territory, the

Osage would enjoy a permanent government factory (to sell merchandise and provide services like blacksmithing), annual stipends of $1,500, and renewed protection under the powerful arm of the U.S. government. A major amendment, included by Governor Meriwether Lewis, called for the Osage to cede land north of the Missouri River (which would include the modern-day Missouri counties of Clay, Platte, Buchanan, and others). For whites who hoped to settle on the frontier, this monumental treaty was a boon, and houses cropped up around the fort. Although Fort Osage was evacuated from 1813 to 1815 as a result of the War of 1812, it remained a central site of American dominance until its abandonment in 1827. Another Osage treaty in 1825 encouraged further settlement by opening up a twenty-four-mile-wide belt of land along the western Missouri border.[24] In addition to the American influence, some French creoles, having maintained a presence in eastern Missouri and Saint Louis, spread westward into other places within the Missouri River valley.[25]

The steady influx of new settlers into Missouri necessarily dictated discussion over when the territory might be eligible for statehood. On January 8, 1818, the Speaker of the House of Representatives presented the first petition for Missouri statehood. The ensuing debate over slavery's extension and Missouri's place in the Union continued unabated for more than two years. Missouri's admission as a slave state would grant the South an advantage, a proposition that vexed Northerners. After a succession of heated debates, Congress finally approved the Missouri Compromise of 1820, a collection of bills masterminded by statesman Henry Clay. This compromise attempted to solve the controversy over slavery's extension to the benefit of both North and South. Southerners would gain Missouri as a slave state, and a new free state (Maine) would be created out of Massachusetts's land holdings, preserving a tenuous balance in Congress. Another key stipulation was that slavery would not be sanctioned in the Louisiana Purchase north of the 36° 30' parallel, with the exception of Missouri.[26] The compromise's passage ensured slavery would safely exist in Missouri. As a result, slaveholders throughout the Upper South continued their emigration into this new western state, bringing bondspeople alongside the white members of the household.

Statehood in 1821 brought change to the border region, as it did elsewhere in Missouri, including a dramatic increase in the state's white and black populations. The esteemed French trading dynasty of the Chouteaus, which had dominated the Missouri River fur trade during the late eighteenth century and had already established a secure footing in the West, set up a major trading post that would prove a locus of settlement on the border. In 1821, François Chouteau established Chouteau's Landing in modern-day Kansas City, near the junction of the Missouri and Kansas Rivers. In the 1820s, the fur trade and its related kinship networks engendered a stable trading economy that dominated this area, and today the Chouteaus are recognized as the earliest settlers of Kansas City.[27] The Chouteaus relied on bondspeople not only for their business enterprises but also for subsistence agriculture and personal comfort. Maximizing profit by using slave labor in a business context was no different than embracing its economic benefits in agricultural pursuits. Their economic future lay in the West, and they saw no reason for slavery to be excluded. Mobility for white trappers and traders was likewise central to their economic success, and enslaved people moved throughout the Missouri River valley in conjunction with the whites and natives tied to this powerful family.

As historian Anne Hyde describes the Chouteau trading empire, each post operated much like a modern franchise, with a command structure centered in Saint Louis but some autonomy for post heads on the far reaches of white settlement.[28] Earlier, in 1819, François built the first fur-trading post on the Kansas River, about two and a half miles east of present De Soto, Kansas, a joint effort with his cousin Gabriel.[29] The governor of Spanish Louisiana had granted François's father, Pierre Chouteau, and his uncle, Auguste Chouteau, exclusive trading rights with the Osage; thus François grew up learning the fur business and soon commanded an impressive influence over the region surrounding the confluence of the Kansas and Missouri Rivers. In 1819 François married Bérénice Menard, also of French descent and a slaveowner herself, and in 1821 the young couple traveled on a pirogue down the Missouri River with their two young sons and one slave. They settled near François's primary fur warehouse at what became known variously as Chouteau's Landing, Kawsmouth, and Randolph Bluffs. The Chouteaus accumulated several more slaves over the course of their marriage and enjoyed an almost unparalleled status in the environs. The Chouteaus' world was a diverse one, with this western fur enterprise the locus of contact between local natives like the Osage and Kansa, English and French speakers from the east, and African Americans both enslaved and free.

Although there are no records of Chouteau slaves left in their own words, other records illustrate some details of their everyday experiences and access to public and private spaces. The 1830 census shows three slaves within the François Chouteau household.[30] The Chouteaus employed enslaved labor in a variety of tasks, ranging from business endeavors, to agricultural labor, to work within the home. Some slaves were their legal property but others were hired; for instance, in 1829, an enslaved man named Joseph worked alongside a mixed-race man François had hired to pilot the boat transporting furs back to Saint Louis.[31] At least one—likely more—of the male slaves worked in the warehouse. These warehouses were typically quite large, storing not only the pelts brought east from the Rockies but also trade goods such as cloth, blankets, guns, sugar, coffee, beads, and other trinkets that would be traded for fine pelts. After an incoming shipment was unloaded from the canoe or wagon and negotiations for pay had concluded, Chouteau and his workers (including both enslaved and paid employees) inspected, sorted, and pressed the pelts and skins before wrapping them into packages.[32] Presumably, slaves and employees were also responsible for keeping an accurate inventory of the European goods in addition to helping with other essential elements of the commercial enterprise. A flood destroyed the Randolph Bluffs warehouse in 1827, and Chouteau relocated nearby to a new, massive warehouse and a steamboat landing that served as a gathering point for trappers, traders, and locals for miles around. At the height of his influence, François supervised five trading posts (including those of his brothers Cyprien and Frederick, in Indian country). As he traveled between the posts and Saint Louis, some of the enslaved men at these posts likely traveled alongside him.[33]

Other bondspeople worked within the Chouteau household, either as house servants or in the fields. The 1830 Missouri census showed an adult female slave and a young girl who worked in the large frame house and lived in slave cabins located nearby.[34] Bérénice Menard Chouteau, François's wife, also purchased an enslaved girl named Nancy (of unknown age) in 1837 as a playmate and personal attendant for her young daughter, Mary Brigitte. Presumably, Nancy helped out around the house doing domestic chores and consequently contributed to the family's well-being in a concrete way, as well as a psychological one, since in the early years Bérénice was often left alone when François traveled on business.[35] The specific nature of this owner-slave relationship remains undocumented, but as historian Thavolia Glymph reminds us, slaveholding women had significant power within households, which were both economic and political spaces. This had profound implications for the experiences and identities of enslaved women.[36] Women's labor, whether black or white, was integral to this household's success as well as the productivity of the Chouteaus' fur empire. As such, the stakes for Nancy's labor may have been high, and François's frequent absences likely exacerbated any tensions that existed within the household.

Sustaining a high standard of living was a time-consuming task for the enslaved individuals in this household. According to his brother Frederick Chouteau, François and his family lived in a two-story home with a large wraparound portico, located a short distance from the freestanding kitchen, smokehouse, and other outbuildings, including slave quarters. After their first home was destroyed in the same flood that claimed the warehouse, the Chouteaus built another grand house, likely constructed by slaves. In addition to owning cattle, chickens, and hogs that foraged along the water, the Chouteaus ran a large farm in the bottomlands near the river. This was initially a source of staple crops for home consumption more than for commercial use, although by the 1840s it included around one hundred acres of hemp, suggesting that high hemp prices lured the Chouteaus into expanding their operation.[37] This expansion is also referenced in a letter from 1833, where François noted that he bought a "mulatto. . . . He is very expensive but he is skillful and a good farmer and we have the greatest difficulty obtaining men here."[38] This need for reliable labor points to the Chouteaus' varied economic enterprises, their obligations (and perhaps preoccupation) with the fur trade and not agricultural endeavors, as well as the nature of life on a frontier where basic amenities and comforts were difficult to procure without significant commitment.

The enslaved residents of Chouteau's Landing, living at a busy crossroads where trappers, traders, government officials, and local citizens congregated, had regular contact with other enslaved people and local natives. This borderland provided ample opportunities for slaves to test boundaries on their mobility, even though slaveholders like the Chouteaus monitored and utilized slaves' movements for their own ends. Some visitors were slaveholders who brought slaves with them as they conducted business. For example, in 1832, a Methodist minister from Tennessee, James Porter, came west to aid in ongoing missionary efforts among the emigrant Indian tribes. He left his family, livestock, and thirty slaves at Chouteau's trading post while he procured land and a residence, finally settling in the Westport area on the Missouri side of the border.[39] The slaves who worked for the Chouteau family undoubtedly had much contact with native tribes as well, since at least some of the male slaves spent time working at the warehouse. Warehouses were abuzz during the spring and summer when local Native Americans, French trappers, and white locals congregated to do business. Likewise, Frederick Chouteau,

François's brother and partner in the fur business, had several posts, including one near the first Shawnee Methodist Mission, in Indian Territory. Although Frederick did not own slaves, his brother did, strongly suggesting that François's slaves may have had contact with slaves who worked at the mission. African labor (whether slave or free) proved central to the fur trade in the West. French-speaking African creoles, free and enslaved translators fluent in native languages, and other black tradesmen often worked side by side with their American, French, and native compatriots. In a profession where mobility was essential to success, many of these male laborers found themselves with unprecedented opportunities for travel and a level of professional respect not unlike that of at least some of their white competitors. Enslavement placed concrete limits on how enslaved men and women accessed the landscape, but the heterogeneous flavor of life on this frontier opened up a realm of new possibilities.[40]

The French style of slave management emphasized a relational, paternalistic attitude that drew its power from the now-defunct *Code Noir*, which still shaped the enslaved experience. These practices can provide some insight into the slave-owner relationship. For instance, in 1840, Bérénice wrote a letter to her father, Pierre Menard, on behalf of a slave named Alexi, stating that Alexi "was looking for a master before my arrival from down there [Saint Louis]. . . . He greatly desires to come and stay with me for four or five years—that he will serve faithfully. But that he needs to leave from where he is living. I beg of you to see Polite [Hippolyte] on that subject and to write to me." Apparently this slave felt comfortable enough to express his discontent, and he seemingly found an ally in Bérénice. Bérénice's motives were not purely charitable, however, since earlier in the letter she also stated that she desperately needed men to work on the farm.[41] The case highlights not only how mistresses managed household affairs but also how their paternalistic attitudes continued, and were perhaps informed by American expansion, which embraced similar principles.

Sometime after François's death in 1838, Bérénice moved to Westport, in Missouri, and the Chouteau warehouse was no longer a major staging area for the fur trade, having been damaged in the regular floods that plagued the Missouri River. Gradually the influx of Anglo-American settlers on the Kansas-Missouri border made the French influence seem a distant reality.[42] Nevertheless, prior to the mid-1840s, French traders like the Chouteaus were well known and highly respected members of the community, signaling the power and influence that came with slaveholding. These ethnically diverse worlds, and the syncretic proclivities of the French worldview, were one victim of the ideological and demographic shift toward American settlement. Changes were coming to this borderland.

As the Chouteaus had continued to enlarge their healthy share in the Western fur trade in the 1820s and 1830s, other white settlers also looked westward for fresh land and opportunity. Environmental incentives, combined with the continued subjugation of native tribes like the Osage, made the new state an appealing prospect for settlement. For farmers from the Upper South, the soil in their native states often lacked nutrients due to overuse and uneducated farming practices; fresh land in the West held the potential for recovering any previous losses and stabilizing their household finances. They were well accustomed to diversified agriculture and its labor requirements. Most of these emigrants had never participated in plantation culture and had practiced small-scale, diversified farming of crops like hemp, corn, and tobacco. Trade drove the border economy, particularly in its early years, but it was growing into its place as a heart of agricultural production.

Therefore, the composition of Missouri slaveholders in the border region and elsewhere in the state correlated with the establishment of the family farm as the predominant agricultural unit. Whereas slaveholders in the Deep South relied on the plantation system to run their extensive cotton, rice, or sugar enterprises, the average slaveholder in the Upper South—Missouri included—owned ten or fewer slaves. These slaveholders moved to Missouri because their smaller model could be reproduced in Missouri much more easily than in the cotton belt of the American Southeast. As Aaron Astor has outlined, this generally led to a proportionally higher number of slaveholders than in the Deep South, albeit with a smaller and more dispersed slave population, which indicates that more whites were tied to slavery and invested in its continuation than might appear at first glance.[43] Although nonslaveholders emigrated to Missouri from Midwestern states such as Illinois and Indiana, as did nonslaveholders from the South, the majority of white settlers entering the border counties in these early years came from regions where slavery was well established. These men and women understood slavery to be a labor system that reinforced a strict racial hierarchy that privileged all whites, not just those who owned human property. The political culture of this region, then, was one that embraced slavery and its attendant benefits for white society, reinforcing in word and deed slavery's key place in shaping the border's social geography.

The settlement process in western Missouri, within the counties included in this study, demonstrates both the Southern flavor of this borderland and bondspeople's centrality to varied economic ventures. On the north side of the Missouri River, several key settlements grew into centers of business in the years immediately following statehood, thanks largely to slaveholders' capital investments. Clay County, with its county seat in Liberty, was founded in 1822 and touted as prime agricultural land on the fringe of Little Dixie, the region along the Missouri River that would prove to be the most important hemp, tobacco, and livestock-producing country in the entire state. The county census two years later listed 1,861 white residents and 231 slaves.[44] Within just a few short years, the county boasted several mills, a tan yard, numerous merchants, a saddle shop, and a rapidly growing population of both farmers and entrepreneurs eager to build roads, schools, and other improvements. Slaveholders operated several of these businesses, and many of these earliest emigrants hailed from the Upper South.[45] By 1830, there were 5,338 residents of the county, with 882 enslaved residents making up 17 percent of the population.[46] Although this information was not available in the 1830 census, examining just one township in Clay County in the 1850 census (the first to record state of origin) demonstrates that among white adults over the age of eighteen who were born outside Missouri, a vast percentage came from the Upper South. White residents from the states of Kentucky, Tennessee, Virginia, and North Carolina composed 88.5 percent of the population there in 1850 (see Table 1).[47]

Neighboring Platte County, which was unofficially settled by many residents of Clay County even before its incorporation into Missouri, saw a similar demographic makeup. Prior to the 1830s, the so-called "Platte Country" belonged to both indigenous tribes and emigrant tribes such as the Potawatomi, Sauk and Fox, and Iowa, although the border between Indian lands and Missouri remained porous, and squatters faced little resistance in their trek across the line.[48] With the realization that economic success lay westward, the ongoing march of American business pursuits essentially doomed these Indian possessions. Leading Missouri senators, including Thomas Hart Benton, called for annexing the region and convinced the Missouri legislature to extinguish Indian claims therein. Thus, in 1836, commissioners signed treaties with these tribes to cede this fertile land along the Missouri River.[49] What became known as the Platte Purchase included the current Missouri counties of Nodaway, Holt, Buchanan, Andrew, Atchison, and Platte. The ensuing flood of newcomers came primarily to farm, with many emigrants

Table 1. State of Origin Statistics for Washington Township, Clay County, Missouri

State of Origin (excluding Missouri)	Number of White Emigrants	Percentage of Population
Kentucky	198	45.0
North Carolina	98	22.3
Tennessee	50	11.4
Virginia	43	9.8
Ohio	7	1.6
Indiana	5	1.1
New York	4	0.9
South Carolina	4	0.9
Maryland	3	0.7
New Jersey	3	0.7
Alabama	2	0.5
Pennsylvania	2	0.5
Florida	1	0.2
Georgia	1	0.2
Unknown/Illegible	19	4.3
Total	440	100

U.S. Bureau of the Census, *Seventh Census of the United States*, 1850, Population Schedules (Washington, D.C.: Government Printing Office, 1853).

hailing from Southern states,[50] H. Jason Combs's work on the Platte Purchase demonstrates that of these counties, Platte County had one of the highest percentages of settlers from the Upper South, resting at 65 percent.[51]

The major Platte County towns of Weston, Platte City, and Parkville supplied army garrisons and native communities in the vicinity, fostering their own trade enterprises. The first American settler in what became Platte City was Zadock Martin, who moved there in 1828. Martin, his sons, and several enslaved men built living quarters out of "hewed lynn logs . . . two shed-rooms were added, making a house of four rooms," with slaves living in the shed rooms. Martin's first business endeavors were to operate a ferry, run a tavern, and farm in the fertile bottomlands.[52] Parkville was located on the Missouri River, and in the

1830s, it was known as English's Landing; it was not platted until 1844, four years after the first lots were sold in Platte City. The first American settler to arrive in Weston was an army officer from Fort Leavenworth named Joseph Moore, who settled on the current site in 1837, although the town was not chartered until 1842.[53] Like Independence and Westport a few miles south, Weston was a station for emigrants and traders heading west. It also lay on the Missouri River, and according to a later reminiscence by local historian George Remsburg, "had a splendid wharf, with big warehouses, where hemp and other products were stored and eventually shipped in great cargoes to St. Louis."[54] From its earliest days, Weston was a proslavery town. By 1840, Platte County had almost nine thousand residents, including 858 slaves valued at $223,620 (approximately 60 percent of the total assessed value) and comprising 9.6 percent of the population.[55] Slavery was well established in this part of the newly opened Platte Purchase.

Northwest of these settlements, in what became Buchanan County, lay Blacksnake Hills (now Saint Joseph). This community was far enough away to establish some autonomy, but as a growing hinterland, it was still tied to the larger economy developing on the border. Since sometime in the late 1820s it had served as a trading post commanded by Joseph Robidoux III, a slaveholder. He began as an agent of the American Fur Company and then worked independently, overseeing a family-run empire that stretched into the Upper Missouri and down to Santa Fe. Most of these early settlers were French-speaking traders from Saint Louis, where Robidoux was born and where his father had gained influence in the fur business. His relationship with the Chouteaus alternated between collegiality and competition, since their French heritage and chosen profession granted them common interests and many mutual acquaintances. Robidoux sought independence for his posts when possible, but his work could not be separated from the lines of credit, suppliers, and other associates that drove the trade, illustrating the deep business and personal connections that defined the trading dynasties of Saint Louis. Thankfully for Robidoux, the Chouteaus headquartered elsewhere in the border region. His small settlement at Blacksnake Hills primarily had contact with local natives, trappers, and traders, since this land originally belonged to the Iowa and Sauk and Fox tribes, and it was not part of Missouri until the Platte Purchase.[56]

It is unclear when Robidoux acquired his first slaves, but he placed an order with Jean and Pierre Laffite in 1818 requesting twenty slaves (including women, men, and children who could speak French), in addition to other supplies, including muskets, blankets, sugar, and knives.[57] In a later letter to the Laffite brothers, he extolled the virtues of African slave labor, as Indian slave labor was too arduous and complicated to be of use to his enterprise, and "much material and slaves will be required for this task" of building posts on the Missouri. If these slaves did arrive as expected, the men likely helped make improvements to the post.[58] His wife, Angelique, remained at their estate in Saint Louis for the duration of their marriage, and any enslaved women he acquired would have possibly remained with her to assist with childcare, housework, and other domestic tasks.[59] By the 1820s, he had at least one male slave with him named Hypolite or Poulite, who had some responsibility in both the trading post and the mill, being fluent in French himself.[60] Given that Robidoux had several white men working at the post handling various affairs, it is possible that other enslaved men and women contributed to his business endeavors as well. While the experiences of enslaved members in his household are difficult to discern due to the paucity of sources, their labor no doubt contributed to his successes.

The only glimpse available into Robidoux's slaveholding practices comes from a freedom suit filed in the Saint Louis Circuit Court in 1822. In *Jeffrie v. Robidoux*, this sixteen-year-old enslaved man and his grandmother Rachael Camp sued Robidoux "for assault and battery and false imprisonment." In October of 1820, while in Saint Louis, Robidoux had "beat, bruised, and ill treated" Jeffrie to the extent that he feared for his life. Robidoux then "imprisoned" him for two years. Robidoux's defense hinged on the fact that Jeffrie was his slave and such punishment was normal in the daily affairs of managing one's slave property. Jeffrie appealed, and the case dragged on for almost fifteen years.[61] Court records do not state how the case concluded, but a mixed-race man named "Mr. Jeffre" appears in Robidoux's business correspondence from the 1830s in reference to trade with Indians. At some point, it appears that Jeffrie (now Geoffrey Dorwin, or Deroin) had established a competing enterprise, to the great annoyance of his former owner. By Robidoux's account, Dorwin was working with two other men who were either African or mixed race, trading in liquor and various goods they had procured in Clay County. Dorwin acted as a free person, so at some point during the protracted legal battle in Saint Louis he had escaped or somehow loosened his proverbial bonds to Robidoux, and according to records of the Iowa Subagency, he worked for part of that period as an interpreter. He may have succeeded as an interpreter because he had spent time on this very border while under Robidoux's control, learning the tricks of the trade and establishing networks with local tribes. While at the agency, General Andrew Hughes, the Indian agent, somehow negotiated Dorwin's freedom. Robidoux was more displeased about the business competition, but his correspondence also references attempts to circumvent his former slave's free status.[62] This fascinating, though convoluted, case illustrates the mobility of slaves and former slaves involved in the fur trade, as Dorwin moved about independently, and there is no mention of his race being a barrier, though his legal status was subject to debate. Slaves and free blacks like Dorwin shaped life in Buchanan County, even before the county was officially organized.

The county's population grew rapidly after the Platte Purchase became part of Missouri in 1837. Approximately 51 percent of these white emigrants, including both slaveholders and nonslaveholders, hailed from the Upper South.[63] Many moved to what became Saint Joseph, a promising spot for the overland trade that lay adjacent to rich farmland and plentiful timber.[64] Rudolph Kurz, a Swiss artist who traveled throughout the American West in 1848, noted that Saint Joseph was showing "evidences already of a rapidly expanding and flourishing city. . . . Upon my arrival the principal streets were much enlivened by fur traders and immigrants on their way to regions, as yet little known, in Oregon and California."[65] According to the founding documents of the county, there were also 263 slaves.[66] In addition to labor in businesses, enslaved residents worked in agriculture, especially hemp, which as one historian has commented, "proved an unqualified success."[67] Some old timers also remained. Robidoux, known today as the father of Saint Joseph, successfully navigated the changes in border society and remained in Missouri to coordinate his business ventures, where he also operated a flour mill and a private ferry.[68] He wielded significant authority over local affairs, and his home became a central meeting place, serving as the first circuit court of Buchanan County.[69] Like other communities on the border, the fur trade that had dictated the rhythms of frontier life for many natives and newcomers was giving way to agricultural pursuits and increased trade with overland emigrants.

To the south, in Jackson County, rural hamlets and larger communities like Independence (founded in 1827) and Westport (platted in 1834) cropped up and expanded in the 1830s. Of the total population of Jackson County in 1830 (numbering 2,823 souls), there were 193 slaves and sixty slaveholding households. Roughly 6 percent of the adult white population in 1830, and 12 percent of adult white males, were slaveholders.[70] This relatively small number belies the influence, however, of slaveholders who maintained key positions of power within these communities. James Shepherd, a slaveowner and cousin of William Clark, brought a group of emigrants out in 1821 to what was then open prairie. In a letter to his cousin, Clark had described the area favorably, noting that "this is a beautiful land with fine soil, all the timber you would need for generations, high-growing grass for your cattle. . . . Time is running short and settlers are pouring in and I beg you to come early."[71] Among these early families were future pillars of the Independence community, some of whom owned slaves. Samuel C. Owens, a Kentucky transplant who owned six slaves in 1830, was the first circuit court clerk in the county and later served as a representative to the state legislature. Two out of three of the county's first judges, Abraham McClelland and Richard Fristoe, were slaveholders. Fristoe, who served later as a member of the state legislature, had moved to the border in 1818 with his family and slaves.[72] Not every emigrant came from the South, nor did every white Southerner support slavery on principle. However, there was a critical mass of Southerners that at the very least shaped the political and business contours of the region.

The enslaved population of Jackson County, though lacking a political voice and legal status as free people, played an integral role in shaping this frontier landscape. Tom, an enslaved member of the McCoy household, helped build the town of Westport, which was founded and platted by his owner, John Calvin McCoy. McCoy was born in Indiana, but he came west in 1830 with his parents, Isaac and Christiana McCoy, who served as missionaries in Indian Territory. It is unclear when he first acquired slave property. According to a later reminiscence by McCoy's daughter Nellie McCoy Harris, Tom was told to "take a yoke of oxen, and a plow, and open up through the timber and hazel-bush, a road from the store, the nearest way home."[73] The aforementioned store was one of the first buildings in Westport. The enslaved men on James Shepherd's farm built both a temporary log house and a more permanent brick structure, in addition to their work at the Shepherd and Maxwell warehouse, a business that Shepherd began with his cousin Lucien Maxwell. Here slaves sold yokes, harnesses, and other equipment procured in Saint Louis, as well as handmade rawhide whips that Shepherd had trained the slaves to make from leather received in the Indian trade.

Although white entrepreneurs dominated the outfitting business, African Americans both enslaved and free were central to this growing trade economy, serving as craftsmen who supplied resources to those traveling overland. Robert Weston's shop in Independence had several outbuildings, including a wagon shop and plow factory, with much of the work being conducted by slaves. Both Samuel Owens, one of the most established traders on the Santa Fe route, and his associate, Josiah Gregg, were slaveholders who owned several trade centers in Jackson County and neighboring Clay County. Robert and James Aull ran the Liberty (Clay County) branch of Owen's business, and since the Aull brothers were slaveholders, it is likely they used slave labor in their business ventures.[74] All in all, enslaved people working in businesses such as these enjoyed greater opportunities for mobility, working in a world where the vagaries of commerce encouraged adaptability and flexibility on the part of slaveholders. Of course, enslaved craftsmen's legal status remained unchanged despite their talents. They may have been lauded for their handiwork and economic contributions, and perhaps enjoyed increased autonomy, but such accolades were patronizing and reinforced white racial superiority in the minds of white locals.

An important component of the county's founding, as with other border counties, was the strong kinship ties that slaveholders used to tighten bonds within the community, cementing their influence through intermarriage. One of the first settlers in Jackson County, James H. McGee, moved west in 1821 at the behest of his brother-in-law Samuel Fry, settling briefly in Clay County before relocating to Jackson County in 1828. There he purchased about four hundred acres, eventually establishing a farm, mill, and distillery. In the 1830 census his household included two slaves. His parents-in-law and sister-in-law, who had emigrated alongside McGee, his wife, and their seven children, remained on a farm near Liberty.[75] Other families developed densely woven kinship networks upon arrival. One such family was the Hudspeths. The patriarch, William Hudspeth, sought to re-create his native Kentucky by bringing slaves, hunting dogs, and racehorses when he emigrated in 1828. In the 1830 census, his household included twenty-five bondspeople, including fourteen children under the age of ten. The Hudspeths had kinship ties to the Hambrights, another family that settled nearby, and they lived near other slaveholders, the Chiles, all forming a small settlement a few miles from the now-abandoned Fort Osage.[76] Chain migration, while a source of disruption for the enslaved men, women, and children it affected, might also ensure that slaves were reunited with loved ones in the West. The effects of such migration, while inextricably tied to the shifting social geography of the Upper South, illustrate how often slaves' movement was the result of their owner's wishes and not their own desires.

Both Westport and Independence saw increased emigration after the original start of the Santa Fe Trail, farther east in Franklin, Missouri, fell victim to the rushing waters of the Missouri and pack trains turned to Independence and Westport for outfitting. Missouri's statehood coincided with government attention to its strategic geographic location at the crossroads of East and West, attention encouraged by traders such as William Bucknell. Mexican independence in 1821 and the relaxing of their protectionist trade policies fostered a lively trade with Santa Fe, making the Santa Fe route a superhighway of the early nineteenth century. This trail connected the United States with neighboring Mexico, stretching over eight hundred miles of prairie and desert, a journey that took two to three months of often-strenuous travel.[77] In particular, the route became popular among autonomous traders with limited capital. From 1822 to 1843, approximately $3 million worth of goods made the trek into the Southwest, and somewhere between $100,000 and $200,000 entered the state annually thanks to the goods procured in Mexico.[78] The opening of the Oregon Trail in the 1840s only increased business. This trade contributed significantly to Missouri's economic development, not just the settlement and success of the border region. Westport and Independence were a syncretic world of American, Mexican, and native cultures, in some aspects not dissimilar to the world of the Chouteau fur empire. As one resident described it, Westport was "an animated scene; handsomely dressed citizens, family carriages, the freighters' big wagons, Mexican dons, picturesquely apparelled teamsters, coaches with three or four spans of mules, with a sprinkling of Indians, in civilized or native dress, all made a picture hard to describe."[79] However, this description leaves out the seemingly invisible labor of bondspeople in this frontier town.

Outfitting freight trains was big business. As Perry McCandless has noted, "the[se] towns, their promoters, and the services offered by the townspeople spearheaded the opening, settling, and developing of new regions and served as the economic, social, and political centers of their surrounding areas."[80] As such, communities like Westport and Independence steered the future of the border region in ways that neighboring communities could not. Independence, which served as the county seat of Jackson County, contained everything necessary for outfitting, including blacksmiths, wheelwrights, saddle makers, and wagon makers, as well as other businesses, such as grocers and apothecaries, where travelers could purchase medicine, foodstuffs, and whiskey. A number of these businesses benefited from slave labor. According to an 1837 gazetteer of Missouri, "The regular and healthy growth of this place presents strong evidence of the great value of the country around it. . . . The traders and their hands generally reach Independence destitute of everything in the list of food and clothing. The necessities of these people bring to this frontier town singular advantages."[81] Westport's rise came partly at the expense of Independence, since Independence lacked direct access to the Missouri River, while Westport boasted a natural river landing. Leaders of the community included John B. Wornall, John C. McCoy, William Henry Chick, and Alexander Majors, who were all slaveholding emigrants from Southern states (namely Kentucky and Virginia). Chick and McCoy, along with other investors, also helped found the City of Kansas in 1839, adjacent to Westport and near the former Chouteau property.[82] Within each of the disparate communities rising from the prairie, the majority of settlers hailed from Upper South states, signaling slaveholders and nonslaveholding Southerners' faith in the West as the future of the nation.

Of course, not everyone heading to Jackson County was affiliated with the Santa Fe trade or Oregon Trail; as the westernmost settlements in the United States (save Texas), other adventurers and explorers used Westport as a point of departure. William Fairholme, a British military officer and adventurer, traveled throughout the West in 1840 and kept a detailed journal. Among references to the flora, fauna, and native peoples he encountered, he also recorded that his expedition included "a black fellow, named Henry, whom we have hired from his master, as Cook." Henry appears at several other points in Fairholme's narrative, including a section where Fairholme recounts hearing from Henry some "stirring incidents of Indian warfare," thanks to his experience living among the Western tribes of the Rocky Mountains.[83] Henry's noteworthy mobility across vast regions may have been the exception rather than the rule, but his story illustrates the extraordinary contexts for blacks to move (even somewhat independently) through the western landscape. Although African Americans in the West often receive little attention from historians, they nevertheless figured strongly in nineteenth-century perceptions of the West as a multicultural environment and exemplified the flexible, and as yet uncalcified, boundaries of black mobility.

Beginning in the 1820s, settlers from Jackson County and elsewhere in the country began expanding south into Van Buren County (what is now Cass County, Bates County, and Vernon County), some bringing slaves with them. When the federal census was taken five years after Van Buren was officially organized in 1835, there were 4,693 residents in the county, with approximately 1,400 of them working in agriculture and 214 slaves (5 percent of the total population).[84] Further boundary adjustments came in the 1840s, dividing it into three separate counties. This region enjoyed especially fertile soil, and the earliest white settlers focused their efforts on staple crops that provided food for their families, such as corn and wheat, and animal husbandry. None of these counties contained a sizeable population center or significant trading posts, aside from the county seat of Harrisonville in Cass County. They remained agricultural hubs that transacted business in communities to the north, serving as a hinterland to what would become a major metropolis later in the nineteenth century. This had been Osage country until 1825, leading to a more gradual influx of white settlers, who could only gain title to land after the Osage moved to Indian Territory that same year.[85] The few squatters in the region and the leisurely pace of settlement have made the earliest history of these counties spotty.[86] The only sanctioned settlement during the Osage years was the Harmony Mission in modern Bates County, founded by the United Foreign Missionary Society.[87] Among the counties that make up this borderland, these counties would remain on the periphery, given their distance from population centers and the perils of overland travel in these early years.

Past Missouri's western border, the land controlled by native tribes like the Osage and Kansa also saw increased American development in the 1820s, including slaveowners who emigrated from the Upper South. As white settlers continued to flow into western Missouri unabated, the U.S. government became more concerned with protecting citizens and guarding American interests, particularly after Fort Osage's abandonment in 1827. A new military outpost in the border region would solve this dilemma. This they found where the Missouri River turned northward, at the site of a military post as far back as 1744 when the French had erected Fort de Cavagnial. That fort was abandoned sometime in the late eighteenth century, but in 1827 Senator Thomas Hart Benton of Missouri sought permission for a new garrison just past the Missouri border.[88] A later observer noted, "the situation of the fort is very beautiful [with a] commanding view of the river and subjacent country for many miles around. . . . Indian settlements & Villages, indeed we are quite in contact with the Indians whome we meet on every occasion on going out the proper limits of the fort."[89] The first post commander was Colonel Henry Leavenworth, the fort's namesake, who was tasked not only with protecting freighters on the Santa Fe Trail but also with serving as liaison between native tribes and the U.S. government, preventing the sale of liquor among these tribes, and guarding the fur trade on the Upper Missouri.

As with all military installations, mobility among the various infantry, dragoon, and cavalry units—combined with the requisite Indian visitors and traders providing their services—meant that Fort Leavenworth was geographically important. In 1834, the new Trade and Intercourse Act granted military officers in the territory unparalleled power over tribal boundaries and other matters, making them and their cultural mores significant to the shaping of this border society. Its significance also testifies to the integrated nature of this borderland, where movement across the western border of Missouri was uncontested and common-place. Slaveholding within what would become northern Indian Territory, whether within native, white, or mixed-race households, centered on strategic points where mobility was the norm, and Fort Leavenworth served as one locus of the slaveholding and enslaved communities.[90]

Slaves were present early in the fort's history. Some army officers periodically hired slaves from neighboring Missouri, but at least two prominent figures at the fort—Colonel Hiram Rich, the post sutler, and Major Sackford Maclin, the pay master—owned slaves themselves. Rich moved from Liberty, Missouri, to Fort Leavenworth in 1841 and had extensive contact with native tribes and outposts as far away as the Rockies.[91] Sutlers, who were responsible for supplying general goods to the military and civilians living at the fort, sometimes acting as an informal banking system, were "king over all territory tributary to a military post."[92] According to a newspaper article in the *Leavenworth Times*, Rich "knew everybody in the Platte Purchase and every Missourian who came to this side never failed to call on the Colonel."[93] He served the fort's inhabitants in this capacity until his death in 1862. As sutler, Rich controlled the flow of material goods and was central to the fort's success.[94] It is likely that enslaved members of his household worked primarily in business or the home, although perhaps he also operated a small farm, as it was common for sutlers to develop diversified enterprises. Maclin was from Arkansas and was active in land speculation and the Leavenworth town association. He entered the Confederate army in 1861.[95] A bondsperson in a household like Maclin's would likely have worked as a personal servant, and given the army's inherent mobility, it is certainly possible that this enslaved individual enjoyed greater mobility than an agricultural laborer. While no surviving records describe slavery's earliest presence at this frontier fort, leaving us only conjecture, Fort Leavenworth's position at a bustling crossroads nevertheless illustrates slaves' role in building an American community on the western border.

Further changes would come to the western side of the border after the passage of the Indian Removal Act in 1830. The Indian Removal Act relocated Native American tribes from the eastern United States into a newly designated Indian Territory situated just west of white American settlement, with the northern portion of that territory lying adjacent to Missouri. Per the language in the act, the "United States will forever secure and guaranty to them, and their heirs or successors, the country so exchanged with them," a promise that would ultimately go unfulfilled.[96] The government also expected these natives to become "civilized," which included learning English, adopting Christianity, wearing American clothing, practicing agriculture, and eating American cuisine. Although most studies of Indian Territory and the removal process ignore the existence of northern Indian Territory, focusing solely on the southern portion (the new homeland of the Cherokee and other southern tribes), there were in fact emigrant tribes stretching from modern-day Oklahoma to Nebraska. At least twenty-five tribes totaling over ten thousand

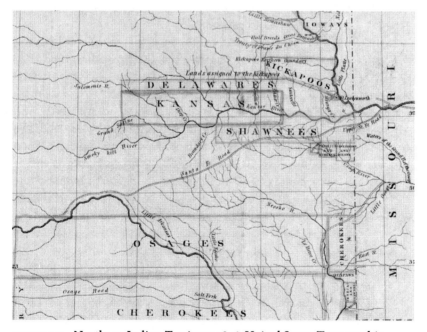

FIGURE 2. Northern Indian Territory, 1836. United States Topographic Bureau, "Map Showing the Lands Assigned to Emigrant Indians West of Arkansas and Missouri," 1836. Courtesy of the Library of Congress, Geography and Map Division.

people, coming primarily from lands near the Great Lakes and in the Midwest, received land in what is today eastern Kansas.[97] These were in addition to the Osage, Kansa, and other tribes who already called this region their home.

The tribes granted lands in this region were diverse. The first tribes to arrive were the Delaware and Ottawa (coming from Ohio and Missouri) in 1829 and 1830, followed by the Kickapoo, some Quapaw from Arkansas, the Citizen Band Potawatomi, and some Shawnee (including Tenskwatawa, the "Shawnee Prophet"), all before 1835. Between 1835 and 1854, more Potawatomi arrived in addition to the Sauk and Fox from Iowa, Seneca of New York, Miami from Indiana, and Wyandot from Ohio.[98] For the U.S. government, Indian Territory would serve as an outlet for these eastern Indians, where they could exist on the margins of white development under heavy supervision from the Bureau of Indian Affairs. By 1853, there were just under seventeen thousand native peoples living in Kansas, with about 60 percent being members of these emigrant tribes.[99] For natives, this relocation harbored new challenges and opportunities, as each tribe settled into what they believed would be their permanent homeland on this border.

Some emigrant natives had adopted white understandings of slavery, either because of the civilization program's emphasis on assimilation or the influence of mixed-race tribal members, who bore the cultural heritage of both white Americans and indigenous peoples.[100] At least three tribes—the Shawnee, Potawatomi, and Wyandot—had members who owned slaves. In this way, Indian removal facilitated slavery's spread. The often painful adjustments that were part and parcel of the civilization and removal processes meant that some native peoples developed a set of cultural values that blended Native American social practices with white concepts of racial difference. For native and mixed-race slaveholders, slavery became a sign of material wealth and privilege. The ownership of slave property signaled not only an embrace of white cultural mores but also a means of bringing economic and political influence to the tribe. This is not to say that native slaveowners embraced all aspects of American culture, or that slaveholding whites considered them social or racial equals, but despite their differences slaveholders of all races could sometimes find common ground. Native people did not universally accept slavery, however, and the mission presence on the border meant that denominational rifts among the Baptists, Methodists, and Presbyterians over the slavery issue manifested themselves within native communities in the 1840s.[101] Still, for proslavery residents, slaveholding among natives was a sign of their impending assimilation into white culture. After removal, it became increasingly vital to assuage any lingering white doubts about natives' fitness for inclusion in the American polity, and slaveholding became one avenue for demonstrating such allegiance to American labor ideals.

Key leaders within these relocated native communities developed close ties to Protestant missionaries and businessmen both in the territory and across the border in Missouri, further extending slaveholding mores and situating slavery at key geographic crossroads. One such leader was Joseph Parks, who came with the Hog Creek band of the Shawnee to Kansas from Ohio in 1833.[102] Parks, reportedly of mixed-race heritage, served as an interpreter during treaty negotiations, and the United States handsomely rewarded him for his cooperation; he received a 640-acre land grant in Ohio and assumption of leadership within the tribe after arriving in Kansas.[103] The Shawnee—who relocated in fits and spurts—came from various bands across Missouri, Arkansas, and the Old Northwest Territory and had diverse allegiances. Shawnee slaveholding practices in Missouri existed as far back as the eighteenth century, when Louis Lorimier, a French trader, married Pemanpich, a mixed-race Shawnee woman. Their slaveholding household remained in southeastern Missouri after his death in 1808 and reportedly was one of the wealthiest families in the state.[104] Likewise, the Hog Creek Shawnee, of which Parks was a part, recognized slaveholding, although a majority of the four bands that relocated to the territory did not support the system.

According to one of Francis Parkman's travelogues, Parks owned a trading establishment in Westport, Missouri, in addition to his large farm of nearly seven hundred acres and "a considerable number of slaves."[105] It is unknown exactly when he first purchased human property, but by 1843 he owned at least one slave, a sixteen-year-old man named Stephen who worked as a blacksmith at the Fort Leavenworth agency.[106] Henry Harvey described Parks as an "intelligent man who had long been engaged in public business. . . . His house has been the resort of all classes and the sums he bestowed on his people constituted a fortune, yet he remained a wealthy man."[107] In the postremoval period, Parks fostered connections with local officials, became a Mason, and joined the Methodist Church, using these relationships to aid his tribe. Parks's role as chief also required that he handle relations between the Shawnee and the U.S. government. He worked as an interpreter at Fort Leavenworth, despite his lack of felicity with most native languages, and traveled to Washington, D.C., to negotiate more benefits for the Shawnee.[108]

Parks's experience garnered him a great deal of influence within West-port and surrounding white communities, although among the Shawnee the shift from hereditary leadership to government chiefs like Parks could engender internal disputes. These disputes sometimes resulted from his close cultural, religious, and business ties to Indian agents like Richard Cummins and missionaries like Thomas Johnson (both of whom were slaveholders), who failed to respect native autonomy. As Stephen War-ren observed, "more than any other Shawnee leader of the time, Joseph Parks epitomized the growing divide between the Shawnee people and their leaders. Moreover, his success demonstrates the extent to which most Shawnees, Christian and non-Christian alike, lost access to lead-ers representing their needs."[109] He remained a chief until his death in 1859. His ability to engage effectively with the white community, and assimilate into slaveholding society on the border, led to his success as a Shawnee leader. Surviving sources do not explore his relationship with the enslaved individuals in his household, but his power within the tribe ensured that slaveholding would remain a signal of status and power in Indian Territory.

Like Parks, Mackinaw Boachman (or Beauchemin) was a slave-owning, mixed-race Indian who developed close ties to the slavehold-ing community in Indian Territory and western Missouri. Boachman's diverse background as the son of a Chippewa woman and French fur trader, who was raised in the Potawatomi nation before allying with the Shawnee, exemplifies the syncretic nature of native-white relationships in northern Indian Territory. He worked for the American Fur Company and formed both business and personal relationships with the Chouteau dynasty of Saint Louis. He allied with the Shawnee after marrying Polly Rogers, whose father, Henry Rogers, was a slaveholder. He also converted to Methodism and served as an interpreter for missionary Thomas John-son, living a short distance from Johnson's Shawnee Methodist Mission (in present-day Johnson County). He later became a preacher himself and missionized among the Wea, Chippewa, and Sauk. Boachman owned two slaves and operated a way station that provided mules and horses to emi-grants, which likely meant his slaves worked either in the home or the sta-ble. These two enslaved individuals probably had significant contact with slaves at the nearby mission.[110] It is also likely that the enslaved residents of the Johnson and Boachman households enjoyed some mobility elsewhere in the region, traveling alongside their owners for business or pleasure.

The Wyandot, who had slaves and slaveowners in their midst, entered the territory later, in 1843. A powerful leader within their community was a mixed-race chief named William Walker, who had received an English education and worked as an interpreter and merchant. He converted to Methodism while in Ohio thanks to the witness of a free man of African and East Indian descent, John Stewart. Despite the multiple religious disputes that engulfed the tribe in later years, William Walker maintained close ties with the Shawnee Methodist Mission. Walker became principal chief in 1836, after serving as one of five Wyandot representatives tasked with investigating their new land holdings out west.[111] While Walker's personal convictions regarding slavery have not survived, nor have any sources from the bondspeople in his household, it is clear that the Wyandot were divided in their racial attitudes. Some Wyandot adopted white, Christian values and argued that Africans came from the devil, a belief that might have been used to justify enslaving people of color.[112] Walker's use of slave labor aided in the establishment of this labor system in the West, and his prominence within the community as a mediator between native peoples and white officials garnered great respect.

Slaveholders and nonslaveholding white Southerners, sharing in the prospect of creating a slaveholding society out West, gained an advantage with the Indian Removal Act's passage, which granted them new avenues for personal enrichment. The relocation of thousands of native peoples—some who were removed by force—was a massive undertaking. This act and its related bureaucracy ushered in a new emigration of Indian agents, military officers, traders, and Christian missionaries, including some who were proslavery and who contributed to slavery's continued existence in the region. Because the government strictly regulated non-native settlement in Indian Territory (although squatters certainly evaded detection), the number of white emigrants remained small between 1830 and 1854, confined to Indian missions, trading posts, and military stations like Fort Leavenworth (and later Fort Scott). Frontier society's transient nature dictated that no population statistic can be absolutely accurate, but according to William Cutler's 1883 history of Kansas, there were approximately fourteen hundred white inhabitants in northern Indian Territory, including about seven hundred military men and a comparable number of civilian traders, missionaries, and other personnel.[113] The exact number of slaves and slaveholders living in the territory will never be known, but in terms of cultural impact, slavery existed here and shaped the territory's development. Unlike the political environment present on the Kansas-Missouri line during Bleeding Kansas, these slaveholders brought slaves as a convenience to themselves and their families, and it remained a very small-scale system. The prospect of expanding slavery did not go unnoticed, but at this point it was as yet unclear whether or not Indian Territory would pass away to make room for further white settlement.

Some of the most influential slaveholders within Indian Territory were white Protestant missionaries charged with the duty of caring for Indian souls. From 1832 to 1869, there were twenty-seven operating Protestant missions; with the exception of two missions, all of these were founded when this was Indian country. The most well known of these missionaries was Thomas Johnson, a Virginian, who set up the first Methodist mission to the Shawnee in 1830. In 1839, Johnson moved the mission to its present location (in modern-day Fairway, Kansas) and enlarged its ministry to include a manual labor school for Indian children that would form the basis of a thriving community.[114] Johnson owned at least three slaves, who worked in his home and around the mission. Johnson's mission and school physically embodied a version of American civilization that supported slavery wholeheartedly, and his significant influence over local politics and the Methodist denomination made his mission's environs a central site for the slaveholding community.

Another missionary, Samuel Irvin, ran a mission school at the Nemaha agency for the Sauk and Fox tribe, and at some point Irvin hired an enslaved woman from Missouri as a cook. According to a white neighbor's reminiscence, Irvin purchased this woman and freed her; this most likely occurred after 1854 because Irvin appeared in the first territorial census with one slave in his household.[115] Although doctrinal disputes shook Indian Territory in the 1840s, in the earliest years of native resettlement, missionaries wielded significant power within the local community. When those missionaries owned slaves, it normalized this labor system and helped establish human bondage on the western side of the border.

Indian agents who served as liaisons with the government also shared in slavery's establishment within Indian Territory and neighboring Missouri. Two of the most influential Indian agents within the territory were Richard Cummins and John Dougherty, and both were slaveholders. Richard Cummins lived on a farm adjacent to the Shawnee Indian Mission and Manual Labor School and employed at least a dozen slaves.[116] Cummins was officially the agent of the Shawnee tribe, although later he was placed in charge of all the Indian agents in the territory. According to a later reminiscence, Cummins's "large experience, tact, and influence with the Indians often made his services invaluable to the government."[117] As Indian agent, Cummins assisted missionary Thomas Johnson in setting up the

Shawnee Methodist Mission both at its original site and at its current site. Cummins also supported the civilization process, which demanded that native tribes abandon their traditional ways and embrace white cultural mores. For some Indians—including those in Kansas and other tribes farther south, like the Five Civilized Tribes—becoming fully assimilated into white culture entailed becoming an active part of the slave system, and as a slaveholder himself, it is plausible that Cummins supported natives' efforts to acquire human property.[118] He had close ties with slaveholders like Joseph Parks and Thomas Johnson, and in later years he expressed concern that abolitionism was gaining a foothold, signaling his dedication to re-creating a Southern racial order on this border.[119]

The other prominent slaveholding Indian agent was John Dougherty, a Kentuckian who came to Fort Leavenworth in 1828. Over the course of the next ten years, Dougherty attended to Indian business at Fort Leavenworth in addition to his work in Saint Louis, headquarters of the western division of the Bureau of Indian Affairs. He later moved across the river to Clay County. Dougherty (and Cummins) were intimately involved with settling emigrant tribes on their new lands, mitigating land disputes, cracking down on alcohol trafficking, distributing annuity payments, and corresponding with the Superintendent of Indian Affairs, William Clark (of Lewis and Clark fame). According to a reminiscence recorded by Lewis Dougherty, John Dougherty "had a great influence with the Indian Tribes from the Missouri [River] to the Columbia [River] and assisted the United States in making many treaties. His Indian name in English was Controller of Fire Water, among his agency Indians."[120] In a land dominated by a Native American presence, Indian agents wielded measurable power as government representatives and liaisons with families like the Chouteaus, who required trading licenses and other endorsements from the United States. These agents were leaders of the border community.

These white Americans—missionaries, traders, military men, and Indian agents—brought with them their dedication to the Southern slave system in the form of enslaved African Americans. So did the native slaveholders who had become acquainted with the slave system. Although records do not detail the enslaved residents' experiences in their own words, it is clear that the enslaved residents of Indian Territory lived at geographically and socially strategic locations, and the power and prestige of their owners, combined with kinship and business networks, possibly afforded them additional opportunities for movement. This borderland, despite its cultural and racial diversity, was becoming deeply tied to slavery and Southern influences.

In the years before 1840, what would become the Kansas-Missouri border was a zone of transition. It was in many respects a nexus for the broader concerns that captured Americans' attention in the early nineteenth century, particularly motivations for western expansion and the challenges of navigating the diverse and syncretic world that residents found already in place. Although the rationales for relocating to the frontier were varied, most early white emigrants into this region came from elsewhere in Missouri or from Upper South states like Tennessee and Kentucky, seeking continuity between their past lives and their new ones. Slaveholders and their white allies ascribed to the slaveholding cultures of their home states, planning to transplant those values out west. The enslaved population, meanwhile, sought familial stability and cultural continuity but usually lacked the ability to maintain such connections. Likewise, emigrant tribes who espoused slaveholding brought their own belief systems as they settled in northern Indian Territory. Slaveholding was inseparable from American expansion.

This was also a world that valued mobility. This mobility lay central to the lived experience of enslaved people, who made their way west in the Second Middle Passage, and whose labor served as a primary context for their movement across the landscape. These enslaved men and women built homes and outbuildings, constructed roads and ferries, worked as tradesmen, assisted in business endeavors, and labored within the home to care for children and attend to their owners' personal needs. As a liminal space, there was potential for some fluctuation of racial boundaries, since the relative geographic isolation of the region sometimes illustrated how out-of-sync old values were in this new territory. However, as slaveholders wielded considerable power over this fledgling world, their attempts to bring coherence and stability worked in tandem with slavery's establishment. As this society settled into its own, its former heterogeneity would dissipate and life here would begin to resemble life in the Upper South. This world would both restrict black rights and afford new opportunities to the enslaved community—opportunities for gaining marketable skills, for building community, and for resistance.

2 / Becoming Little Dixie: The Creation of a Western Slave Society, 1840–1854

Sometime in the early 1850s, a teenaged enslaved man named Larry Lapsley came to western Missouri from Danville, Kentucky. His owner, Samuel, an undisciplined and irresponsible ne'er-do-well, had brought him out west, no doubt hoping to make a prosperous new life in what would become known locally as Little Dixie.[1] Larry worked on a farm on the Little Blue River in Jackson County until Samuel purchased shares in a livery stable near Pleasant Hill, in Cass County, where Larry later recalled he "was always at work." After his owner succumbed to overwhelming debt in 1859, Larry was sold to Samuel's brother-in-law William Bunor. As he recalled later, "One day he said to me, 'Larry, I want you to go over to my brother Wills for a few weeks and do some work for him as he wants you.' Not thinking anything strange by this command, I readily obeyed."[2] Later, Larry discovered in a conversation with other slaves that he had become Bunor's legal property; he confronted Samuel on the matter but did not receive a straight answer. Larry remained on the border until 1861, when Bunor took his slaves to Texas at the outbreak of the Civil War. While down south, he escaped and wound up in Salina, Kansas, after a harrowing journey through the brambles and brush of Indian Territory.[3] Larry Lapsley's experiences in Jackson County and Cass County illuminate the important role African Americans played in building settlements on the Kansas-Missouri line, as well as the contours of a small-scale system where slave mobility was not uncommon.

Until the late 1830s and early 1840s, the border had been on the rugged outskirts of what white and black Americans generally considered to be untamed wilderness. Circumstances changed after American emigration increased rapidly, the Platte Purchase opened for settlement, and most of the Eastern emigrant tribes affected by the Indian Removal Act had resettled in Indian Territory, including some who owned human property. Although this region is not normally associated with Southern influences, in reality life on the border was becoming so deeply entwined with slavery that in many respects it closely resembled more established slave societies in the Upper South.[4] For instance Jackson County, one of the more populous counties on the Missouri side of the line, saw a sharp increase in its slave population after 1840, which corresponded with an increase in personal wealth so significant that by the next decade the county enjoyed the highest aggregate wealth in the state.[5] Meanwhile, in neighboring Indian Territory, where slavery also existed, several leaders within both the white and native communities owned slaves and developed close ties with slaveholding communities in Missouri. Contemporary maps may have demarcated a clear boundary, but in reality there were kinship networks, business connections, religious affiliations, and political relationships that bound together slaveholders and slaves on each side of the border and encouraged (in theory, at least) some continuity of experience.

The only significant distinction between slaveholding in this region and slavery elsewhere in the United States (particularly the Lower South) was one of scale. Small slaveholdings' prevalence meant that slavery in Missouri and Indian Territory took on a different cast than the plantation complex that developed on cotton, rice, or indigo plantations in the Deep South.[6] Slave hiring, diverse forms of employment, abroad marriages, and close contact between slaves and slaveowners were common. Small-scale slaveholding was dominant in the Upper South by 1860, and this was likely true in 1840, although aggregate data is not available since earlier censuses did not note the number of slaveholders. In 1860, the average slaveholding household in the seven border counties of Missouri included 4.1 slaves; the highest average came from Clay County, at 5.3 slaves on average in each slaveholding household, and the lowest came from Vernon County, with 2.5 slaves per slaveowner. Small-scale slaveholding, as historian Diane Mutti Burke has successfully demonstrated, was common in Missouri, where 80 percent of slaveholding households owned fewer than twenty slaves.[7] Since there was no census of Americans in northern Indian Territory, there is no statistical data available for west of the border, which in the 1840s had around fourteen hundred legal, non-Indian residents and approximately ten thousand native peoples from relocated tribes. There were likely a few dozen enslaved

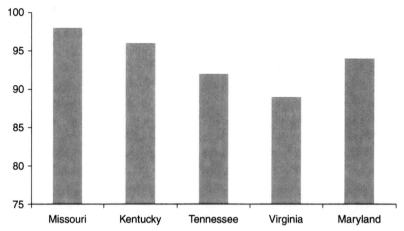

FIGURE 3. Percentage of Slaveholders Owning Fewer Than Twenty Slaves, 1860. United States Bureau of the Census, *Eighth Census of the United States*, 1860, Slave Schedules (Washington, D.C.: Government Printing Office, 1864).

people.[8] Small-scale enterprises flourished on the border due to white migrants' cultural background as Upper Southerners, the region's proximity to free territories and states, and because the system was moldable to slaveholders' diverse and changing needs.

Slaveholders carried over social, economic, and political values prevalent elsewhere in the Upper South in their attempts to concretize slavery's relevance in the region, but the continued development of this small-scale system was no easy process. This borderland was evolving from a fledgling society with slaves to a maturing—though not fully mature—slave society. Slaveholders' desire to write slavery onto the landscape both literally and metaphorically hinged on the formation of a slaveholding border elite with cultural capital and social dominance. Once ensconced in powerful positions, slaveowners could ensure slavery's continued existence by controlling key public and private spaces through the successful commercialization of agriculture and animal husbandry, a reliance on domestic help, broadening connections to business markets in Saint Louis and elsewhere, and the codification of slavery through the law. Yet, at every juncture, slaveholders' efforts to do this were met with resistance. African Americans also laid claim to contested spaces, extracting limited control from the slaveholding elite whenever possible. The contours of this small-scale system illustrate the competition for control over place.

Small-scale slavery was unlike the developed plantation complex, which had its own spatial orientations, but agricultural landscapes still remained central in this nineteenth-century agrarian society.[9] Settlers in the earliest days of American settlement on the border primarily practiced subsistence agriculture, reserving most for home use, since the time and financial commitment necessary to set up agricultural enterprises was daunting for newcomers. Wheat, corn, or oats could be used to feed one's family and livestock, or they could be bartered for goods at the local general store when specie was in short supply. After weathering the "seasoning" period in their first years, as well as periodic financial crises such as the Panic of 1837, farmers on the border could embrace a more commercial attitude, and those who were slaveowners regularly employed slave labor in agricultural contexts.

Slaveholders turned to two crops cultivated solely for profit: tobacco and hemp. Upper South farmers often had previous experience with tobacco cultivation and processing. Tobacco cultivation in Virginia and Maryland had been closely tied to slave labor from a very early date, and such labor was considered essential to the tobacco farm's economic well-being, with one slave potentially bringing in nearly fifty dollars per acre.[10] Slaveowners who could not afford to purchase additional slaves could hire labor for peak periods of growing, harvesting, and processing the leaves. According to local farmers, tobacco was superior to other crops, not only because planters benefited from plentiful returns, but also because it had the potential to stimulate the local economy. One newspaper article stated that "if the Farmers of Clay would go into the raising of Tobacco extensively it would induce 'Stemmers' to locate among us. Glasgow [Chariton County] and Camden [Ray County] are reaping great advantages from their Tobacco Manufactories."[11] In the 1840s, as more and more slaveholding (and nonslaveholding) farmsteads increased their tobacco production, it became clear that the local economy would continue to benefit from enslaved labor.

Tobacco required a great deal of care for planters to make a noticeable profit, attention that bondspeople (and sometimes slaveholders) provided. As nineteenth-century planters were well aware, tobacco depleted essential nutrients in the soil, and leading scientific agriculturalists of the day agreed that crop rotation, fertilizer, and letting fields lay fallow would help farmers gain profitable returns.[12] Since diversified agriculture was common on the border, no doubt many planters maximized their tobacco output in this way. Tobacco was a tedious, labor-intensive crop. The field needed to be plowed and fertilized in January so the crop could be sown in early spring. After planting, slaves covered the seeds with brush to protect the imminent seedlings from any impending frost. Once the plants had grown to several inches high, they could be replanted into the fields, with watchful slaves hoeing, fighting off insect infestations, weeding out new growth, and topping off the terminal buds. Harvest began in the middle of September. In order to produce the finest leaves, the plants needed to wilt and hang dry, have their stems removed, and be protected from humidity. As soon as the leaves reached the desired color, enslaved workers packed them into hogsheads, which were barrels that could contain approximately a thousand pounds. From there the tobacco was ready for shipment.[13] Slaves might accompany their owner to the dock in Liberty or Westport, where the tobacco would be loaded onto steamboats for either local markets (like in nearby Saline County) or more distant cities.

New Orleans and Saint Louis trade routes extended into the border region, where eager buyers encouraged farmers to raise tobacco that could be sent down the Missouri and Mississippi Rivers to be sold on the international market. Provided that the tobacco was carefully processed, it could sell for $3.50 to $5.50 per hundred pounds in the antebellum period.[14] Not all tobacco met such standards, though, as tobacco warehouses in Saint Louis sometimes published instructions for improving product quality in local newspapers. These open letters reminded readers that "buyers regard the character of the cask, not less than the quality of the *tobacco*," reprinting the 1845 regulations for tobacco inspection as a not-so-subtle reminder.[15] Despite the apparent inattention to detail, tobacco warehouses still advertised in newspapers like the *Liberty Tribune* and promised superior service, and Missouri tobacco farmers placed high hopes on their ability to compete in national markets. Commission men who ran tobacco purchasing houses in major markets like that in New Orleans actively encouraged further tobacco cultivation in western Missouri, and some farms even became large-scale commercial enterprises.[16] By all estimations, tobacco was simply good for business. Tobacco cultivation increased throughout this period and became central to the establishment of slavery on the border and in the rest of Little Dixie.

Hemp, the other commercial crop in the region, was well suited to the local environment and was commonly grown in Upper South states like Virginia and Tennessee, the very same states that contributed greatly to the border population. Although tobacco was the first major cash crop in western Missouri, hemp quickly joined it as a favorite. After the cotton boom of the early nineteenth century, cotton planters increasingly needed hemp rope to bind their cotton bales; cotton cultivation there-fore necessitated a complementary increase in hemp production. Also, in 1841, the United States passed a stronger protective tariff that limited Russian imports of hemp and encouraged domestic cultivation. There was talk in Congress of encouraging contracts with the navy to purchase domestic hemp, although this saw limited success as it required a special process less common in the region (water rotting), and the quality of Little Dixie hemp sometimes fell below the navy's standards. In any case, these factors combined to encourage hemp production in Missouri. By 1850, farmers statewide were producing over sixteen thousand tons of hemp, and prices remained high until the late 1850s, with most of this the result of slaves' hard labor.[17]

Planters were not always able to earn consistent profits, however. Hemp cultivation was a time-consuming investment that demanded adherence to high production standards, and it was especially suscep-tible to market fluctuations. Prior to the mechanization of farming, most of this work had to be done by hand, and slaveholders called upon their slaves to furnish that labor. Slaves sowed seed, thinned out the seedlings, gathered seed needed for the next season, plowed, hoed, and maintained the fields until August. During the harvest, on average each slave could complete one acre per day, using a scythe to cut down hemp stalks that ranged from six to eight feet tall. Through the rest of the autumn months and into the early winter, the hemp was gathered into stacks to dry and then spread again on the ground so that the woody stems could rot and allow easy access to the fibers within (called the dew-rotting process, the preferred method in Little Dixie).[18] In order to extract those fibers, slaves often used a device called a hemp brake, which had flat wooden boards that pounded the hemp until the fibers separated from the woody stalks. Hemp breaking was extremely difficult and taxing work that did not appeal to white laborers.

Thus, hemp cultivation shaped the border landscape by providing yet another incentive for planters to use slave labor.[19] When an enslaved man exhibited a special knack for breaking hemp, that was a considerable asset. In 1849, a slave trader in Platte City, G. P. Dorriss, placed a hiring advertisement for twenty-five slaves, stating specifically that there were "hemp breakers" among them.[20] Whoever read and responded to this notice most likely did so because they realized that hiring slave labor for the hemp season was a sound investment. Hemp cultivation bolstered the fledgling economy on the border, becoming a profitable enterprise for many Missouri farmers and their neighbors within Indian Territory.

The agricultural economy in this borderland was heavily dependent on bondspeople's labor, and slaveowners used commercial agriculture to defend slavery's continued existence.

Especially in Clay, Platte, and Buchanan counties, hemp was central to the local economy and connected these western folk to broader markets. Special commission houses cropped up throughout Missouri, including ones in Weston (Platte County), Saint Joseph (Buchanan County), and Liberty (Clay County), and each facilitated an easier transfer of product to market. As historian Miles Eaton has concluded, a third of the towns that served as freight headquarters were located on the western border.[21] Furthermore, commission houses in Saint Louis frequently posted advertisements in western counties like Clay and Jackson, promising "to pay the strictest regard to the interests of those favoring him with their Business."[22] According to R. Douglas Hurt, in the early years of hemp cultivation the crop could sell for as much as $170 per ton in Baltimore and $225 in New York, making distant markets leaders of the industry and tying them to Missouri until western markets matured. However, by the 1840s and 1850s, the market was flooded and prices dropped; by the middle of the 1850s, hemp cultivated in Missouri could only bring about $85 per ton in Saint Louis.[23] As the nineteenth century progressed, hemp cultivation declined rapidly.

In addition to cash crops like tobacco and hemp, slaves in Missouri and Indian Territory cultivated staple crops that provided food for the household or for trade. The most profitable and sustainable form of agriculture was diversified, with a mix of subsistence crops and others for commercial markets. Bill Simms of Osceola, Missouri, stated in his narrative for the Federal Writers' Project that on his farm they "raised cows, sheep, cotton, tobacco, corn, which were our principal crops."[24] Zadock Martin, a slaveholder and founder of Platte County, had at least four fields of corn, including one near his homestead, one near Weston, and another in the Missouri River bottoms.[25] Other enslaved people, like those on the farm of Smallwood Noland in Jackson County, tended to large fruit orchards.[26] Local newspaper advertisements noting farms for sale often described the acreage and improvements and are an interesting source for examining diversified agriculture. For instance, in 1851 Thomas Morton of Clay County listed an advertisement for his 480-acre farm, which consisted of "300 under fence, of which there is 75 in blue grass, 53 in hemp, 20 in clover well set, 20 in timothy and the balance in wheat and corn." The property also included an orchard, wells, a house, outbuildings, and "negro quarters."[27] Some counties in the region focused their efforts on growing corn, wheat, or oats instead of commercial crops. This was most common in Cass, Bates, and Vernon counties, all located south of the larger population centers. Unlike hemp and tobacco, wheat and corn cultivation was less amenable to slave labor, thus these counties contained a smaller slave population than those farther north.[28]

Livestock raising was also common on the border, providing a complement to agricultural pursuits. It became a massive commercial enterprise in the 1840s and beyond. In the early years of American settlement, hogs were particularly important to settlers' welfare; according to R. Douglas Hurt, "swine became their chief cash source for paying mortgages and other frontier debts."[29] Packed pork could be sold locally for around $.02 per pound, and there was enough demand that the *Liberty Tribune* posted a brief note encouraging locals to establish a butchery in Liberty to help the industry.[30] Once steamboats began plying the Missouri River, farmers could also send their hogs to market "on the hoof," packed in barrels, or in the form of smoked meat. In the early 1850s, a farmer might receive between $3.50 and $4.50 per hundredweight for packed pork.[31] Hogs were also essential for the household's well-being, since hogs provided bacon, ham, and lard. Copying the customs of animal husbandry that existed in the South, farmers on the border let their hogs roam wild, keeping track of their drove by using notches or holes cut into each pig's ear. While slaves regularly tended to other livestock as part of their daily routine, hogs required almost no care. Zadock Martin's hogs foraged in the densely overgrown brush along the Missouri River and "his hog-killing was done with dogs and guns."[32] Sometimes these hogs were far too wild to corral, and white farmers worked alongside enslaved men to tramp through the dense woods and hunt down their stock.

In addition to tending the semiferal hogs, slaves on the border were responsible for other livestock, particularly sheep and cattle. Sheep were especially important during the first years of white settlement, since many frontier families depended on wool for their clothing. Unlike hogs, most sheep were kept for household use, not for trade. A. H. F. Payne of Clay County, who owned five slaves in 1840, imported seven hundred Saxony sheep in 1847 to improve his stock.[33] With such a large number, enslaved members of the household undoubtedly worked alongside Payne during sheep-shearing season. Animal husbandry, even on smaller farms where the commercial nature of stock raising was less pronounced, meant enslaved people had to take on additional responsibility for managing the farm landscape.

Enslaved women, particularly those who labored in domestic contexts, were an important part of the slave labor force. As part of their attempt to establish cultural hegemony, as well as the need for household labor, slaveholders encouraged the use of enslaved women and children as domestic servants. Slaveholders on the border generally adhered to gender conventions when assigning tasks to slaves. There are some accounts of women working in fields, but most references to female labor place women firmly in the home. Tildy, who worked for the Samuels family in Clay County, had a variety of responsibilities as housekeeper. According to the reminiscence of John K. Samuels, her white owner, she "cooked the meals on the old cast iron wood stove, and did the laundry by hand on a copper washboard and copper washtubs."[34] At least one of Joseph Parks's female slaves worked as a cook at his home in Indian Territory; in 1848, she was accused of poisoning a small child and "Parks had her sent away at once."[35] Young girls might work within the household as a nurse or playmate. Former slave Margaret Nickens left her home in northeastern Missouri when she was eight years old to serve as a nurse for the two children of Georgia Ann Dawson, who lived in Clay County. Potentially, the white mistress and older female slaves in the household could focus their energies on other tasks, trusting that Margaret would keep young children from being underfoot. Childcare was an age-appropriate task for younger children, who learned their household roles at a very young age.[36] The household was a workplace as much as it was a private space.[37]

For the most part, descriptions of border slavery do not mention enslaved men working as servants, but they do occasionally place young boys in the home. Septimus Scholl, a slaveholder from Kentucky who emigrated to Jackson County in 1844, promised his seven-year-old grandson Edward, who lived in Kentucky and suffered from a chronic bone disease, "a little black boy to wait on him, to gear his horse and drive his carriage."[38] It is likely that Scholl would have sent a young male slave close to Edward's age. No doubt some enslaved men worked within the household, but by and large this work was noted as children's or women's labor, holding to the gendered conventions of the late nineteenth and early twentieth centuries when many such accounts were recorded.

Gendered notions of domestic labor are also apparent in slave hiring advertisements and sale notices that appeared in local newspapers. These often refer to the slave's capabilities or skills in addition to the standard descriptions of their age or physical features. In 1848, a posting from an unknown seller in the *St. Joseph Gazette* offered a twenty-one-year-old woman and her five-month-old baby for sale, explicitly stating that "the woman is a good house servant."[39] A few months later, another article appeared in the same newspaper, this time seeking to hire six men and "a Negro Woman who has no children, and is a good house servant."[40] These advertisements were usually quite short; the person posting the notice believed that these qualifications were worth mentioning, even given the limited space. As Diane Mutti Burke has noted, such gendered divisions of work were more common in regions where small-scale slaveholding predominated, although slaveholders were not opposed to sending women into the fields if the extra set of hands would speed up the harvest.[41]

Although slavery's small-scale nature dictated that enslaved men and male slaveholders had regular contact (absenteeism was uncommon), enslaved women still bore the brunt of the intimacy between white and black. Female slaves had their closest contact with the mistress of the household, who directed and trained them in specific tasks. Depending on labor demands, white women may have worked alongside enslaved women in the kitchen or main house. There were many tasks to be completed, including gardening, canning, and cooking, as well as mending, washing, and cloth production, not to mention childcare. As Bill Simms noted in his later reminiscence, slaves "made our own clothes, had spinning wheels and raised and combed our own cotton, clipped the wool from our sheep's backs, combed and spun it into cotton and wool clothes. We never knew what boughten clothes were."[42] Thavolia Glymph's excellent study of Southern households observed that "the constancy and intimacy of contact between enslaved women and mistresses gave a particular cast to their relations. In the kitchens, bedrooms, and parlors, where mistresses were expected to rule, no parallel division of slave management offered the kinds of buffers masters enjoyed through the employment of overseers."[43] Although small-scale slaveholders rarely employed overseers, her point about intimacy remains true.

Despite the fact that households were generally feminized spaces, however, enslaved women living and working in close quarters with whites also had contact with male slaveholders. Enslaved women were both a labor force and targets for white men's sexual desires, suffering from rape, sexual assault, and other abuses. Of course, slaveholders publicly emphasized that female slave labor mattered most because it eased the workload of white Missouri women, making no reference to their own sexual proclivities. Domestic help allowed small slaveholders to present the image of wealth, improving (or solidifying) their family's social standing, thus providing their household with additional social capital.[44] This was a major contributor to slaveholders' goals of strengthening slavery, because with that social capital came the privileges of a growing border elite.

Although farm and domestic labor were certainly the lot of many slaves, in the 1840s this region also became a center of Western business. Although the Santa Fe Trail had opened in 1821, and businesses in Independence, Westport, and Liberty were already participating in outfitting these freighters, such businesses flourished even more after the Oregon Trail opened in the 1840s and gold was discovered in California in 1848. From 1840 to 1854, approximately 230,000 emigrants embarked on a journey to Oregon, California, or Utah, with the majority leaving from western Missouri.[45] Slaves were often at the center of the booming business of outfitting pack trains, assisting families in their covered wagons, and providing other services for the crowds of men, women, and children who flooded these towns. Trading establishments provided a variety of services, including wagon repairs, horse trading, and general merchandise.[46] Saint Joseph, farther north in Buchanan County, had a busy wharf. Once white settlement in the area increased in the 1840s, it became a natural departure point for the gold fields, thanks to its boosterism in newspapers and a better geographic proximity than Independence.[47] Slaves worked at the docks unloading steamboats, carting goods to the warehouses, or doing other miscellaneous tasks necessary to keep business progressing at a rapid pace.[48] Slave labor also powered other businesses in the region. Sam Shepherd, an enslaved man in the household of Edwin Hickman, worked at the saw and grist mill in Jackson County that Hickman built in 1847. In addition to the mill's daily business, Shepherd conducted "considerable repairs" to improve output.[49] The increasing border population, and the resulting urban growth, made slave labor in businesses crucial to the local economy. Access to these public spaces may have come at the behest of slaveholders, but thanks to prominent roles in business, these enslaved men had contact with many community members, both black and white.

The demand for blacksmiths, wheelwrights, coopers, carpenters, and brick masons also opened up opportunities for some male slaves to acquire specialized skills. According to more than one secondhand account Jim Shepherd, an enslaved man, hewed the logs for the first courthouse in Jackson County.[50] One of the earliest settlers in Independence, Jones Flournoy, was a slaveholder; the enslaved members of his household built a brick home near the town square. According to a local historian, they "excavated for clay to make bricks. The slaves stacked the sun dried bricks and piled wood over them to burn. After the bricks were burned and cooled the slaves constructed a four room brick house with a fireplace in each room."[51] Independence also had an iron foundry where slaves forged items like stoves, kettles, yokes, and agricultural implements.[52] A striking example is that of Hiram Young, a former slave born in Tennessee around 1812. Thanks to his skill in carpentry, he earned extra money that he saved to purchase his wife, Matilda's, freedom. This made their future children free (since a child's slave status followed that of the mother). After purchasing his own independence, Young moved to Liberty in Clay County and then later moved to Independence, where wagons and oxen yokes were in high demand.[53] By the end of 1851, he had opened up his own wagon business with a free African American named Dan Smith. They used hired slave laborers who received wages, and Young gained a reputation as one of the best carpenters in the area.[54] The varied, mobile professions of enslaved and free black men in these transportation hubs signal not only the importance of skilled labor in the region but also demonstrate the ways that enslaved and free black individuals affected the social geography of this borderland.

Many of these business endeavors, as had been the case in the years of fur trade dominance, relied heavily on movement across the border between Missouri and what was then Indian Territory. Close business and personal ties between native tribes who owned slaves—particularly the Shawnee, Wyandot, and Potawatomi—and their Missouri neighbors illustrate the cross-border contact. The Oregon and Santa Fe trails passed through native lands, thus freighters felt compelled to develop healthy relationships with any local tribes who had the power to affect their bottom line. Native people ran ferries across the Kansas River, provided other services (like blacksmithing), and established successful farms that sold corn, wheat, and other foodstuffs to Missouri locals and emigrants.[55] Enslaved people in the territory would have assisted in these endeavors. According to one Kansas City pioneer, the Wyandot "created quite a trade for the new town of Kansas City, and in a few years some of their prominent men opened business," including Joel Walker, whose brother William Walker was a slaveholder.[56] Some natives also established trading posts at key crossroads in Indian Territory, such as Potawatomi stores on the Oregon Trail at Uniontown, near present-day Topeka, which had previously been the site of a Chouteau fur-trading post with the now-displaced Kansa. Uniontown's founders included slaveholding Indian agent Richard Cummins.[57] Uniontown serves as one example of how significant economic exchanges both helped native tribes like the Potawatomi integrate into the border economy and potentially allowed enslaved individuals greater access to the extensive landscape.

Other strategic sites for the slaveholding community on that side of the line, and sites where slaveholders exploited slaves' mobility for their own ends, were the few white businesses operating in the territory. One of the first sutlers at Fort Scott was Hiero T. Wilson, originally from Kentucky, who hired slaves and later purchased human property. Fort Scott was founded in 1842 as part of a network along the Fort Leavenworth–Fort Gibson road intended for frontier defense.[58] As noted earlier, sutlers were civilians who received government contracts to provide supplies that might not be available through the army quartermaster. They generally carried a diverse inventory that served the needs of both military personnel and locals; in this case, those locals included white missionaries, Indian agents, and native peoples. Sutlers sold goods from back East that were desperately needed out West, and thus Wilson controlled the flow of goods into this region. The Fort Scott post's store may have been staffed by enslaved labor. According to Wilson's daybooks, he hired a slave named Louis in November 1844 at the rate of seven dollars per month, and less than a year later he hired a woman named Nancy at six dollars per month from Lieutenant R. E. Cochran.[59] At some point he probably acquired slaves of his own, as the first census of Kansas Territory showed seven enslaved members of his household.[60] No direct information remains from enslaved people who lived at this bustling fort. Still, with a relatively small permanent population, and a constant circulation of visitors like Indian agents, Native Americans, and travelers, enslaved people likely had some access to public space that might have been less common on self-contained plantations. This was still a world where mobility, regardless of ethnicity or legal status, was central.

While the commercialization of agriculture and business pursuits shaped and strengthened border slavery, slaveholders also used their privileged status in the community to build strong connections to national markets, including the interstate slave trade. Without the slave trade, slavery on the border would have declined, and there would have been wider economic implications as well; as Adam Rothman has noted, enslaved people were viewed in monetary terms and thus existed "as both the principal source of labor and the principal source of capital available to slaveowners in the American South."[61] This was particularly significant for western communities that often suffered from a shortage of capital, with whites benefiting in myriad ways from better commercial connections. Of course, a local slave trade also existed on the border, although on a smaller scale than in cities like New Orleans or Saint Louis (the closest large market). Both the local market and this broader market in slave trading were mechanisms for the slaveholding population to grow and maintain their workforce, increase their wealth, and ensure white supremacy.

Slave markets also illustrate how enslaved people involuntarily experienced movement across the landscape. According to Michael Tadman's calculations, somewhere between 60 to 70 percent of slave movements came from the interregional slave trade.[62] This trade disrupted slave communities, shuffled the enslaved population across state boundaries, and introduced bonded labor into new regions, serving as a central component of the South's westward expansion. The story of slave mobility in this case was one where that mobility was the result of forces beyond a slave's personal control; there were opportunities for resistance, to be sure, but this was an involuntary migration. The internal slave trade that connected eastern states like Virginia and western states like Missouri provides one example of how the enslaved population was subject to slaveholders' whims and had little control over their own movement.

One of the cruelest aspects of slavery was the insistence that slaves were commodities, in what Walter Johnson has referred to as "the chattel principle": the belief that a human being could, because of their legal identity, be evaluated according to the same terms as one would evaluate livestock. Slaves had a simultaneously dual nature as human and as property.[63] Under this principle, an enslaved person's monetary worth was determined by his or her fitness for work, skill set, physical strength, age, and sex. Slave reminiscences, newspaper advertisements, and slaveholders' financial records all recorded the monetary value of these human beings. Historians too have tracked this human capital. Historian Harrison Trexler has concluded that there was a rise in slave prices in Missouri during this period before the Civil War, which rings true based on national statistics and on anecdotal evidence.[64] Understanding slave prices illuminates the central role slavery played in local economies and why slaveowners were so loathe to end slavery and transition to free labor. For modern eyes, it also codifies the dehumanizing nature of enslavement.

Some probate records, like Richard Fristoe's, provide points of reference for how this chattel principle appeared in practice. Fristoe, a native of Tennessee, died in 1845. The first inventory of his estate, most likely conducted in that same year, lists eight slaves according to gender, name, and value. Eleven enslaved individuals appear in an 1849

Table 2. Enslaved Property Values in Richard Fristoe's Probate
Inventories, 1845–1849

Name	Sex	Age in 1845	Value in 1845	Age in 1849	Value in 1849
Cordelia/ Dealey	F	7	$200	11	$250
Elizabeth	F	—	—	3	$150
Ellen	F	15	$500 (w/child)	19	$500
Henry	M	—	—	5	$175
Isora	F	—	—	2	$125
Jacob	M	43	$350	47	$400
Juley	F	—	$25 ("not sound")	—	—
Julian	M	—	—	9	$200
Lewis	M	—	—	3	$175
Martha	F	19	$500 (w/child)	23	$500
Peter	M	—	$500	—	—
Priscilla/ Percella	F	37	$250 (w/child)	41	$200
Susan	F	3	$150	7	$200

Joanne Chiles Eakin, ed., "Richard Fristoe: Administration of His Estate in 1848,"
Kansas City Genealogist 39, no. 1 (Summer 1998): 22.

inventory. Each of the three older women was listed jointly with a child in
1845. It is likely that these children were too young to be separated from
their mothers. If this is the case, in at least this instance, Fristoe and his
administrators sought to keep family groups together. Given the paternalistic language that often appeared in slaveholders' correspondence, some
slaveholders—perhaps unconsciously, perhaps consciously—recognized
this dual nature of slavery by acknowledging parent-child relationships
even as they treated enslaved people as commercial objects.[65]

Other notes filed alongside the Fristoe inventories further reveal this
duality. Nancy Campbell, one of Fristoe's children and an heir, received
Ellen and Lewis; although the note is undated, Ellen would have been
in her late teens and Lewis was a toddler. Mary A. Tally, another of
Fristoe's daughters and heirs, received Martha (in her early twenties),

Susan (about seven years old), and possibly other slaves (the note's punctuation makes it difficult to interpret). Both of these appear to be family groupings, once again implying that Fristoe's administrators preserved the black nuclear family to at least some degree.[66] This does not, of course, imply that the harsh realities of life as a slave could be entirely mitigated, but it does illustrate that the slave-owner relationship was a complicated (and nuanced) one. These individuals were both property and people.

There were various financial reasons behind an administrator's or slaveholder's decision to sell slave property, but all of these had the same result for the enslaved individual: separation from one's familiar surroundings and the slave community (varying to some degree based on the specifics of the sale). A common justification for slaves' sale was to divide the assets of a deceased slaveowner's estate. Often wills dictated how slave property should be distributed, or the court or administrators tended to that themselves, but in other instances enslaved men, women, and children faced the auction block instead of being divided among the deceased's heirs. In 1852, Permelia Jackson and her guardian informed her siblings that four of their father's slaves—Bets, Sean, William, and Frances—would be sold "for the purpose of distribution amongst us."[67] With seven heirs and four slaves, there was no other means for an equal division, making it necessary for the "proceeds of said sale be divided amongst your petitioner [Permelia] and the said other children."[68] The slaves' reactions to this impending sale are not known, but one can surmise that they were distraught at the prospect. After Septimus Scholl's death on August 11, 1849, his slaves found themselves at the mercy of the courts and Septimus's heirs. Several, including a child, were sold. Three slaves were hired out until the estate could be finalized. A woman named Harriet went to Septimus's widow for the cost of twenty-five dollars.[69] A slaveowner's death was a common reason for selling enslaved property, not only because the slaveholder's will or administrator dictated such a sale in order to distribute assets more easily, but also because the deceased sometimes left debts that needed to be repaid.

Slaves also found themselves on the auction block for other reasons. Bill Simms, from Osceola, near Bates County, stated in a reminiscence that if a slaveholder "got hard up for money, he would advertise and sell some slaves, like my oldest sister was sold on the block with her children."[70] Since slaves functioned as a major source of capital, such financial motives were quite common. On occasion slaves faced an impending sale after a court ruling. On December 1, 1847, the sheriff of Buchanan

County put up for sale "one NEGRO GIRL named MARTHA, a slave for life," to be sold on the courthouse steps in Saint Joseph.[71] The circumstances surrounding her sale are unknown; since the decree came from the Circuit Court of Chancery, which handled lawsuits (among other things), it is possible that her sale came about as a way to resolve a business or family dispute that could not be settled in regular court. Regardless, Martha's fate lay in the hands of her white owner.[72] Other enslaved people were sold because they resisted their owner or attempted to escape. Henderson Davenport of Platte County was sold multiple times; his last sale reportedly occurred because "he got rather disobedient." He remained, however, in the border region and was able to maintain family relationships and an abroad marriage to Lucy Dearing, who had lived across the street from him when he lived in Parkville.[73] Although slaves sometimes manipulated the system, the slave trade made little room for acts of resistance, particularly in situations where the legal system was involved.

Enslaved women and their infants were usually sold together, a practice that was also common elsewhere in Little Dixie. Slave traders and slaveholders were nothing if not practical; until a child could be weaned, there would be no point in separating him or her from the mother. In Saint Joseph, George Grimes's estate administrator offered a thirty-four-year-old female slave and her seven-month-old baby "to be sold together," but "a Likely Boy 11 years old, and a Girl 8 years old" went up for sale at the same time, with no apparent stipulation that they be kept together. The historical record sheds little light on the situation, but the 1840 census shows that George Grimes owned six slaves, and the age distribution shows that the only woman of childbearing age in 1840 (seven years before this sale) was between the ages of twenty-four and thirty-six. There is no way to be sure that all the children listed on the census (three boys and one girl) were this woman's offspring, but it is a possibility. The implication being, of course, that while this woman and her nursing infant remained together, she was separated from two of her other children.[74] Slave sale advertisements that listed both women and infants (with their ages) did not always explicitly state that the mother and child would be sold together, perhaps because stating the slaves' ages made such a caveat unnecessary.[75]

Slave traders and those who purchased slaves rarely paid attention to family groupings, so it was not uncommon for older children to be torn from loved ones or mothers to be sold away from their children. Former slave Jerry Myers's reminiscence, recorded in 1940, called to mind "the day his spirited mother was sold to a half-breed from Wyandotte" (in Indian Territory).[76] The reasons for her sale are unknown, although his description of her as "spirited"—which implies she resisted her owner's will—may hint at a possible explanation. A slave who showed spirit had the potential to stir up dissent within the enslaved community. As Myers learned firsthand, the separation of parents and children was common. Matthew Salafia noted in his study of slavery in the Ohio River valley that "in the upper South approximately one of three slave children suffered separation from their families through sale."[77] The close contact between slaves and slaveholders, common in small-scale systems, did not necessarily translate to an increased concern for the makeup of slave families.

Each of these instances involved the local slave trade on the micro level, but the interstate slave trade also existed on the border, linking western Missouri and Indian Territory to Saint Louis and New Orleans markets. Slave traders from Saint Louis, such as Corbin Thompson, posted advertisements in newspapers throughout the state, including the *Western Journal of Commerce* printed in Kansas City. Others kept their main offices in towns like Saint Joseph, where the firm Wright and Carter used a building on Second Street. Thompson McDaniel was headquartered in Independence, and G. P. Dorriss worked out of Platte City.[78] John Doy, a free-state settler who spent time in a Platte County jail in 1859, also mentioned another trading firm in Weston, called White, Williams, and Co.[79] These traders acquired human property from a variety of sources, ranging from estate sales to private transactions. Sometimes slave traders captured fugitives and, if never claimed, these slaves entered a holding cell in the slave trader's auction house or local jail until their sale. This situation was convenient for the slave trader, but these men and women often endured intolerable living conditions and violence during their incarceration. Samuel Ralston, a slaveholder in Jackson County, recalled in a letter that "the Negroes that ran away last fall have all been taken, and their owners have sent them to N. Orleans, this will deter others from a similar movement."[80] Slave traders on the border maintained business connections with firms in New Orleans and Saint Louis, which had a booming trade in human beings during the antebellum period as the largest slave market in Missouri.

In addition to selling local slaves "down south," slave traders brought slaves from other Southern states to Missouri. In 1849, G. P. Dorriss, a slave trader in Platte City, advertised the sale of twenty-five young men and women between the ages of twelve and twenty years old, who "have just arrived from Old Virginia, under the best discipline, bought with care, sound and healthy, and titles good."[81] The regular importation of slaves reinforced, for slaveholders, that the system was here to stay. One can only guess at the heart-rending stories behind each of these sales; each individual had been separated from family or other loved ones before coming to an unfamiliar part of the country, on the edge of American settlement, which was surely an experience fraught with uncertainty, fear, and loneliness. These men, women, and children physically embodied the border elites' dedication to building a slave society out west, thus altering the physical landscape (through their labor in fields, businesses, and households) as well as the social geography that privileged white slaveholders' power. For those who experienced the horrors of this Second Middle Passage, they were an unwillingly mobile class.

This chattel principle is also evident in the business of slave hiring, which was integral to small-scale systems like that in Little Dixie. Slave hiring was significant because it aided the slaveholding elite's attempts to strengthen the institution while also leading to increased mobility for bondspeople.[82] Slave hiring allowed greater flexibility because settlers who could not afford to purchase slaves had an opportunity to temporarily enter the slaveholding class and gain access to the benefits of slave labor.[83] This forged a clear connection between the use of slave labor and wealth; it also showed how slaveholders could set limits on the availability of labor by controlling the hiring market. Conversely, it provided opportunities for enslaved people to move throughout the border landscape. "Dual mastery," as Diane Mutti Burke observed, "worked to the advantage of some slaves as they negotiated their relationships with hirers."[84] The hirer-slave relationship, then, did not entirely mirror that of the owner-slave relationship. Slave hiring was so prevalent that the chances of being hired out were three to five times greater than the chance of being sold, and in Missouri, the hiring of both men and women occurred with some regularity throughout the antebellum period.[85]

For those in the white community, there were several advantages to slave hiring. Both slaveowners and nonslaveowners rented slave labor to increase efficiency on the farm or in their business, especially during peak times like the harvest. The existence and popularity of slave hiring in this region makes clear that renting out one's slave yielded clear economic benefits for the slaveowner, and for the nonslaveholders who gained temporary access to this labor, becoming a slave's master (albeit briefly) could bring some of the comforts of life in the eastern United States out to the frontier. One advantage of hiring out one's slaves—as opposed to selling a slave—was that if a slaveowner went into debt and needed additional income, renting out slave labor could be the difference between financial solvency and bankruptcy. It was also relatively common after a slaveowner's death for the estate's administrator or the widow to hire out slaves in order to pay the family's debts. Samuel Reed of Bates County stated in his will that he wanted "the earnings" of Tamar, a female slave, divided among his widow and heirs, and that five years after his death Tamar be freed.[86] In such situations, slave mobility worked to benefit slaveholders' bottom line, and more broadly, to assist in the entire white community's financial solvency.

In a typical slave hiring contract—many of which were drawn up informally on a scrap of paper—the individual who received that slave's labor was only a temporary master and was generally responsible for the hired slave's food, clothing, lodging, and medical bills. Often the term of hire was a full calendar year, starting on New Year's Day, but for farmers who only needed extra hands during the harvest season the term might be only a few months. As was the case with slave sales, hiring prices depended on the slave's gender, age, health, and ability to perform manual labor. For example, a healthy enslaved man in Missouri might be hired out for anywhere between $75 to $125 (for a full-year term). Women usually hired out for a lower rate, due to factors such as their maternal obligations. In Boone County, in central Missouri, the typical rate of hire for men was between one-seventh and one-eighth of their total value, while the hiring price for female slaves averaged about one-sixteenth of their value.[87] The ratio in border counties was likely similar. Regardless, women were hired out regularly if one goes by advertisements and other sources from this period.

Slaves found themselves hired out in a variety of situations. Enslaved men who worked as carpenters, blacksmiths, brickmasons, or in some other artisan trade had a particular skill set that was often in high demand. As noted earlier, the first courthouse in Jackson County was built out of logs hewed by an enslaved man named Jim Shepherd, who had been hired out to the courthouse's contractor, Daniel Lewis.[88] Shepherd was well known throughout the area for his talents, and in fact this courthouse remains standing today. Slaveholders also hired out female slaves. In 1848, a schoolteacher at the Shawnee Indian Manual Labor School in Indian Territory, Ann Archbold, described her students and her living arrangements in a letter. She stated "I never had better accommodation anywhere. My washing is done in the best style by a black girl hired on purpose to wash for the Teachers and Preachers of the Institution."[89] Hiring female domestics was relatively common, as evidenced by the number of hiring advertisements in local newspapers. In 1848, a posting appeared in the *St. Joseph Gazette*, seeking to hire six men and "a Negro Woman who has no children, and is a good house servant."[90] Hiring an enslaved woman for domestic purposes could introduce nonslaveholding whites to slave labor, since domestic servants' labor aided in the household's maintenance and also brought status to the white family by demonstrating their financial success.

Although the hiring market benefited the white community, whether slaveholders or nonslaveholders, hiring arrangements also provided opportunities for enslaved people to move throughout the border landscape. Ann Davis Shatteo's reminiscence, recorded in 1875, proves an excellent example. Ann Davis was born free in Illinois but was kidnapped as a child. Her kidnapper, Green Crisp, had a difficult time selling her since he could not produce the necessary papers proving ownership. As a young girl and teenager, she was hired out to a Mr. Fuller at the Harmony Mission in Bates County, established in 1825. While there, she bore three children of unknown paternity who were taken away to Texas. These offspring may have been the product of sexual abuse or an illicit relationship with a white man, since the enslaved population in the county remained quite small and she did not mention an abroad marriage in her reminiscence.[91] Crisp apparently "disposed of her conditionally" to George Douglas of Bates County, where she stayed for seven years, but she ended up with Crisp again, after repeated attempts to use the legal system to gain her lawful freedom. Green Crisp then turned her over to John Crisp.

Sometime in the early 1840s, Ann Crisp, as she was then known, crossed the border and entered the household of Hiero Wilson, the sutler at Fort Scott in Indian Territory, where she was allowed to keep some earnings and work toward purchasing her freedom. Hiring out one's own time occurred with less frequency than traditional hiring arrangements, but this situation provided enslaved laborers with opportunities to earn money and to control their own mobility by dictating their daily schedules and sometimes moving into another household. Within a short time, she began working for Samuel Lewis, a trader who operated a post on the Neosho River, not far from the Catholic Osage Mission in modern-day Neosho County, Kansas. Shatteo most likely worked in the trading post and at home. Although gendered divisions of labor generally allowed men more access to public spaces, while women remained in the household, the small-scale nature of slaveholding and social geography of this borderland likely meant she was regularly amid the hustle and bustle of mission business.

Shortly thereafter, Shatteo went with Lewis to Uniontown, a new trading post on the Kansas River, when the Potawatomi moved to their new reservation near both their Catholic mission and the Oregon Trail. Here Shatteo, and two children born in the interim, would eventually acquire their freedom in 1849. While in Uniontown, she also married Frenchman Claymore Chattilon (or Shatteo), who was a former employee of the American Fur Company.[92] After her manumission, Shatteo ran a boarding house and restaurant to feed the many emigrants passing on the Oregon Trail. When Uniontown fell into disuse, she moved to the outskirts of Topeka and purchased a tract of one hundred acres, where she was residing at the time she shared this reminiscence. Her ability to regulate her own movements and choose her own employers, combined with her residence at key geographic locations in Indian Territory and western Missouri, epitomize the ways in which hiring could affect the contours of this borderland.

For those who were enslaved, sometimes the increased mobility that came with the slave-hiring system had far-reaching benefits on a personal level. Jackson Dempson was sold at auction in Plum Creek, Missouri, to Thomas Johnson, the head missionary at the Shawnee mission and manual labor school in Indian Territory. After Dempson joined the Johnson household, he hired himself out to work as a cook on various Missouri River steamboats. This allowed Dempson an extraordinary degree of movement across the border landscape and provided opportunities for him to travel outside his own community. According to Thomas Johnson's son Alexander, who was also a slaveholder, this easy mobility allowed Dempson to find a wife who was enslaved on a farm in Howard County, Missouri, near the center of the state.[93] Dempson later settled at the mission with his wife. Slave hiring could foster opportunities to travel and form relationships with individuals who might not normally be accessible, in this case a pleasant side effect of knowing the region's social geography.

Slave hiring could have advantages for bondspeople, but such arrangements could not circumvent all of slaveowners' attempts to control public and private spaces. The border elite shaped the legal system and used other authoritarian mechanisms to maintain white supremacy, because doing so both regulated the enslaved population and ensured slavery's continued existence. Slavery's initial legality drew from the terms of the Louisiana Purchase, which protected inhabitants' property, including slaves.[94]

Missouri's General Assembly, Supreme Court, and state constitution all supported a racial hierarchy that privileged whites. The legal system in Missouri was an apparatus designed to support property rights (including the right to own human property), protect the white population from insurrection, and ensure the implementation of justice. The Missouri state slave code, which was based largely on the Virginia and Kentucky codes, recognized slaves as both persons with certain legal rights and as property.[95] Those legal rights were limited, but they included the right to sue for one's freedom if held illegally (as argued in the famous case of Dred and Harriet Scott) and to have a trial by jury (though not a jury of one's peers). Furthermore, unlike other slave states, Missouri offered some protections for slaves convicted of a crime, such as the guarantee of an attorney.[96] Still, slaves could not testify in court against a white person, raise their hand against a white person even in self-defense, hold property without their owner's consent, congregate together, or obtain a marriage license. As the nineteenth century progressed, new statutes and legislation prohibited the sale of alcohol to slaves (1835), the emigration of free blacks into the state (1835), and the education of slaves (1847), among other restrictions. Slave codes hinged in many cases on whether or not enslaved people had access to public spaces or amenities. Municipalities and counties were also allowed to establish slave patrols to curtail escapes and limit slave mobility, with more attention being paid to this as the century progressed.[97] The punishments for violating these codes might come through extralegal channels, such as private punishment on the farm or plantation, or lynching, but other crimes did enter the court system. Slaves who committed a serious crime—such as murder or rape—and were put on trial faced stiff penalties if convicted.

Since slaveholders dominated the judicial system and municipal governments, white communities on the border also passed their own local ordinances. These maintained white authority and limited slave mobility, in addition to enforcing state slave codes. In 1844, slaveholder Samuel Ralston noted that his community in Jackson County had established a patrol, even at this early date noting that "in consequence of our border location" slaveholders feared for their property.[98] By the early 1850s, the Liberty Tribune's published list of county expenditures stated the costs of patrols. In May of 1850, John Morris received $8.50 "for services as patrol of Liberty," and in August of 1851, Gabriel Cathcart, William W. Woods, and Thomas McQuiddy each received $12.50 for patrolling Liberty Township and Gallatin Township, respectively.[99] According to one early county history, a patrol existed prior to 1850 in an informal capacity.[100]

Although few references to slave patrols have survived, their existence demonstrates the white community's desire to curb the mobility of the black population and maintain white control over public spaces.

In addition to contact with slave patrols, some enslaved residents of the border had contact with the judicial system at various levels. In 1848, a slave named Anderson and another enslaved man had a falling out in Liberty, and, possibly while intoxicated, Anderson killed the other in a fit of passion. Anderson was apprehended and put before the circuit court in Clay County where he pled guilty, and he was convicted and sentenced to suffer thirty-nine lashes before being exiled from the state for a period of twenty years.[101] This incident illustrates the judicial system's attention to black-on-black crime, not because of any true concern for black lives but because troubling cases like this could potentially affect the white community and hurt slaveholders' bottom line, since murdering a slave deprived an owner of their property. In fact, in this case, the owner of the deceased slave sued the perpetrator's owner, John D. Ewing, for damages and won the case. Later, in 1850, the Missouri Supreme Court ruled that owners would not bear responsibility for criminal deeds committed by their enslaved property.[102]

Other slaves were accused of crimes against whites. Frank, an enslaved man living in Clay County, was indicted for rape in 1847. Although the records are spotty, he pled not guilty. Even though a woman named Jane Belcher was called as a witness (perhaps the victim herself), the jury could not agree and the circuit court attorney chose not to prosecute the case any further.[103] The reasons for this decision are unclear, but it is possible that there were inconsistencies in witness testimony or an overall lack of evidence. Similar crimes (both alleged and proven) occurred at other times and in other border counties, but as Harriet Frazier has noted, many offenses were not brought before a court. This might be for one of several reasons, including financial disincentives. Since the accused slave's owner was required to pay all court costs if the slave were convicted, such situations might have been handled by other means. In cases of rape, the court's punishment was sometimes castration, which would decrease a slave's resale value.[104] Whether convicted, sold, or punished in other ways, enslaved men who were accused of committing a crime, especially the rape of a white woman, felt the weight of the law.

Civil cases also entered the court system, including a case in Platte County where a store clerk named Baker illegally sold alcohol to Willis, a slave of Sarah Hughes.[105] One crisp winter day in 1849, Willis took some grain to the local mill and adjacent store. While waiting for the grain to be ground, he purchased a quart of whiskey and spent time chatting with some white employees, eventually becoming quite intoxicated. He left the mill at dusk and apparently wandered along the path for a short spell, since the next morning he was found facedown in the road, stiff and nearly frozen to death. Sadly, the damage to his body was severe, and he survived only a few more days. Hughes sued the clerk and the owners of the store, Skinner and Shepherd, for damages, yet another example of the chattel principle in action.[106] It was apparently known about the community that Baker often failed to obtain owners' consent prior to sale, which was illegal according to an 1845 statute. Hughes won the case and was awarded Willis's monetary value of $900. The storeowners appealed, and the case went to the Supreme Court of Missouri in 1850, which upheld the lower court's ruling. They argued that "we regard the death of the slave as the natural consequence of the act of the defendants in providing him with the means of intoxication." It also likened liquor sales to slaves as similar to "placing noxious food within the reach of domestic animals," a disturbingly offensive reference to our modern ears.[107]

There are several interesting components to this story. The fact that Willis was able to run errands independently and to manage his own time speaks to the general mobility of the enslaved community, their access to public spaces, and the apparent trust Sarah Hughes placed in him individually. That he enjoyed this pint of whiskey with white companions implies that socializing between white laborers and slaves was a natural occurrence, as none of this court summary suggests such behavior was out of the ordinary (and the store clerk sold liquor to slaves on many occasions). The leisurely nature of these black-white interactions, while signaling Platte County slaveholders' open attitude toward racial mixing among the lower classes, is contrasted with the Missouri Supreme Court's perspective. These justices were concerned about the sale of liquor not solely because it violated state law but also because it threatened the lives of slaves, legally considered property. Their statement that this was no different than placing spoiled food in a pig trough or cow pasture outlines in stark relief their denial of slaves' humanity, placing responsibility in the hands of whites and rejecting enslaved people's agency. Likewise, Sarah Hughes, who filed suit in the first place, looked for culpability and compensation where she could, from her white neighbors; although, unlike the Supreme Court, her motivations seemed to be financial rather than ideological. Her gender and presumed status as a widow likely made her even more invested in recompense. Willis's death and the ensuing court actions illustrate how slaveholders shaped the legal system to meet their own ends. Moreover, it shows how enslaved men and women pushed back against statutes and laws by traveling without white supervision and enjoying alcohol from time to time, a freedom that might have gone unnoticed under different, less fatal, circumstances.

While enslaved people chaffed at slaveowners' control of public and private spaces, they nevertheless built an active black community which served as a staging ground for resistance. Of course, their interactions with other African Americans might have been hampered as a result of both small-scale slaveholding (which led to more isolation from other slaves and more contact with whites) and sparse settlement patterns that prevailed during the antebellum period. But slave neighborhoods did exist. Evidence of neighborhood boundaries can be seen in pension case files for black veterans of the Civil War, with affiants who often belonged to the former soldier's neighborhood attesting to the nature of the soldier's prewar marital relationships, character, employment status, and disability. In these affidavits, both white and black neighbors (including former owners) described the close emotional and physical connections among enslaved people. For instance, in Roy Davis's pension application, which included a number of affiants from eastern Jackson County who had remained in the area since emancipation, the enslaved people on the farms of Daniel Cushenberry and William Chiles "were very intimate."[108] In a different pension case, George Norman testified that despite the fact they belonged to different owners, he and his brother Ed Cockerell lived "in the same neighborhood" and saw each other once a week.[109] According to historian Anthony Kaye, "every neighborhood was a place of kinship as well as discipline, of both work and amusement, of collaboration and strife, of spiritual sojournings and brutal exploitation, of loves and hatreds, of contempt and fellowship, of admiration and indifference, each in myriad forms."[110] Although few direct sources exist to delineate these communities' boundaries, it is clear that here, as elsewhere, communal bonds saw slaves through the trials of separation from family, childbirth, and the arduousness of everyday life. Slave communities were significant to both the physical and social boundaries of this western society.

On larger farms or plantations, or in urban areas, enslaved people sometimes lived apart from their owner with some degree of independence, an important component to building a separate sense of identity, creating community, and allowing for subversive actions. In Jackson County, Jabez Smith, who at his death owned multiple farms spanning 3,470 acres and 311 slaves, had slave cabins built on each farm, and his probate inventory grouped enslaved property by farm and also family group, signifying that his heirs and perhaps the local community understood the boundaries (both familial and physical) that formed in the neighborhood.[111] As the largest slaveholder on the border, he did not fit the normal small-scale paradigm. His main farm in Independence also had a large grouping of slave cabins known locally as "Nigger Hill."[112] Zadock Martin, in Platte County, reportedly had "shed-rooms" added onto his log house, which could have served as slaves' housing during their first few years on the border. However, at some point he did order the construction of slave "cabins scattered around on his lands."[113] This phrasing implies that there was some physical distance between Martin's home and those of his enslaved workers. Judging from photographs of surviving slave quarters elsewhere in Missouri, it is likely that these cabins were of varying quality, but they nevertheless allowed for separation from prying white eyes.

Community formation was not a given, however. As many historians have argued, slaves in Missouri were often in closer contact with the white family, thanks to the nature of small-scale slavery. According to Eugene Genovese, "the argument for the greater humanity of the small slaveholders turned, to a great extent, on the fact of greater intimacy, of rough camaraderie, and of mutual sympathy born in common quarters"; this had adverse effects, however, and did not mitigate the system's horrors.[114] When the entire household unit only had one house, slaves lived inside the house alongside the white family, which could limit opportunities for building an autonomous community. This was especially true for house servants, who were expected to be at their owner's beck and call, even at odd hours of the night. According to Howard Marshall's study of Little Dixie architecture, domestic slaves often lived in the main house, usually in an attic space or in a loft above the kitchen.[115] Some slaveholders may have expressed greater compassion after being so intimately connected to their slaves, but close quarters often caused additional problems for bondspeople. Diane Mutti Burke's research points out that this close physical proximity had the potential to foster additional abuse (especially that of a sexual nature), since slaves in these situations had little to no privacy.[116] Overall, the relationship to the white slaveholder in many ways determined the quality of life for Missouri's slaves, as evidenced by the vagaries of individual experiences. While the small-scale slaveholding paradigm had the potential to expand bondspeople's physical and social reach, it could also limit the building of a cohesive slave community necessary for support and protection.

As with most sources on slavery, those addressing slaves' community and family lives are tantalizingly brief, and many of these are filtered through a white lens. Yet, there are some elements of this slave community that can be pulled to the foreground. One example is marriage and courtship. Abroad marriages—unions where the man and woman lived on different farms—were a common feature of slave life on the border. In her analysis of WPA narratives and Civil War pension records, Diane Mutti Burke found that "a full 57 percent of Missouri slave marriages were between men and women who lived on different holdings," a statistic that was likely reflected on the western border as well.[117] This trend was a side effect of small-scale slaveholding, since men and women would likely need to look past their home to find a suitable partner. Maria and Jack Seals lived in separate households—Jack near Platte City and Maria in Liberty. They had been married in slavery by a white Baptist minister named Benjamin Riley, a relative of Maria's owner, and then became legally married after the war.[118] Louisa Bowler's parents also lived separately in Clay County, but as was typical in the region, their owners permitted them to see each other and to consider themselves husband and wife.[119] Enslaved men and women, regardless of their physical proximity to each other, found and maintained contact with their spouse in at least limited ways.

Civil War pension file affidavits are one source for discerning how these enslaved men and women viewed marriage and also how pension examiners and white communities in the postwar years described these unions. Deponents and claimants generally referred to marriages prior to emancipation as "slave marriages" to distinguish them from legal marriages that occurred during or after the Civil War. Both the neighborhood and local custom recognized such unions, seeing the enslaved couple as man and wife even if marriage was illegal. Most were conducted in front of a minister, sometimes an African American. Since proven marital status was necessary to receive a widow's pension, widows' application files often include rich details explaining these relationships. Henderson Davenport and Lucy Dearing, both of Platte County, lived "across the lane" from each other in Parkville, and after their marriage they continued to reside separately, since they had different owners. The short walk of a few hundred yards was no inconvenience, and as the only slave in the Dearing household, Lucy lacked a private cabin. However, after Henderson was sold to George Crowbarger, who owned a farm twelve miles away, their marriage became strained. On at least one occasion, Lucy (who took the last name Crowbarger) was allowed to take a horse and visit her husband for the weekend, after rumors circulated that he had "taken up" with another woman. When questioned about her attitude toward marriage, she told the pension examiner that "as long as he lived I considered him mine." Despite her fidelity, the examiner wrote in his summary statement that slave marriage "was always a loose bond."[120] This bond was difficult to maintain, as many spouses discovered. All in all, abroad marriages illustrate the challenges of maintaining contact with loved ones, the ways in which these unions broadened slaves' access to movement, and also how despite the lack of legal underpinning, such marriages were binding in slaves' eyes, though not perhaps in those of pension examiners.[121]

Although less is known about the more intimate details of slave marriages and courtships, other primary sources at least partially uncover this story. Sometime in the early twentieth century, Robert Withers, whose grandfather Abijah Withers had been a slaveholder in Clay County, Missouri, shared some of his family tales about the local slave population with a newspaper reporter. According to Withers's family lore, an enslaved man in the household, George, "was terribly smitten with a girl in town and as soon as he got his supper nearly every night he would hit the path to go see her."[122] This was a complicated situation because another slave, Ned, was also interested in this woman (her name is unknown). Ned belonged to Dr. W. T. Wood, a man well known within the community who mentored young doctors and in the course of his medical career had acquired a human skeleton. One morning, after the other slaves began the day's work, George came out to the fields and spoke with his owner, Abijah. According to George, "Dat no account niggah Dr. Wood's Ned waited 'til I had gone to town last night and den he tuck and hung dat skelpin on a limb of a tree right ovah de path. Ah started home in plenty of time to git da but when ah seed date skelpin ah jess natcheley had to go outn mah way a little to get around het."[123]

While the details of this story were surely embellished for the white reader's amusement, this account does raise interesting questions. Clearly Robert Withers's acceptance of racial stereotypes makes this incident out to be an example of how slaves were uneducated, superstitious, and irresponsible. Like other reminiscences of this period, Withers begins his account by stating that Missouri slaveholders were always benevolent, and that even when his grandfather was "a little rough," these slaves "recognized his justice and they all loved him."[124] Both slaveholders and their descendants often argued that slavery was a benign institution, or at least, that some slaveowners treated their slaves well. It is also noteworthy that Withers's story ends there, with no mention of George's punishment or lack thereof.

The true particulars may be beyond our reach, but under the surface several stories are at play. It is clear that George was having some sort of relationship with this woman, although the nature of that relationship is unknown. Not only do we know nothing of her perspective, but the entire account was filtered through a white lens, making it that much more difficult to parse. The frequency of George's visits ("nearly every night") implies strongly that he was committed to the relationship; Withers's account leads us to believe that these two people were not married, but it is certainly possible that they did indeed view each other as husband and wife. George's frequent visits may also point to the woman's interest in pursuing the relationship, since she could have discouraged his affections if it were only a casual friendship. Of course, it could also be true that he did not visit her on each trip and instead used that free time for other pursuits, making her his cover if anyone inquired about his whereabouts. It is clear that the relationship was apparently public, and this love triangle was no secret within the local community, white or black. The fact that Abijah Withers knew part of this back story—and passed it down to his children and grandchildren—points to the fact that white slaveowners had at least limited knowledge of slaves' romantic relationships. Since Ned was also aware of George's feelings, to at least some degree, it is likely that the black community in town and in the country had an active communication system.[125]

Another intriguing element of this story is that it provides a glimpse of the relationship between slaveowners and the enslaved. There was a give-and-take relationship between George and Abijah Withers, at least in Robert Withers's retelling. As long as the field hands were ready to work each morning, their free time was their own. This meshes well with what historians know about slavery in Little Dixie, where abroad marriages were the norm, so it is certainly possible that there was an element of negotiation, an implicit understanding that governed the owner-slave relationship. So did the central motif in this story—Ned's attempt to scare George with the skeleton—really occur? That is anyone's guess. If nothing else, this story gave George an excuse for coming to work late that morning, an excuse that apparently seemed plausible to Abijah Withers. While this story provides more questions than answers, it nevertheless hints at the workings of courtship in the slave community. Robert Withers intended for the story to be a humorous diversion for the white readers of the newspaper, when in actuality it is a testament to slaves' ingenuity, as they cleverly played into racial stereotypes to reach their own purposes. It also demonstrates the mobility within the local community and the tacit understanding among whites that enslaved people would use the landscape in their own ways and with their own motivations.

Slave communities, such as that which allowed for courtship, also served as meeting places for religious and social gatherings. A powerful force in these neighborhoods was the church. Although slaves spent most of their waking hours at work, for some slaves there were also opportunities for religious instruction. In frontier settlements, most churches began as home gatherings. If a slaveowner supported slaves' Christian education and opened up their home for the service, then the slaves within that household would most likely have been included (at least to some degree). The largest mission in Indian Territory, and a central site of slaveholding power in the region, was the Shawnee Methodist Mission, where missionary Thomas Johnson's family held slaves. At this lively mission there were frequent Sabbath services, with the native schoolchildren, some of their parents, and some slaves in attendance.[126] In 1843, there were at least ten black children listed as members of the mission. By 1848, there were at least three black members of the church, with that number remaining steady into the 1850s.[127] It is not clear who these people were—or if this number is accurate—but based on the Methodists' desire to convert unbelievers, it is likely that some slaves were among their parishioners. Some church meetings, however, were segregated. According to one white woman's reminiscence of an early meeting in Westport, there was a separate "part of the house reserved for the servants in all white people's churches."[128] Slaveholders' attitudes spanned a wide spectrum, from complete indifference to a steadfast commitment to educating slaves about God's mandates for racial hierarchy. Throughout the antebellum South, slaveowners used their interpretations of scripture to justify slavery and impose these beliefs on bondspeople, hoping to undermine resistance.

Slaves, on the other hand, embraced the New Testament's egalitarian message and formed their own approach to Christian life. In Missouri, as in other Upper South states, slaveowners attempted to counteract this practice by passing laws that restricted slaves' movements and their access to black-sponsored church meetings. Placing limits on slaves' mobility was a central component of slaveholders' attempts to assert hegemonic control over public spaces. For instance, in 1847, the state legislature passed a law stating that "no meeting or assemblage of negroes or mulattoes, for the purpose of religious worship, or preaching, shall be held or permitted where the services are performed or conducted by negroes or mulattoes, unless some sheriff, constable, marshal, police officer, or justice of the peace, shall be present."[129] Law enforcement, whether formally or informally, also had the power to "suppress" these meetings. Undoubtedly slaves found ways around this, and the law was likely enforced sporadically, but its passage points to slaveowners' fears that Christianity's message would lead to slave resistance.

In addition to church meetings, slaves assembled in other social gatherings. When a slaveowner planned a festive celebration, slaves were expected to contribute their labor. However, this could also be an opportunity to socialize with slaves on neighboring farms who might be brought along to help out with the event. One white woman's description of Westport illustrates the attention to detail and time-consuming work that went into the most lavish parties. One particularly onerous task was food preparation. She wrote that "turkey and hams, chickens, roast pig, saddle of mutton and sometimes venison and buffalo were served. . . . In the center of each table was placed a large stack of pyramid cake, and sometimes one at each end."[130] Although no slave reminiscences from this region refer directly to their involvement in preparations, it is likely that slaveowners took advantage of slave labor in these situations. In some cases, enslaved people were excluded from the festivities, but even when tasked with planning events there could be opportunities for enslaved people to relax and enjoy a few moments of rest.

Slaves did not partake in these activities to the same degree as whites—most slaveowners made clear that these parties were white spaces—but slaves could occasionally hold their own celebrations. Community events were significant moments in the borderland, since enslaved people could use their mobility with limited white interference. Some gatherings took place without a slaveowner's approval. One family history detailed how Wilhelm Kroll, a German immigrant who settled in the Kansas City area in 1853, rented the top floor of his business for one such party. According to the story passed down by Kroll's family, "one young slave girl, attending, evidently without her master's permission, was there. During the evening, the girl's master entered the hall with a blacksnake whip, which he proceeded to use on the poor girl."[131] At this point, Kroll intervened on the girl's behalf, and apparently he continued to let the local black community hold functions there until the building was later destroyed by fire.[132] This event's location may have been unorthodox, but it illustrates how slaveholders worked actively to restrict slaves' access to each other, trying to proscribe and confine slaves' movements.

For suspicious whites, any social function that drew a crowd of slaves and free blacks could be a breeding ground for dissention. An ordinance in Independence prohibited slaves from gathering on the streets and sidewalks, and if a large group of slaves chose to ignore this regulation they could be detained in the jail until their owner paid the fine. Those found in violation might also face physical punishment, since slaveowners generally did not appreciate having to pay such penalties.[133] Whites understood that some social gatherings would always occur outside their purview, and that there were limits on their ability to monitor slaves. However, despite the fact that there were no slave rebellions on the border, fears of uprising and resistance encouraged watchfulness among white neighbors.

A significant challenge to the cohesion of the enslaved community was the prospect of protracted separation from loved ones. As has already been discussed, slave sales were a regular occurrence, and no enslaved person was entirely untouched by human trafficking. Separation occurred, though, in various other arrangements, often stemming from a slaveholder's death. William H. Stratton of Bates County dictated in his will that he wished for his slaves to be divided among his nieces and nephews "and that none of my said slaves be sold." If his nieces and nephews had not reached the age of majority at the time of his death, "the said slaves of which I may be possessed at my death shall be hired out for the benefit of said children."[134] Hiring out was more temporary than sale, but the prospect of being separated from loved ones surely lingered in the minds of the slaves who would be affected by Stratton's death. A resident of Buchanan County, Missouri, William Williams stipulated in his will that his wife, Esther, have "during her natural life or widowhood her choice of the slaves."[135] The remaining slaves and livestock (which he grouped together) were to be divided among his children. As was common in slavery, a slaveowner's death could thrust slaves into a state of turmoil even if none faced sale as a result.

As the cases above illustrate, being divided among the white family members might permit an enslaved person to maintain some connection with their own kin. White family members may share a word or two about "their people" in letters to distant loved ones, which would in turn be passed along to any black relatives seeking news from home. These fleeting snippets of news were precious. Bonds between slaves and slaveholders, likewise, would have facilitated greater opportunities for mobility, since calling on neighbors was a common practice in the nineteenth century; slaves who were considered family might participate and visit their own families and friends. White members of the same family might also live in close proximity, making it easy for enslaved people to maintain relationships in more informal ways. This was certainly the case with Sam Denny and Melinda Denny, who were given to Harriet Marsh Denny upon her marriage, separating them from their mother, Maria Seals, who belonged to Patsy Marsh, Harriet's mother. However, both the Denny and Marsh families lived in Liberty and stayed in contact.[136] The strength of these connections between enslaved people, however, was generally contingent upon the cooperation of white slaveholders and family members, who might write letters only infrequently, refuse to include news about their slaves, or prevent slaves from visiting family who lived close by. The implication, then, was that there was significant variation among households and no sure guarantee that slaves could maintain stable relationships with their own kin.

Informal arrangements also separated slaves and disrupted the physical and social landscapes of these border neighborhoods. Slaveholder Septimus Scholl wrote many letters to his son-in-law, Rodney Hinde, that provide insight into slaves' separations. In a letter dated January 1, 1849, Scholl described where his slaves were living: Kit, Betty, and Jane were all living at his daughter Eliza's house, Evaline was "at town" (probably hired out), Bob was with his son Nelson, and the remaining slaves stayed at home.[137] Since some of these slaves were still living within the extended white family, it is very likely that they were able to see each other on a regular basis, but the fact remains that they were not living together. Loose arrangements like that of the Scholl family were not uncommon. Margaret Nickens was separated from her mother when she went to live with the Dawson family in Clay County, which was several days' travel from her home in Monroe County. Her memories of their farewell exemplify the sadness that prevailed in these situations, when enslaved parents could not change their children's fate. According to Nickens, "when we was fixing to leave, dere was lots of people standing 'round. My mother had to stand dere like I wasn't her's and all she could say was, 'Be a good girl, Margaret.'"[138] Recalling their parting was clearly an emotional experience for Nickens. There is no evidence that she was sold, so this arrangement was engineered to assist members of the white family on a temporary basis.

The most permanent form of separation from loved ones, and the sharpest injury to the slave community, was death. For both enslaved African Americans and white settlers living on the border, the threat of disease, fatal accidents, or violence made death an ever-present force in everyday life. Diseases like cholera made no distinction between free and slave, and when a frightening cholera epidemic swept through the border region in 1849, the slave community was hard hit. According to William Harris, in Westport "deaths occurred so rapidly it seemed for a time the entire population was doomed. People sickened and died within a few hours; few families were spared and some were completely wiped out."[139] Although his retelling of this epidemic's effect only describes how white settlers were affected, it can be inferred that members of the black community faced a similar situation. Somewhere between one hundred and two hundred enslaved individuals who belonged to Jabez Smith, Jackson County's largest slaveholder, died during this outbreak; according to Doctor Leo Twyman, the first case in the county was "a vigorous and previously healthy negro man, the property of Jabez Smith."[140] Other lethal diseases were common during the antebellum period, here as in the rest of the United States. In 1847, Missouri slaveowner Septimus Scholl lamented the death of Peter, a young enslaved boy who had contracted measles.[141] Scholl's letter mentioning Peter's death may have been motivated by Scholl's personal sadness or simply by his displeasure at losing a financial asset. Regardless, Peter's family surely felt his loss much more deeply.

In addition to fatal illnesses, slave families and neighborhoods also dealt with deaths caused by accidents. In another letter to his son-in-law, Scholl described a seriously injured "little negro boy of Kit's four or five months old which fell out of his mother's lap [into the fire], she being asleep, and is so badly burned very little hope of recovering, the burn entirely [covering] his face."[142] The child, whose name is never given, only lived for two more weeks.[143] Kit had lost another child only eighteen months prior (the same Peter mentioned above). While this is filtered through a white lens, and Kit's personal reactions are not preserved in the historical record, there is no doubt that she struggled to overcome the grief caused by two children's deaths in such rapid succession. Other members of the local slave neighborhood doubtless felt these blows in addition to the sorrow sweeping through Scholl's household.

Slavery was a coercive and brutal system—a fact that cannot be neglected—but on the border (as elsewhere) slaves continually pressed against restrictions on their liberty and carved out a limited degree of autonomy. The slave community that developed in the region in many ways engendered such opportunities. Resistance included nonviolent forms of questioning white authority, such as breaking tools, feigning illness, or other indirect means of dissent. It also included resorts to violence, whether in self-defense or not, and organized actions that directly challenged white control over public spaces. In recent historical studies, these everyday forms of resistance, which were far more commonplace than open rebellion, have received significant attention from scholars. Indeed, as Stephanie Camp noted, "it was in the daily tug-of-war over labor and culture that power and its assumptions were contested from below."[144] These were also the contexts where the importance of space and place came into sharpest relief.

One form of nonviolent resistance that relates to these spatial boundaries was when Missouri slaves escaped into Indian Territory, Iowa, or some other location. For slaveowners, this was deeply concerning, particularly since Missouri was geographically bound on two sides by free states: Iowa to the north and Illinois to the east. Samuel Ralston mentioned as much in a letter from January 1844, writing that the residents of Jackson County had a patrol that would "ensure perfect safety to the owners of Negroes, and will encourage many persons to become citizens of our county who hitherto have been afraid in consequence of our border location."[145] This physical boundary—inscribed on a map but porous in reality—held a psychological power over slaveholders. Indian Territory to the west was neither officially slave nor officially free, but since slaveowners resided there without government interference or noticeable public censure, it was in practice a territory open to the possession of human property. Yet, there were many nonslaveholders and some abolitionists among native tribes in the region, who no doubt assisted escaped slaves. Although the thoughts of the enslaved community are not readily available in the written record, they no doubt recognized a different psychological power of this border, the power to lead them to freedom.

Slaves in Indian Territory escaped as well, perhaps with greater success given the territory's small slave population. Stephen, a slave of Joseph Parks, fled in 1848 with a free black companion named John Scott, having stolen two horses and a mule from the Shawnee Mission—presumably Stephen escaped from Indian Territory, then, and not Parks's residence or business in Westport. In the runaway advertisement he posted in the *Liberty Tribune*, Parks noted that Stephen could speak Shawnee well and that a gunsmith was robbed at around the same time, and it is possible Stephen would have sought refuge with sympathetic Indians. The ad also notes that John Scott had spent time in Santa Fe, granting him experience that would likely prove useful to the fugitives.[146] Both this free man and Stephen had various connections that could have aided in their successful escape, thanks to prior opportunities for mobility and the existence of a black community.

Slave escapes occurred with some frequency in Missouri, and the state government instituted several laws regarding fugitive slaves. For instance, before the passage of the Fugitive Slave Law in 1850, Missouri's General Assembly issued an act in 1849 stating that if proof could be made that a fugitive slave within a free state or territory was the legal property of a Missouri slaveowner, the Missouri governor had the power to request "that such Slave may be arrested and delivered to his lawful owner; and that the public officers of such State or Territory may be directed to aid in the capture, safe-keeping and redelivery of such Slave to his owner; and in resisting and defeating all unlawful efforts to rescue the slave when taken."[147] The Fugitive Slave Law of 1850 stated that slaveowners could pursue escaped slaves into Northern states and both law enforcement and civilians were obligated to help those slaveholders retrieve any fugitive. Strict laws such as these demonstrate that slave escapes were a worrisome issue that concerned both slaveholders and any nonslaveholders who sought to perpetuate the system. Slave escapes were enough of a concern to Jackson County slaveowners that they commissioned a patrol fence guarded by men on horseback, proving that local government bodies also involved themselves in the prevention of slave escapes.[148] There is no concrete evidence that such a fence existed, but whites' desire to construct such a barrier, at what would have likely been great cost, attests to their investment in limiting escapes.

Although abolitionist sentiment was not robust on the border prior to Bleeding Kansas, there was a real concern among slaveholders that abolitionists and free blacks would encourage escapes. Bill Simms noted this in his later reminiscence of slavery days, stating that "slaves were never allowed to talk to white people other than their masters or someone their master knew, as they were afraid the white man might have the slave run away."[149] The Missouri General Assembly passed a law in 1837 that prohibited antislavery activity, hoping to limit abolitionists' influence, meager though it already was. By the 1850s, it was primarily an influx of German settlers, particularly in the center of the state, and the growing cosmopolitanism of Saint Louis that brought abolitionist feelings to attention.[150] In western Missouri, there was little abolitionist agitation, aside from the well-publicized Missouri Mormon War of the late 1830s, where locals expelled the Mormon population partly due to their antislavery beliefs. The free black population was also small; the General Assembly had passed a law in 1835 stipulating that free African

Americans had to obtain a permit and post a bond if they wished to remain in the state.[151] In the 1850 census, there were only 108 free blacks in the Missouri border counties of Clay, Platte, Jackson, Buchanan, Cass, and Bates, and likely some additional free black men and women across the border at military posts like Fort Leavenworth.[152] Nevertheless, in a precarious geographical position, slaveholders worked to ensure that the enslaved population would not learn of abolitionist feelings, and escape because of them, a goal that would be challenged during the political and social turmoil of Bleeding Kansas.

In addition to nonviolent resistance like escape, at times bondspeople adopted more violent means of asserting their autonomy and defying slaveholders' power. Although the survival of the system was predicated on some element of negotiation, there were times when traditional means of relating to each other simply broke down. In Platte County in 1853, an enslaved man named Abe Newby resisted a beating from Dan, a slave foreman, by pulling out a knife and stabbing Dan to death. Dan, in this case, was a stand-in for the owner's authority. Newby was arrested, tried, and sentenced to death by hanging. His hanging drew a large crowd and was later remembered as the only judicial slave execution conducted in the county.[153] Sam and Dill, both enslaved members of Samuel Ralston's household, told Ralston that they no longer wished to live with him, which angered him greatly, and in response he attempted to whip them into submission. The two men fled, but they returned the next day. When Ralston saw them that morning he determined to maintain discipline and, together with a Mr. Hill, he attempted to "take them" (and also another enslaved man, Riley). In response, Sam picked up an axe, and when Ralston drew his pistol, Sam then pulled out a knife. Sam and Riley were unable to fend off the attack—they were whipped—but Dill escaped.[154] Ralston's letter describing the situation is not followed by additional correspondence on the matter. From the enslaved men's perspective, however, this was a valiant attempt to resist their owner's authority, even to the point of violence, and it signaled the breakdown of a relationship that perhaps (prior to this) had been based more on negotiation.

Female slaves sometimes used violent means as well, including Annice, an enslaved woman from Liberty who apparently attempted to murder her mistress, Dinah Allen, in April 1850. Allen had been attacked while in her bed at night, having been "struck across the face with— from every appearance—an axe or a large knife," and she stumbled into her sons' bedroom, bleeding profusely.[155] Interestingly, the first mention

in the local newspaper made no mention of Annice as a potential cul-
prit, but eventually the community concluded that this was the work
of Allen's "negro woman." Another source states that Annice confessed
to planning the murder with a white man, and since her testimony was
inadmissible in court, both were lynched as punishment.[156] The black
community's reactions to the murder are unrecorded, but Annice's
lynching was both an act of personal retribution and a warning to other
slaves who might contemplate resistance.

There is scant information within these already biased sources, but the
Liberty Weekly Tribune reporter's response sheds light on white attitudes
toward such offenses. His article promotes the benevolence of the slaveholding community by casting this, and an unrelated attack by another
enslaved woman, as the "murderous propensities of a capricious and
vindictive slave." This was an unsurprising, but nonetheless disturbing,
refusal to recognize the evils of slavery. More significantly, the article
frames these acts not as aberrations but as the inevitable result of lax laws
and poor investigating by law enforcement; the author asks, "is not the
public warranted in exhibiting its indignation in such a manner as will
deter all slaves from attempting to commit hereafter like atrocities?"[157]
This plea for community intervention defends lynch law and illustrates
slaveholders' precarious attempts to maintain control. It also reinforces
the rhetorical power slaves could marshal in their assaults on slavery in
the region. These women, if they did indeed commit such acts of violence, struck a blow to slaveholders' confidence and called into question
the power of the law. Their resistance demonstrated discontent within
the slave community.

Despite slaves' resistance, the western Missouri frontier and adjoin-
ing Indian Territory were becoming a fledgling slave society by the early
1850s. Slaveholding whites attempted (sometimes successfully) to assert
hegemonic control over the enslaved population, hoping to restrict
blacks' access to public spaces. Slave labor was central to major cash
crops like hemp and tobacco, but it was also a vital force behind local
business endeavors, household affairs, and community life, touching
every facet of the frontier experience. Bondspeople pushed back against
these restrictions, at times negotiating more freedoms and at other times
challenging slaveowners' control over slave mobility by running away.
Slave hiring and abroad marriages, which were regular occurrences on
the border, were important contexts for slaves' access to the landscape.
The small-scale slaveholding that flourished on the border at times took
on a different cast than slavery elsewhere in the South, but in terms of

whites' dedication to perpetuating a racial hierarchy, slavery here was not unique among other Upper South states. Part of what made this system successful—from slaveholders' economic standpoint—was its flexibility. By 1854, however, change was on the horizon. The events that followed the Kansas-Nebraska Act of 1854 and the violence that blossomed in its wake promised to irrevocably alter a slave system that had, to this point, been continually strengthened by slaveowners and their allies within white society.

3 /   Contested Ground: The Enslaved Experience
            during Bleeding Kansas, 1854–1857

In July 1855, a thirty-nine-year-old enslaved woman named Lucinda reached her breaking point. Suffering abuse at the hands of her owner, Grafton Thomasson, she escaped and found peace in the hereafter when she drowned in the Missouri River near Atchison, Kansas Territory.[1] After her body washed ashore by the ferry landing, it lay undisturbed for nearly three days, a silent, ominous testament to slavery's abuses and a warning to both abolitionists and other slaves who might be inclined to resist white authority.[2] The local community of Atchison, a notoriously strong center of proslavery sentiment, buzzed with gossip. Had she taken her own life? Was she mad? What had happened within Thomasson's household to inspire such a final act of desperation? Perhaps she had been sexually assaulted; as the only enslaved woman in the Thomasson household, she would have been vulnerable to such treatment. Or, maybe she resisted her owner's will, carving out a limited sense of personal autonomy through resistance that ultimately proved unfruitful. An abolitionist lawyer originally from Cincinnati, J. W. B. Kelly publicly denounced the treatment of her body and hypothesized that Thomasson's cruelty and alcoholism had led to her demise. In retaliation, Thomasson and other proslavery locals stripped off Kelly's clothes and whipped him. Kelly was then banished from the territory, never to be heard from again.[3] Lucinda's apparent suicide, and Kelly's abuse at the hands of a vigilante mob, acts out in stark relief the fact that slavery existed in Kansas in 1855. But now, unlike earlier generations, slaves and slaveholders here were at the center of a nationwide contest between slavery and freedom. When Kansas bled, enslaved people and white citizens like Kelly found themselves drawn into a conflict that would foreshadow the events of the Civil War.

Americans living in the 1850s were a generation torn by sectional strife. The United States' recent victory in the Mexican-American War brought over 525,000 square miles of western territory into American hands.[4] This reignited long-standing—though temporarily muted—national debates surrounding slavery's expansion, federal power, and political liberties. White Southerners, regardless of their status as slaveholders or nonslaveholders, generally desired a West open to slave labor, not only for practical purposes but to protect white Southern interests. White Southerners wanted their fair share of Manifest Destiny's spoils. White Northerners, by and large, sought a West founded on the principles of free white labor. Black Americans, whether free or enslaved, Northern or Southern, hoped for a nation without slavery altogether, a more ambitious and far-reaching transformation that was not yet in the cards. The Compromise of 1850 addressed these land cessions and brokered a deal to appease both Northerners and Southerners, while not conceding victory to either. For instance, it included California's admission to the Union as a free state, a concession to Northerners who opposed slavery, but it also included a revised fugitive slave law that made it easier for slaveholders to retrieve their lost "property." The fragile peace it promised disintegrated almost immediately, and the Second Party system collapsed. Northern distaste for the new fugitive slave law manifested, as one example, in Harriet Beecher Stowe's publication of the best-selling book *Uncle Tom's Cabin*, a powerful piece of antislavery propaganda.[5] Many Northern whites harbored intense racial prejudices, considering abolition anathema, but their commitment to a "free soil" ideology grew. Political and social turmoil shaped this decade.

This ideological and political conflict over slavery's expansion also affected those out west. Residents on the Kansas-Missouri line saw a breakdown of the demographic, cultural, and ideological cohesion that connected those in Indian Territory (soon to be Kansas Territory) with those across the line in Missouri. Slavery had existed here for decades, the residue of an Upper South culture that inscribed slaveholding values on both the physical and metaphorical landscape, shaping the region's social geography into one based largely on slave labor, not free labor. This was, of course, despite continual action on the part of the enslaved community to challenge the system's integrity. It had also been a region of racial mixing and diverse peoples who remained resilient through a number of adjustments, including the acquisition of the Platte Purchase, the opening of the Santa Fe, Oregon, and California trails, and the establishment of Indian Territory as a result of the Indian Removal Act. Through it all, slavery had survived, and thrived, albeit in a small-scale form. And yet, deep sectional divides served as a portent that could not be ignored.

In 1854, the Kansas-Nebraska Act and its advocacy of popular sovereignty magnified the peculiar institution that existed on the border and projected it onto the national stage. It created Kansas and Nebraska territories out of the Louisiana Purchase, opening them to white settlement. Both were the current home to indigenous and Eastern emigrant tribes, since this had been the northern part of Indian Territory. By 1854, however, the commitment to a permanent Indian reserve could no longer resist the push of whites' westward expansion and continued agitation on the slavery question. This act also superseded the Missouri Compromise, which had prohibited slavery north of the 36° 30' parallel, as a concession to Southerners in Congress.[6] However, it circumvented Congress's authority over slavery's expansion by emphasizing local control through popular sovereignty, which left slavery's existence to the will of the people residing in these territories. Popular sovereignty's implementation proved a formidable challenge. As Chris Childers has observed, the architect of the act, Stephen Douglas, gave "credence to [two] interpretations—that territorial legislatures could prohibit slavery before statehood or only when a territory drafted a constitution and sought admission to the Union."[7] The former interpretation remained popular in Northern circles, while Southerners preferred the latter. In practice Kansas's popular sovereignty was a referendum on whether the nation's future should be fashioned by free white labor or by coercive labor. This contest devolved into violence, giving Kansas's territorial period from 1854 to 1861 the nickname "Bleeding Kansas." This was a contest between political, social, and economic systems that had far-reaching implications for all of nineteenth-century America.

The ensuing flood of emigrants from all parts of the United States (as well as Europe) meant that the line between Missouri and Kansas—a previously liminal space—took on a new form. Even before the territory officially opened for white settlement on May 30, 1854, interested parties throughout the United States hoped to influence Kansas's future status as either a free or slave state. Southerners believed Kansas was in a strategic location, as evidenced by numerous newspaper articles, pamphlets, and other sources created from Virginia to Louisiana. If it became a slave state, free-soil resistance to slavery in other regions of the West might be curbed. Slaveholders fully understood that Missouri's propensity for small-scale slaveholding could easily be replicated here. An unidentified newspaper stated that "if Slavery, as indicated by the infallible test of the market-price of slaves, is, to a marked degree, prosperous and profitable in the western Counties of Missouri, it must be equally so in Kansas."[8] Western identity also played a role. Missourians specifically—in contrast to emigrants from Midwestern states such as Illinois and Indiana—believed that slavery was a normal, even necessary component of Western development. Progress was the cement binding them to the West. As historian Christopher Phillips has noted, Missourians fundamentally "saw Kansas as a gift—to them."[9] This was a political fault line, certainly, but with such a groundswell of support for slavery in the Upper South, there was no doubt that if slavery could succeed in Kansas it would closely resemble the slave system in Missouri.

Slaveholders and proslavery supporters in Missouri were well suited for a rapid emigration into the territory, thanks to their close proximity and eagerness to make Kansas a slave state. The attendant social and economic risks of moving to Kansas might be minimal; with its close proximity to a slave state, slaveholders could easily beat a hasty retreat to safer territory only a few short miles away, should their rights or property be threatened. Making Kansas safe for slavery would not only protect Missouri slaveholders' property, it would also bolster Southern interests in Congress by altering the balance between free states and slave states. An observer writing from Fort Leavenworth stated in July 1854 that "strenuous efforts will be made, and are now making, to legalize its introduction and to place it on a firm foundation. Those eminent Senators who predicted that Slavery would not exist here, will I fear be confuted."[10] Joseph Anderson, a member of the first territorial legislature, made a similar prediction in his minority report on "An Act to exempt Slaves from execution." He argued that this bill would "bolster up the institutions of slavery," but that this was unnecessary, since "the wild, fertile and beautiful agricultural lands of this territory afford sufficient inducement to southern men to bring their peculiar property to this country when they emigrate."[11] Anderson's perception of the situation seemed correct during 1854 and 1855, when influential proslavery emigrants were slaveholders themselves who assumed powerful positions within the fledgling territorial government, legal system, and law enforcement.

In the first years of settlement—up to 1856—Missourians made a strong showing in terms of population numbers. Governor Andrew Reeder, the first territorial governor, issued a call on November 10, 1854, for a census of inhabitants; this would be used to determine the number of eligible voters for the first election to select the congressional representative from Kansas.[12] There was also another election scheduled to vote for representatives to the territorial legislature. The census noted the names of all family members and enslaved individuals in the household along with their ages and status (with columns labeled "Negro," "Slave," and "Voter"). This first census listed between 186 to 193 slaves present in the territory, approximately 2.3 percent of the total population.[13] Of the slaveowners whose entries are legible, the average slaveholding consisted of 2.5 slaves. The largest slaveholder listed, B. H. James, owned ten slaves. According to historian Gunja SenGupta, there were sixty-three slaveholders in the census who could be conclusively identified in terms of nativity, and of that number, forty-six were from Missouri. Fifty-seven (90 percent of slaveholders) came from all Upper South states including Missouri, Kentucky, Tennessee, Virginia, and Maryland.[14] In sum, emigrants from the Upper South (whether slaveholders or nonslaveholders) made up roughly 58 percent of the total territorial population, and 97 percent of Southern emigrants came from these border states (including Missouri).[15] The number of slaveholders was small, and with a constant influx of new emigrants, the census quickly became obsolete. Yet at the very least, the Upper South population in the territory enjoyed significant representation, and as was the case in earlier decades, these Southerners brought their values and social mores with them to Kansas.

Though population statistics might support Southerners' conviction that Kansas would be a slave state, what is more striking is slaveowners' public language lauding their superior ability to populate the region. This is not to say, of course, that they never felt threatened by Northern emigration, but at least in their public statements, slaveholders focused on the positive even to the point of exaggeration. A letter to the editor of the *New York Tribune*, submitted by a proslavery Kansan, demonstrated this dedication to making Kansas a slave state. The author boldly stated, "now, mark my words, if you please. We shall beat you. We shall firmly establish slavery in that territory, because it is for our interest to do so. And what is more, we don't care a d—n what the northern people may say. They may wince, but they must swallow the dose."[16] A proslavery convention in Lexington, Missouri, in July 1855 agreed that slaveholders were prepared for a full-scale offensive. Not only was there "no natural boundary" between Kansas and Missouri, but the participants also claimed that "one-half of the entire slave population of Missouri is located in the eighteen counties bordering on Kansas."[17] The proslavery

Squatter Sovereign, published in Atchison, printed an article in July 1855 stating that "we can truly answer that no territory in Uncle Sam's dominions can be found where the slave can be made more secure, or his work command a higher price. Kansas is adapted to slave labor, as all can testify who have experimented in the matter." Interestingly, the author went on to suggest that "situated as Missouri is, being surrounded by Free States, we would advise the removal of negroes from the frontier counties to Kansas where they are comparatively safe."[18] This reeks of bravado, but the conclusion that slavery could thrive here would have struck border residents as a rather obvious observation.

Proslavery residents of the border region spoke so confidently about slavery's inevitable place in Kansas society partly as a way to counteract the free-soil propaganda that flowed freely in the Northern press. L. J. Eastin, editor of the *Kansas Herald* published in Leavenworth, referenced the antislavery media in an April 1855 editorial:

> We have been assured, time and again, nor do we doubt, that there
> are thousands of families in many of the old Southern States, who
> have been contemplating, for months past, a removal to Kansas,
> but have been deterred from doing so through fear of slavery
> not becoming one of her institutions. This obstruction is now
> obliterated, for the infernal machinations of the Emigrant Aid
> societies have been defeated. Abolitionism has been rebuked and
> discomforted. Free-soilism has been crippled and overthrown.
> The Free White State party has been annihilated, and Kansas has
> declared loudly and decisively in favor of slavery. That Kansas is to
> become a slave State will admit of no doubt.[19]

Statements like this illustrate how the pro-Southern propaganda machine responded to charges that Kansas would never become a slaveholding state; their emphasis on the dangers of white free soil, as opposed to slave resistance, places the power in white hands and denies the work of the enslaved population. This overconfident rhetoric may have reassured slaveholders, but it also signaled to enslaved people and their allies that the ties binding the institution together were fraying. The continued emigration of free soilers and other Northerners, establishment of a free-state legislature in Topeka in 1856, resistance within the slave community, and founding of antislavery towns all gave the lie to this Southern rhetoric.

Slaveholders' personal correspondence also attests to white Missourians' eagerness to populate the new territory. John Ralston, writing from Independence in January 1854, hoped to improve his finances and "make

Kansas my home if it comes into the Union as a slave state of which we now have no doubt." He was not the only one, since later in that same letter he stated, "the citizens of Missouri are now making claims in the Territory, and will enter the Land as soon as it is surveyed." Shortly thereafter Ralston did move to Kansas, staking a claim on a tributary of the Osage River (likely the Marais des Cygnes River) about forty-five miles southwest of Independence.[20] For many proslavery Missourians, slavery's expansion into Kansas was a given.

Although both nineteenth-century contemporaries and modern historians have generally been unaware of this fact, slaveholders had a clear advantage, not only because of geographic and demographic similarities between western Missouri and Kansas migrants but also because slavery already existed in Kansas prior to 1854. Slaveholders on the border at times pointed out this very detail, though national rhetoric surrounding Bleeding Kansas often failed to absorb such assertions. Only a few months after the territory opened for white settlement, a squatters association in Doniphan County passed a series of resolutions; the eleventh stated that "we recognize the institution of Slavery as already existing in this Territory, and recommend to Slaveholders to introduce their property as early as practicable."[21] In addition, a well-known slaveholder named Benjamin Stringfellow wrote a letter to several Southern congressmen in 1855, published in the *New York Tribune*. He insisted it was safe to take slaves into Kansas because "slaves are now, and have been for years, in the Territory, so that Slavery, in fact, is already established."[22] Stringfellow hailed originally from Virginia before settling in Missouri. He served as attorney general from 1845 to 1849 while living in Chariton County and then moved west to Platte County in 1853.[23] Interestingly, however, the fact that slavery already existed in the territory did not receive widespread attention in the national media, and this relative silence has remained among some historians and the general public today.

Of course, not all proslavery emigrants owned slaves, and not all emigrants from Missouri supported slavery's spread. Missouri's population was not homogenous in terms of political affiliation or racial attitudes, so those leaving the state would be no different. While records tracing emigrants' political affiliations do not exist in most cases, in some areas we have information about emigrants' nativity and slaveholding status. For instance, in order to help supply relief to beleaguered free-state settlers, the National Kansas Committee (NKC), headed by Thaddeus Hyatt, collected information about several Kansas communities. Sometime in 1857, a representative of the NKC (possibly Hyatt himself) spoke with residents along Big Sugar Creek in Linn County. According to their survey, there were thirty-one free-state households and twenty-five pro-slavery households in the area, including two slaveowners who owned three slaves each. Of these emigrants, the vast majority were Missourians (comprising nineteen heads of free-state households, and twenty-one heads of proslavery households).[24] It is not clear if the political makeup of this settlement indicates a trend within Linn County and its environs, but it illustrates in microcosm how Missouri emigrants divided along political and social lines. Nonetheless, some nonslaveholders from Missouri did support slavery's spread, as was surely the case with some of these Linn Countians, because "it ensured that their status would be protected by an unbridgeable gulf between them and the degraded slaves."[25] This conviction that slavery's existence supported white supremacy also thrived elsewhere in the South. From the earliest years of the republic, white Southerners had constructed a racial hierarchy that privileged all whites, not only those with the means to own slave property.

Despite potential cracks in the system, leading slaveholders who settled in Kansas while it was still Indian Territory remained in the region and continued to support slavery. Richard Cummins, the Indian agent who lived near the Shawnee Methodist Mission, retired just prior to Bleeding Kansas and settled in Clay County with his family and fifteen slaves.[26] Joseph Parks, a Shawnee chief, remained in the territory, as did other native slaveholders like Mackinaw Boachman, although many tribes relocated to modern-day Oklahoma. Thomas Johnson, missionary to the Shawnee and other tribes, was active in the proslavery cause and continued his residence at the mission. The mission complex even served briefly as the site of the territorial legislature, which proslavery supporters controlled in its early years. According to a correspondent from the *New York Tribune*, who traveled through the region in 1855, Johnson's home was "the headquarters" of the proslavery element in territorial politics.[27] Former Indian agent John Dougherty had moved from Fort Leavenworth to Liberty, Clay County, in 1836, and until his death in 1860 he remained opposed to abolition and headed a proslavery association that encouraged fraudulent voting in the first territorial elections.[28] For these slaveholders, slavery in the region had already weathered many challenges, and in their hopes and dreams, it would only continue to thrive.

That said, sometimes a blossoming system required a stiff nudge. In the face of what seemed like overwhelming Northern opposition, proslavery proponents found ways to encourage more Southern emigration into the territory. As an article in the *Kansas City Enterprise* noted, "under ordinary circumstances we would be opposed to any unusual means of effecting emigration . . . [but] in view of all the circumstances attending the settlement of the Territory, a policy of this nature on the part of the South would be suicidal."[29] Several leading slaveholders organized the Jackson County Pro-Slavery Pioneer Association in early 1856 "to aid and assist such persons from this county as desire to remove to Kansas, who are friendly to making the same a slave state."[30] Shortly thereafter, slaveowners in Platte County formed a joint-stock company with a clear agenda: "if the slave-holders of this county, and others less interested, will do their duty in this important matter, this society alone, will be able to plant in Kansas, at least 2,000 good bona fide settlers, and pro-slavery voters."[31] By the spring of 1856, the *New York Herald* stated that there were approximately nineteen hundred emigrants from Southern states, and eleven hundred of those men and women were from Missouri. With these recently inaugurated associations, that number would grow. These emigrants were not entering a territory dominated by abolitionists, even if Northern propaganda implied as much. According to some contemporary estimates, in the first year of emigration (1854 to 1855) four out of every five emigrants had been proslavery.[32]

Other Southern states sent formal emigrant parties to Kansas as well. Perhaps the best-known Southern emigrant organization was Colonel Jefferson Buford's company of South Carolinians, Alabamians, and Georgians, numbering four hundred men, who came to Douglas County and Lykins County (now Miami County) in 1856. Buford, who left from Eufaula, Alabama, sold some of his slave property to finance the venture, a sign of his determination to make Kansas a slave state. His company started off strong, but they suffered from sickness, and Buford became disenchanted as his men scattered and refused to put down roots. Farther south, in Bourbon County, around thirty South Carolinians stopped by Fort Scott in early 1856 and reportedly questioned free-state residents and stole livestock. Later in that same year, a group known as Texas Rangers came, though they left soon after. Clearly, some emigrant organizations did draw from the Deep South, but these efforts never reached their fullest potential.[33] Peter Abell, a slaveholder in Kansas, had argued in 1855 that "if the Southern States now carry out the plans they are resolving, there will in future be no trouble in making Kansas a Slave State."[34] The problem, however, lay in the execution of these plans, and Abell's wish remained unfulfilled. Proslavery emigration from states other than Missouri was much smaller in comparison to both Northern emigration and proslavery emigration from Missouri.

For Northerners, Kansas symbolized an important opportunity to curb slavery's expansion in the West. The nascent Republican Party, founded in 1854 to protest the Kansas-Nebraska Act, embraced a free-soil (or in Kansas, "free-state") ideology that lauded Northern free white labor's centrality in a democratic republic. In fact, as Eric Foner eloquently observed, "the free labor assault upon slavery and southern society, coupled with the idea that an aggressive Slave Power was threatening the most fundamental values and interests of the free states, hammered the slavery issue home to the northern public more emphatically than an appeal to morality alone could ever have done."[35] Northerners, particularly those with other reasons to move west, took up this call enthusiastically. George Moore, a recent convert to the Republican Party, relocated partly to capitalize on business opportunities and make a better home for his family, reasons that no doubt resonated with Northern and Southern emigrants alike. But, Moore also noted his motivations came from "a strong desire upon my part to aid in the conflict for freedom and human rights and against the aggression of the slave-holding power."[36] Because of emigrants like Moore, as the conflict progressed, slaveholders in both Kansas and Missouri became increasingly fearful that rapid growth in the free-state population would undermine the slave system on the border. It was a practical concern but also an ideological one. As Nicole Etcheson has argued, Northerners and Southerners had competing definitions of liberty, with Southerners seeing slavery and freedom as complementary political and economic philosophies, not antithetical ones (a conclusion that baffled many Northerners).[37]

Such sentiments are common in reminiscences, correspondence, and other sources from free-soil settlers in Kansas, particularly in 1854 and 1855 after election fraud, intimidation from government officials, and the military's use of force combined to negate the wishes of the territory's free-soil population and pose a fierce threat to Northerners' political liberty. To aid in populating the state with free-soil views, antislavery advocates throughout the North formed organizations like the New England Emigrant Aid Company (NEEAC) to ensure Kansas's place as a free state. The NEEAC founded key towns in the region, like Lawrence, which would be the target of antiabolitionist violence on more than one occasion in the coming years. Although accurate statistics regarding Northern emigration are difficult to come by, roughly a third of the settlers enumerated in the first territorial census of early 1855 were from Northern states, with only 4 percent hailing from New England.[38] Northerners did not dominate numerically in this census largely because of the distance from Northern states, which prolonged emigrants' travels as compared to emigrants coming from western or central Missouri. But, numerically small numbers belie the North's interest in populating the state and their hope to curb slavery's expansion. Kansas only bled when there were two opposing regional ideologies that could be set into conflict.

Despite growing concerns about the system's stability, slaveholders who entered Kansas took their commitment to the peculiar institution seriously, working hard to make it a viable (though small-scale) system. This began with their very first entry into the territory, since they gravitated to geographically strategic sites adjacent to the borderline, hoping to protect their property rights by remaining relatively close to slaveholding communities in Missouri, being aware of the region's social geography. The eastern third of the territory was the only area populated by any significant white or black presence, and prior to the census of 1855 it was divided into seventeen voting districts. By far the highest percentage of slaveholders moved into the area closest to the border. For instance, Kansas counties located north of the Kansas River and across the line from Saint Joseph and Weston, or across from Westport (especially Districts 14 through 17), attracted a fair number of slaveowners.[39] This likely influenced the territorial legislature's decision to move from the territory's first capital in Pawnee to the Shawnee Mission, in District 17.[40]

Within the counties that arose from these districts, the organization of town companies, appointment of judges, and other political functions allowed slaveowners to dominate powerful positions. One example is Hiero T. Wilson, a slaveowner who had operated the sutler store at Fort Scott since 1843, who stayed at the site and continued his business ventures even after the fort was abandoned (temporarily) roughly ten years later. Once the territory opened for white settlement, Wilson was involved in the organization of the town of Fort Scott. His home served as the polling place for the 1855 election, and he was one of the town's trustees in addition to acting as an officer of Bourbon County. Fort Scott was officially incorporated as a town on August 30, 1855. The town code reflected the values of its founders; Section 8 stated that "the trustees shall have power to collect taxes, regulate dramshops, to restrain and prevent the meeting of slaves, etc."[41] Wilson continued to hold a leading role in the town's future, later serving on the board of commissioners. He was not the only slaveowner in Bourbon County who took an active role in local politics. Thomas Arnett, who ran a hotel in Fort Scott, was a judge during the first territorial election and served on the first board of trustees.[42] Many of these techniques were the same methods whereby

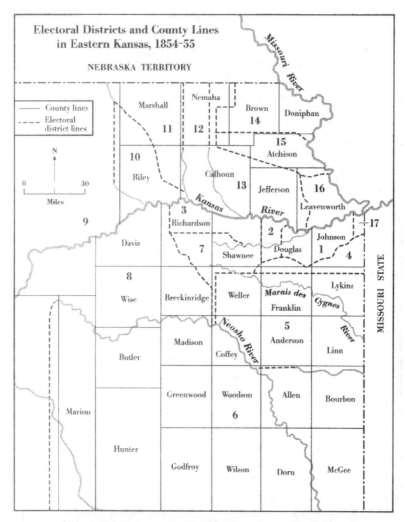

FIGURE 4. Voting Districts in Kansas Territory. Gunja SenGupta, *For God and Mammon: Evangelicals and Entrepreneurs, Masters and Slaves in Territorial Kansas, 1854–1860* (Athens: University of Georgia Press, 1996). Courtesy of the University of Georgia Press.

slaveholders had gained control of western Missouri in the decades before, with one clear difference: the battle for Kansas catapulted the region onto the national stage. Northern and Southern eyes rested on Kansas, and antislavery and proslavery emigrants now lived and worked next door to each other.

In addition to municipal and county politics, slaveholders dominated territorial government. This included the "bogus" legislature that was elected fraudulently in 1855, when proslavery Missourians flooded over the border on election day to vote before returning home to Missouri. These slaveholders and their allies put into office a proslavery legislature and took an active role in territorial politics. Missionary Thomas Johnson and his son Alexander S. Johnson both served as representatives.[43] Hiero Wilson, Milton Bryan, Blake Little, and other slaveholders served as representatives at the Lecompton Constitutional Convention.[44] Since the territorial legislature in the first few years of the territory's existence was a proslavery body, these representatives passed laws that strengthened the slave system (albeit with limited success). In 1855, they passed "An Act to Punish Offences Against Slave Property," which, if followed to the letter, would ruthlessly curb any efforts to promote emancipation. Section II stated that "every free person who shall aid or assist in any rebellion or insurrection of slaves, free negroes, or mulattoes, or shall furnish arms, or do any overt act in furtherance of such rebellion or insurrection, shall suffer death." The following section went even further; any free person who publicized or printed abolitionist material would also be guilty of a felony and would be executed. Additionally, any person who "shall aid or assist, harbor or conceal any slave who has escaped . . . shall be punished in like manner."[45] The law outraged the free-state element in the territory, which protested that this legislation restricted their First Amendment right to freedom of speech and freedom of press.

In practice, the law held little weight, partly due to the growing population of antislavery settlers and the ensuing difficulty of implementing this legislation. The U.S. Army took orders directly from the governor, but it was spread too thin and shouldered the heavy burden of enforcing politically charged and often unpopular policies.[46] Enforcement consequently fell in large part to local militias and roving bands of proslavery settlers. For instance, in 1856, the Atchison Rangers posted a notice on a tree near Stranger Creek, demanding that three men in the Hermon family—John, Henry, and George—must "leave Kansas instantly or they will be hung"; one of the charges was "for decoying and stealing slaves." The Hermons had only ten days to vacate the territory. According to a neighbor, the three men hid in the woods and avoided detection.[47] Although the free-state element in the territory would not allow the full implementation of this law, the Hermons' case does illustrate how proslavery militias—who worked outside the parameters of the law—could

enforce laws that they themselves deemed valid but that free-state settlers considered an abomination.

Efforts to protect slaveholding interests—which centered on limiting
slaves' mobility and curbing free-soil emigration—included some slaveowners (as well as those who were proslavery but did not own slaves) who
organized themselves into vigilance committees. Slaveholders Thomas
Arnett, Blake Little, and Hiero Wilson of Bourbon County took an
active role in their local vigilance committee, whose goal was to "assist
in the better execution of the law, either by the organization of a militia
company or an appeal to the Governor."[48] In Franklin County, northwest of Bourbon, several proslavery citizens and slaveowners formed
the Appanoose Vigilance Committee, and other vigilance committees
appeared elsewhere in the territory.[49] The Platte County Self-Defensive
Association, which formed at a public meeting in Weston on July 20,
1854, policed any "suspicious looking persons" who were distributing abolitionist literature, seeking to make Kansas free, or interacting
socially with either the free black or enslaved communities. Although
based in Missouri, they promoted themselves as a transborder militia
that would protect proslavery settlers in Kansas from impending depredations and harassment.[50] Although these groups served a variety of
purposes for both nascent and established communities on the border,
their emphasis on enforcing law and order was decidedly one sided.

As Kansas slaveholders continued to establish themselves in the territory, on the Missouri side of the line it was as yet unclear, at least in
1854 and 1855, how the events of Bleeding Kansas might impact those
slaveholding populations. Given their prime geographic setting on the
border, cities like Independence, Saint Joseph, and Kansas City would no
doubt serve as key way stations for travelers; as one newspaper boasted,
"Kansas City is the gate to Kansas Territory."[51] The positive side effects
for the local community, thanks to this new flood of emigrants, were
immediately apparent. The region was already quite familiar with the
demands of emigrants, having served the bustling overland trade first
with Santa Fe freighters and then with those heading to Oregon or the
Gold Rush in California. The construction of hotels, general stores, and
other businesses continued amid the partisan strife of the 1850s and
stimulated the local economy, but other deleterious repercussions, particularly in terms of keeping slave labor secure, were of concern.

Although much of that concern came during and after 1856, even in
1855 African Americans' access to public spaces in Missouri was already
under additional scrutiny. In November 1855, Kansas City—one of the

younger communities on the border, having been founded as the Town of Kansas in 1850, then the City of Kansas in 1853—created an ordinance stating that free African Americans required a pass if out between 10:00 p.m. and 4:00 a.m. if they were not "coming from some lawful place of business or assemblage." Any exceptions must be taken up with the mayor. Slaves were also expected to travel with passes, though the ordinance provided less detail on their restrictions. Both free black and enslaved individuals, though, were prohibited from "hold[ing] any assemblage at night without written permit from the Mayor, nor shall they remain at any such assemblage after the hour of twelve o'clock, P.M."[52] It is unclear whether this ordinance was merely modeled on that of nearby towns like Independence and Liberty, working under the assumption that such ordinances would come in handy, or if it was specifically conceived as the result of free-state emigration settlement across the border in Kansas. It was not unlike city ordinances in other parts of the Upper South. Regardless of the motivations, for the black community in Kansas City the effect remained the same: their use of the social and economic landscape was circumscribed, and there were higher stakes for seeking some autonomy. Slaveholders' fears regarding close geographic proximity to potential freedom in Kansas foreshadowed, even in this early stage, the later challenges to slavery's cohesion and enslaved peoples' struggle against such restrictions.

Alongside white emigrants to Kansas—Northerners, Southerners, and a smattering of Europeans—came the enslaved men, women, and children whose presence in the territory has often been ignored in modern scholarship. If the nationwide struggle over slavery's expansion, pivoting on such moments as the Missouri Compromise and the Compromise of 1850, is a familiar story to historians of the antebellum period, this story is not. While the debate over slavery's extension that gripped the nation in the nineteenth century entailed much wringing of hands about the nation's fate—from both ideological viewpoints—one fact cannot be forgotten: Kansas Territory was, at its conception, functionally a slave territory. Slaves on the border may not have participated in the rhetoric struggle over slavery's existence in the West, nor do we have evidence of their thoughts on the partisan violence of Bleeding Kansas. But their experiences illuminate how slavery manifested itself in this period of emigration and intense crisis. In the midst of political turmoil surrounding popular sovereignty, fraudulent voting, competing territorial governments, and widespread violence, enslaved men and women lived and worked in Kansas. Slaves' movement into the territory (as the result of either emigration or sale) demonstrates the cultural authority of slaveholders and other proslavery Southerners who hoped to inscribe their own political and social values onto this new landscape. Slaves' role in shaping the territory's economic and social contours, as well as legislative dictates and slaveholders' extralegal attempts to protect the ownership of human beings, all meant slavery was present and active. At least for the time being. There was no guarantee that slavery would remain viable in the territory. The Southern cultural authority that seemed destined to succeed in 1854 was challenged not only by the free-soil political agenda but also by the actions of the slaves themselves.

Of course, the enslaved population remained small, since most slaveholding emigrants believed that small-scale slaveholding as it existed in Missouri could be (and should be) replicated and transplanted in Kansas. Statistics culled from the 1855 census and surviving reminiscences corroborate the similarities between the Kansas and Missouri slave populations. Each census taker had their own ad hoc system for interpreting the form, and information on the black population fluctuates from district to district, but it does establish basic—if imperfect—parameters of slaveholding in Kansas during this snapshot in time.[53] A detailed age and sex distribution of those individuals who can be clearly identified affirms that this was a young population, with 79 percent under the age of thirty. There was, by and large, a slave community split evenly between women and men, with 47 percent male and 53 percent female (a higher percentage of women than one might expect in a frontier community), and the vast majority emigrated from Missouri. Although census takers were inconsistent in how they recorded data, it appears that fewer than thirty enslaved individuals came from states other than Missouri. As is to be expected, Upper South slaves would have been most familiar with small-scale slaveholding. Other sources point to a larger slave population than that in the official record. In her 1895 lecture on the subject, Zu Adams provided Governor Robert J. Walker's estimate that in 1857 the number was between two hundred and three hundred.[54] John Speer, editor of the *Kansas Tribune* and a devoted free stater, collaborated with a fellow Kansan to count at least four hundred of whom they had personal knowledge.[55] These varied statistics complicate the demographic data available to historians. Still, by all definitions, slavery in Kansas was a small system quite unlike that of the Deep South but not unlike that of the Upper South.

While the majority of those enumerated in the first territorial census emigrated as part of a household, the broader market in human beings also existed in Kansas. Although slave sales were not common in the territory, there were some instances that appear in the historical record. In May 1856, Thomas Johnson of the Methodist mission bought fifteen-year-old Martha for $800.[56] Johnson was already a slaveholder, and his home at the Shawnee Methodist Mission was a locus for the slaveholding community, and by extension the local black community. Only a few months later, in September, William Patton purchased an eleven-year-old girl named Penelope at the cost of $650.[57] According to Pryor Plank, there was a slave auction at Iowa Point in Doniphan County, Kansas, in 1858. He recalled that "these slaves belonged to the estate of Andrew Jasper who emigrated from Kentucky to Doniphan County in 1856 bringing these negro slaves with him. Mr. Jasper died September 15, 1857 and the slaves were sold as above stated."[58] Within this household there were at least two women and an unidentified number of children. Two of the purchasers were from Missouri (Anderson County and Holt County, respectively), illustrating once again the close ties between Missouri and Kansas slaveholders. These slaveowners probably learned of this auction through a newspaper advertisement or word of mouth. This was the only recorded mention of a slave auction of multiple individuals within Kansas Territory.

Whether they arrived in chains or within an already established household, slaves in Kansas encountered the same small-scale parameters that were common on the other side of the line. With the region under close scrutiny from both Northerners and Southerners, these bondspeople existed as either paragons of Western progress (a proslavery perspective) or as evidence of Southern depravity and potential threats to white labor (a free-soil perspective). That said, while the Bleeding Kansas conflict did affect the day-to-day practice of slavery on both sides of the line, there were some aspects of this border labor system that remained constant during this period. Slaves on both sides of the line faced physical hardships and sickness, conflicts with their owners, and separation from their loved ones, experiences that their Southern brethren shared. Even as political debates over slavery dominated the national scene during this period, the challenges that slaves encountered were ever present and not necessarily new.

Surviving sources do not detail the specific contours of the relationships between slaveholders and enslaved people in Bleeding Kansas. It is clear, however, that these relationships were predicated on the same assumptions as elsewhere in the South: slaveholders conceived of their slaves as chattel property, and as such, as commodities to be exploited in the quest for increased productivity. Slaveholders wielded a shocking degree of power over this "property." Still, there were underlying tensions, as slaveholders also realized that enslaved men and women were human beings, with personalities and idiosyncrasies that could not be predicted or fully controlled. Slaves' refusal to act as mere commodities—to assert their own will and test limits—illuminate the elements of negotiation at play. As Walter Johnson has argued, "the contradiction was this: the abstract value that underwrote the southern economy could only be made material in human shape—frail, sentient, and resistant."[59] Of course, in this middle ground, the violence of Bleeding Kansas and increasing antislavery sentiment also shaped the relationships between slaves and slaveowners; despite sharing the same theoretical basis as elsewhere in the South, such local vagaries affected how these relationships played out on the ground level.

A defining characteristic of small-scale slaveholding, and of the growing system on the Kansas side of the line, was slaves' varied forms of employment. While a slave on a large plantation elsewhere in the South might gain expertise in a very specific task, slaves who lived within a smaller system were usually expected to perform many different functions within the local economy. The enslaved individuals within the Bowen household, in Douglas County, likely assisted Bowen in his makeshift general store in addition to their work on the farm.[60] Other slaves worked primarily in businesses. Aranetta, Julia, Bickey, and Daniel came from Virginia with their owner, Mary Brooks, who owned a tavern in Lecompton.[61] Presumably these men and women assisted her by cooking, cleaning, and serving customers. Daphne, a young female slave owned by Fox Booth, worked as a ferry operator. W. H. Mackey recalled years later that "she has rowed me over the raging Kaw many a time." Daphne only remained with Booth until sometime in 1855, when he traded her for a white stallion.[62] An unidentified female slave, owned by Judge Rush Elmore of Shawnee County, was hired out to cook at a hotel in Big Springs, just across the county line in Douglas County.[63] Marcus Freeman, who left one of the few direct reminiscences of the enslaved experience in Kansas, first settled near Kansas City and Westport when his owner, Thomas Bayne, relocated there sometime in the 1840s. They then moved to Jefferson County, Kansas. For two years, Bayne ran a boarding house where Freeman learned how to cook, and later Freeman worked as a printer's assistant.[64]

This diversity of employment is not to say, however, that slaves in Kansas were peripheral to the growing agricultural economy of the territory.

Although Benjamin Stringfellow insisted that "the great staple articles of Kansas must be hemp and tobacco," in fact diversified agriculture was preferred, focusing more on wheat, corn, and staple crops. This is one example of how the labor needs in the territory contrasted with the primary cash crops cultivated in Missouri. Gunja SenGupta calculated that 65 percent of the slaveholding population identified in the 1855 census were farmers, supporting the idea that slaves did play a significant role in agricultural production.[65] Nathaniel Newby, who farmed near Atchison, had at least six slaves; some of these no doubt worked in the fields during the planting and harvesting seasons.[66] John Ralston, who moved to Kansas in 1855, had some of his father's slaves living with him and helping him improve the land. According to a letter his father, Samuel Ralston, wrote on August 31, 1855, "He [John] has some of my Negroes in the Territory, and they work on his claim & mine simultaneously, this is done in order to secure both."[67] Slaves who worked on farms also spent a significant portion of their time caring for stock. Wert, a slave of Judge Rush Elmore, had experience with plowing and driving cattle.[68] Slaves were quite visible within Kansas communities. As a result, free-state settlers who opposed slavery were not just arguing against the system in an abstract, detached way; they had seen slaves at local businesses, working in the field, and elsewhere around town. Kansas slaves' employment in varied occupations is yet another example of how slavery in the territory merely extended the system that already existed on the Missouri side of the line.

Slaves who accompanied slaveholders on business trips were also a common sight throughout the border region. In fact, in small-scale slaveholding regions such as this, slave mobility was often essential to the daily operations of a farm or business. Bondspeople living near Weston regularly drove into town alongside their owners who were running errands or making social calls. Sometimes these individuals were expected to perform labor while in town, but on other occasions they may have been free to socialize with other African Americans and move about town with few limitations.[69] For this reason, some Missouri city statutes that attempted to limit slave mobility in certain contexts (such as at night when the majority of escapes occurred) still contained a provision that allowed slaves to travel without censure if that movement was necessary according to the slave's owner. Such exceptions were economically necessary, and many statutes were not enforced on a regular basis anyway, as slaves regularly traveled without white permission. Enslaved people likely found the ties that bound them to the white community and regulated their movements were relaxed or tightened at a whim, so carving out any ability to build their own neighborhoods was nothing to take lightly.

Travel for business was not confined to towns within Missouri. According to an article in the *Herald of Freedom*, Missourians conducted business in Lawrence on a fairly regular basis, selling produce and other goods raised on Missouri farms, and often they brought their slaves along for the journey.[70] This trade dwindled during the heat of the border conflict, and presumably slaveholders in Missouri became less keen on bringing their slave property into a free-state community like Lawrence, fearing that the slaves might book passage on the Underground Railroad. Nonetheless, bondspeople found ways to cross the border. Jim Daniels, an enslaved man from Vernon County, sought help in 1858 from some abolitionists (including John Brown) across the border in Kansas, crossing over on the pretext of selling brooms. After returning to Missouri, he told his owner that he had spent the day in an Osage Indian camp.[71] The fact that Daniels traveled without prior consent—and that his owner apparently took him at his word—illustrates the independence he carved out for himself while enslaved. According to a later reminiscence, a male slave of Indian agent Richard Cummins had gained his owner's trust implicitly. In one instance, Cummins had loaded annuity payments for the Sauk and Fox into a wagon to transport to the tribe, but at the last minute he was called away on business and simply sent this enslaved man on the errand with no supervision.[72] Such opportunities not only offered slaves some independence but also allowed them to contact other enslaved individuals and perhaps even interact with free-soil settlers, abolitionists, or native tribes who supported emancipation.

Alexander Johnson, who left the aforementioned reminiscence, also noted that his own slaves gained increased independence in the territory. Shortly after Kansas opened to white settlement, Johnson moved his wife and children to Missouri (so she could be close to family while he was away on business), and he left his farm in present-day Johnson County, Kansas, in the care of slaves. At this time he had at least seven slaves, and "it took all they produced to keep them, and I had some expenses to pay besides. . . . They staid there and ran the farm until 1861."[73] Interestingly, these slaves mentioned to Johnson that abolitionists were encouraging them to escape on the Underground Railroad, but the slaves declined the offer. Perhaps their independence and relative freedom from white authority, as sole caretakers of Johnson's farm, gave them enough opportunities to make their own way.

Slave hiring was both a result of the small-scale paradigm and another important avenue for enslaved residents on the border to gain control of their own mobility. A robust hiring system existed there as in other locations in the Upper South. J. P. Howe and George W. Toler, as one example, posted an advertisement in the *Kansas City Enterprise* to "offer their services to their friends and the public generally, as Agents for the Hiring out of Negroes and Renting houses for the ensuing year."[74] A brokerage firm such as this not only provided a service by supplying labor, but its existence attests to the continued importance of slave hiring in the border economy, even during intense political and social upheaval. Benjamin Stringfellow, who had lived in Weston during the 1830s and 1840s before moving to Kansas, understood the importance of hiring and clearly articulated its benefits in an 1855 letter to the *New York Tribune*. He argued that "those who have more slaves than can be profitably employed in opening a farm, can, in the meantime hire out the remainder, including the women and those too young to render much service in the fencing and breaking the ground."[75]

On occasion Kansans—including nonslaveholders—participated in the hiring system. In 1857, Solomon Miller, a journalist and printer from Ohio, settled in Doniphan County. Shortly after his arrival, he began publishing the White Cloud *Kansas Chief* and temporarily hired an enslaved boy to assist him with his business.[76] There were likely many opportunities to hire white labor in Kansas, given the increasing emigration from the North, so Miller's motivations for using slave labor are unclear; he was a dedicated Republican and as such it is unlikely that he supported the spread of slavery into the territory. While these sources did not provide the perspective of enslaved individuals who might be hired out, it is certainly possible that slaves in Missouri welcomed the opportunity to be hired out in Kansas, a state with a developing network for aiding fugitives. Even if this newfound mobility did not ultimately lead to flight on the Underground Railroad, making connections with sympathetic abolitionists and black communities in other locales could increase slaves' access to public spaces and their ability to navigate the social and physical terrain.

In some cases, slaves had the opportunity to hire out their own time, which gave them a right to the income from their labors and allowed them some freedom to choose who they would work for; consequently, these men and women had greater control over their own movement. For example, John, a thirty-year-old barber who belonged to Rush Elmore, reportedly hired out his own time and worked in Lecompton.[77] Buck Scott got a job in Lawrence and used 70 percent of his earnings to reimburse his purchase price to his owner in nearby Lecompton.[78] Marcus Freeman, who had come to Jefferson County in 1855 after some time in Kansas City, returned to the Missouri side of the border, where he "married and rented my time for $200.00 a year for seven years until I was emancipated."[79] It appears that the enslaved members of the Little household, in Bourbon County, had a similar experience with hiring out, though the circumstances are less clear. At some point a neighbor stopped by the Little house and inquired about hiring some of the young men (at least five or six of them) to cut hay, and Dr. Little agreed that "they could go if they wished."[80] Instances such as these were not unheard of, but they were not the norm for most hired slaves; most men and women who were hired out had little or no choice in the matter and did not receive any compensation for their work. Nevertheless, the vigorous hiring market speaks not only to the small-scale nature of slavery in the region but also to the importance of mobility, including sustained movement across the Kansas-Missouri border.

A prevalence of abroad marriages is also, as ably demonstrated by historian Diane Mutti Burke, another result of small-scale slavery, and this was true of the institution during Bleeding Kansas, although there is no surviving evidence of marriages that spanned the Kansas-Missouri line. Bill Simms, a former slave who left a reminiscence of his life on the border, said that "if a slave wanted to marry a woman on another plantation he had to ask the master, and if both masters agreed they were married. The man stayed at his owners, and the wife at her owners. He could go to see her on Saturday night and Sunday."[81] Charity Freeman, who came to Jefferson County alongside her brother, married Robert Skaggs, whose owner, James Skaggs, lived nearby. When James Skaggs took his slaves to Texas in the year just before the onset of civil war, Charity was able to go with her husband.[82] Jennie Hill, a former slave from central Missouri who later settled in Wichita, Kansas, had an abroad marriage with a man who lived on a farm about a mile away. Marriages such as this were not legal, since slaves could not acquire marriage licenses. This did not, of course, mean that enslaved men and women considered these voluntary relationships to be free of obligation or commitment, even if realistically the two parties understood that permanency was no guarantee.[83]

Because the enslaved population remained so small, there were challenges in establishing a coherent slave community on the Kansas side of the line, with the only concentrations being in a few urban areas like Leavenworth, Fort Scott, or at the Shawnee Mission. With slaves in rural areas likely living far from other African Americans, and increased contact between slaveowner and slave that often came about due to close living arrangements, slaves' opportunities for creating such bonds were limited. Since such a high percentage of Kansas slaveholders owned only one slave, according to the 1855 census, it is unlikely that those enslaved individuals had a separate house, particularly since most of the early settlers were working quickly to set up a house for themselves. A lack of privacy would have led to longer work hours (as slaveholders called upon their slaves more frequently), increased supervision, higher odds of sexual and physical abuse, and even more pronounced suspicion of slaves' movements than already existed. Axalla Hoole, who settled in the territory in 1856 with his new bride, Betsy, initially boarded with Paris Ellison, his wife and children, and their four slaves: Sarah, Louisa, Andrew Jackson, and Laura.[84] The Ellison farm near Douglas (a now-defunct town close to Lecompton) consisted of "three log houses built in a row—the middle one of which is the kitchen where the Negroes stay."[85] With four slaves and what Hoole described as "very poor houses," including a separate kitchen facility, Ellison and the white family no doubt kept close to slaves. A slaveholder named Bowen, who lived in a proslavery settlement on Washington Creek in Douglas County, brought ten slaves with him when he emigrated to the territory in 1855. According to a reminiscence recorded later by a free-state settler who lived in the neighborhood, the enslaved residents of Bowen's farm had a two-room log cabin ten rods (about fifty-five yards) from the main house.[86] If all ten slaves—which included about eight children—were crowded into one cabin, there would have been very little opportunity for personal space of any kind.

There were some exceptions, of course. The ten slaves belonging to Rush Elmore gradually built log cabins that were located near the Elmores' house. From contemporary descriptions of these families, there were seven children below the age of fifteen and only two men capable of heavy labor; it is likely, then, that Mike (aged thirty) and Pompey (aged fifteen) were responsible for building these homes.[87] Although a separate house would have allowed the slaves some privacy, the situation still facilitated a close physical proximity between slaves and slaveowners. On a large plantation, such as that of Jabez Smith in Jackson County, most slaves did not see the slaveowner on a regular basis and likely lived farther away in the designated slave quarters; this allowed slaves some autonomy over their work and personal lives, outside the owner or overseer's view. This would have been quite rare in Kansas.

Tight living arrangements were common in frontier settlements, regardless of whether the inhabitants were enslaved or free, and for better or for worse enslaved men, women, and children had frequent contact with slaveholders.

This absence of a strong slave community in most of rural Kansas severely limited opportunities for resistance in these first years, but it did not entirely squelch individual agency. Mike, a slave of Rush Elmore, exhibited "disobedient and unruly" behavior according to white neighbors, and on one particular occasion an overseer named Benjamin Newsom determined to whip Mike. According to a reminiscence left by a white contemporary, "Mike said he wouldn't let anyone whip him but Massa Elmore, and that it was a tight fit if he let him do it. Mike then started on a run for Lecompton and Newsom after him."[88] As Mike was running away, a white neighbor named Emerson noticed the commotion and came to Mike's defense, promising to stay with him at that place until Elmore returned home and could resolve the conflict. After Elmore arrived, Mike "told him that he had better sell him, 'for I won't do you any good here.'"[89] Elmore reportedly let Mike choose his new master, who lived somewhere in Missouri. It is possible that Elmore understood the tenuous grasp he exerted on his slave property and believed that it would be more amenable to simply let Mike leave the Elmore household.

There are three intriguing elements to this story. First, while this account is clearly from the white perspective, it does suggest that Mike was well aware of which whites had authority over him and effectively limited their control over his body. Clearly he was discontented with his situation and used what means he could to resist such strictures. Perhaps the household's settlement in Kansas had separated him from family and loved ones, or perhaps there were abusive relationships within the Elmore home that were triggers. What whites characterized as "unruly" behavior was Mike's attempt to assert some control over his own destiny. Second, white Southern notions of masculinity, which denied black men their manhood while simultaneously fearing black men's physical power, may also have been at play in this interaction. Violence and resistance were one means for an enslaved man to recapture and reframe his identity as a man, thus challenging the mastery of white men. Third, although Emerson's political allegiance and position on the slavery issue is unknown, Kansas slaves were part of diverse communities of both proslavery and free-state settlers, which improved their chances of finding a sympathetic ally. This was one of the unique features of the slave system in Kansas, signaling that the enslaved population took advantage of changing relationships in this borderland. Antislavery allies might live as close as the farm or house next door. Here, instead of supporting slaveholders' power, as might be expected in the South, the influence of local communities might run counter to slaveholders' needs.

Enslaved men might embrace violent resistance, but female slaves who resisted usually eschewed physical violence and used different means. In 1856, two female slaves at Fort Riley, Cely and her daughter Patsy, faced accusations that they had poisoned their owner, Mr. Agness, an ordnance sergeant. According to a white reminiscence, "they were both taken down to the saw mill. The two were set astride the log and the saw started. When the saw got uncomfortably close Aunt Cely declared 'Fo God I is innocent.' The saw was stopped and they were released."[90] Unfortunately, as was usually the case, Cely and Patsy's perspective remains unrecorded. It is possible that they had suffered abuse—sexual or otherwise—at the hands of their owner and were attempting to protect themselves. Or, it is possible that they were innocent of all charges, and when he died "mysteriously" the local white community just assumed Cely and Patsy were responsible. The particulars of this owner-slave relationship are not preserved in the historical record. Whatever the motivations, local whites intervened. Given the staging of this event, as a form of torture with a reprieve at the last moment, it is possible the threat of death was intended not to elicit a confession but rather to send a warning to Cely, Patsy, and any other enslaved residents who might contemplate resistance. Since slave labor was a relatively rare commodity this deep into Kansas, and thus a valuable one, the lynching of these two women might also have had economic repercussions for Agness's heirs or others at Fort Riley.

This story demonstrates two key points about the slave system in Kansas. First, Cely and Patsy's roles within the household clearly involved traditionally female tasks such as food preparation, since their presence in the kitchen implicated them in the affair and made them subjects of the white community's suspicion. If these women had had no interaction with the sergeant's food, they might have remained above reproach. Their fulfillment of gendered expectations of female labor would have provided them the opportunity to slip poison into the sergeant's food (if they were indeed guilty of the accusation). Second, slaves in the territory, like slaves in Missouri, did not receive a fair trial, and a mob's rattled emotions prevailed as the primary means of slave punishment. Bondspeople had no legal standing and no recourse in these situations; they had to rely largely on their own wits and hope for some sympathetic treatment from whites.

Slaves also adopted nonviolent—and consequently less risky—methods of gaining autonomy and increasing the likelihood that they might one day be free. The enslaved members of Bowen's household, in Douglas County, sometimes snuck over to a white neighbor's house only a quarter of a mile away, where Sarah Armstrong taught them the alphabet without their owner's knowledge. When Bowen discovered this fact, he threatened Armstrong, who sought out the local free-state militia for protection. Bowen and these slaves reportedly moved to Westport shortly thereafter.[91] Across the river in Weston, a Northern preacher named Frederick Starr educated several slaves, but after these activities became public knowledge, he was encouraged to discontinue these efforts.[92] Educating slaves was illegal in many Southern states, including Missouri, because slaveowners understood (quite accurately) that being able to read and write gave slaves more marketable skills as laborers and greater opportunities to escape and navigate the free world.[93] Historian William Wilson Elwang noted that Missouri slaveholders "felt with the same class all over the South, that the mental improvement of the slaves meant their dissatisfaction and possible insurrection and rebellion. The submission of the man with the dark skin was secured by keeping his mind dark."[94] Fear of educated blacks circulated throughout the Kansas slaveholding community as well; Bowen's departure for Westport—which was only about fifty miles away—signaled the impending changes that promised to alter the slave system in Kansas. In the eyes of slaveholders, this foreshadowed and reinforced their mounting insecurities about their place in the territory.

Resistance to slaveowners' power continued on the Missouri side of the border as well, as shifting personal conflicts, political intrigue, and partisan warfare were not confined to Kansas. In 1859, two male slaves, Farrel and John, were executed in Lexington after they allegedly murdered their overseer, Henry Nance. According to one newspaper account, the slaves admitted that they had murdered Nance while intoxicated, because he had whipped them and they did not respect his authority. To make matters worse, John did not display the appropriate amount of remorse after the fact, at least in the eyes of the white community. Their execution drew a large crowd composed of both white and black observers.[95] Executions such as this reinforced white authority in the community and sought to discourage bad behavior and violent resistance to slaveowners and overseers, and some slaves were likely told to attend, as a warning. The black response to the execution, as evidenced by the fact that they turned out in large numbers, might also be interpreted as a sign of solidarity for their accused brethren. Even if some enslaved men and women did not condone violence, this particular situation appeared to be a case of self-defense, and there is no doubt that the local slave community spoke among themselves about the appropriate uses of violence as a means of resistance.

Another story of resistance comes out of Saint Joseph, where sometime in 1859 an enslaved man was sold to a slave trader bound for the New Orleans market. This slave trader, identified only as Wright, kept a loaded pistol in his buggy within easy reach. When Wright stepped out of the buggy to water his horse at a roadside spring, his captive pulled out the revolver and shot Wright in the head. Grabbing the reins, he took off in the buggy before abandoning it and running into the brush. A local posse captured the fugitive a few days later, and it was only at a lawman's intervention that he was not lynched. He was tried, convicted, and executed, never getting to share his side of the story in court, since slaves could not testify and had virtually no legal rights.[96] This incident demonstrates slaves' great fear of being "sold south" and their insistence on circumventing the trafficking of human beings by whatever means necessary. His resort to violence might be explained by a fear of the unknown or the threat of future abuse. It also might have stemmed from his impending separation from loved ones, whether literal or fictive kin. Slave sales had profound repercussions for black families, and by extension the slave community. Or, given the violence of Bleeding Kansas, perhaps his knowledge of this political strife gave him additional motivation. Of course black resistance was often, as in this case, met with harsh punishment from white communities that used these incidents to reassert their own authority over black bodies and black movement.

Much has been made of chattel slavery's overall decline in the 1850s, with both contemporary observers and modern-day historians questioning whether it would have survived, had the Civil War not occurred. Although changing emigrant patterns on the border did affect the demographic makeup of the region, these patterns only provide a partial glimpse of potential challenges to the slave system. In Missouri, it is clear that Northern and foreign emigration brought abolitionist sentiments to the fore in previously unprecedented ways, but outside of Saint Louis, or outside ethnically German settlements in central Missouri, proslavery voices generally squelched abolitionist voices. Missouri had never been a bastion of abolitionism, and in its western reaches that affinity did not change in the years preceding the Civil War.[97] Slavery remained central to the state's economy. Even if the slave population had decreased in proportion to the white population over the preceding decades, the net number of enslaved people continued to grow. For instance, as Jeremy Neely discovered in his study of the southern Missouri-Kansas border, "the percentage of households that owned slaves doubled in Bates and Cass Counties. Immigrants from the Upper South, most of them owning a single slave, fueled much of this increase."[98] It cannot be argued that slavery was being strengthened in Missouri, perhaps, but neither can it be argued that—barring the events of Bleeding Kansas—the system faced its impending demise. Some slaves and slaveholders in the region may have recognized cracks in the system, but not every resident enjoyed such foresight.

A number of factors—stretching from demographic, to social, to political—make clear that 1857 was the apotheosis of Southern influence in Kansas Territory and a turning point for slavery on the other side of the line. In terms of demographics, during the first years of settlement, slaveholders and other proslavery emigrants made up the majority of settlers entering Kansas. They also situated themselves in geographically prime positions where they could amass both political influence and social capital. These were the peak years of slaveholding in the territory. However, Southern emigration into the territory began to decline by the end of 1856 and into 1857, at a time when Northern emigration was increasing. Kenneth Stampp argued that by 1857, "Kansas was rapidly being lost to free-state settlers," a date echoed by more recent scholars like James Shortridge and Gary Cheatham.[99] In his study of southern Missouri and Kansas, Jeremy Neely explained that typical emigrants in the late 1850s were Westerners, chiefly from Ohio, Indiana, or Illinois.[100] On the national scene, David Potter has argued that Americans' interest in territorial matters petered off by about 1857.[101] Granted, a lack of detailed records makes it difficult to date this shift with any precision. Although the exact turning point is uncertain, there *was* a demographic reshuffling that affected who controlled the territory, at the same time that the number of slaves (not coincidentally) declined. For slaveholders on the border, this created an increased precariousness, foreshadowing that they would not be safe from interference by abolitionists or from slave resistance. It also made Kansas a progressively appealing target for Missouri slaves hoping to reach freedom.

Social factors also played into the shift toward Northern control over the region. As the population increased, many settlers' attention turned toward the sometimes tedious but vital business of improving farms, establishing towns, founding churches and schools, and weathering the normal challenges of life in a new place. People were moving on. The most significant (and virulent) proslavery mouthpiece in the territory, the Atchison *Squatter Sovereign*, ceased publication in 1858 and was renamed *Freedom's Champion*, which no doubt helped quiet inflamed feelings.[102] Historian Dale Watts's research on politically motivated killings in the territory also attests to the fact that violence in the territory was declining after 1856 and 1857; the bloodiest year was 1856, when there were thirty-eight identifiably political murders, but 1857 only saw six.[103] This statistic does not prove a decrease in Southerners' influence, but it does suggest that social pressures had lessened by 1857, discouraging violent conflict. The worst of the "bleeding" years was over, although a few noteworthy episodes were yet to come, such as the calculated massacre of five free staters near the Marais des Cygnes River in May 1858.

Political instability made the work of settling the territory difficult, providing an incentive for Kansans to put hard feelings aside. By one settler's account from 1857, peace and quiet reigned, since "on every hand I saw Free-State and Pro-Slavery men engaged together. . . . They profess to have buried all animosities and to be animated by the sole desire to live henceforth in harmony and in joint effort to subdue the wilderness and promote the welfare of their common country."[104] Social pressures to focus on community building might have also resulted from increased emigration from Northerners and Southerners who were less invested in the slavery question, lacking passionate free-soil or proslavery ideals. In that sense, then, even though proslavery Southerners remained in the territory, their political and social hegemony—which allowed them to promote their cause, and in the process helped lead to full-blown violence—was waning.

The Lecompton Constitution, a proslavery document up for debate in 1857 and 1858, was another marker denoting the peak of Southern control over the territory's destiny, not only in terms of a Southern presence on the ground but also in light of the federal government's sway over territorial affairs. This constitution stipulated, much to the distaste of free soilers, that "the right of property is before and higher than any constitutional sanction, and the right of the owner of a slave to such slave and its increase is the same and as inviolable as the right of the owner of any property whatever."[105] Furthermore, the state legislature could not issue an order of emancipation without slaveholders' express consent. To ensure that slaveholders did not lose money by bringing slaves into the territory, "any person who shall maliciously dismember or deprive a slave of life, shall suffer such punishment as would be inflicted in case the like offence had been committed on a free white person."[106] The Lecompton Constitutional Convention, which did not represent the wishes of free-state settlers and contained seven slaveholding representatives, put only the sections on slavery to a popular vote in 1857. Free-state men boycotted it on principle because how the election was framed would not allow for the complete end of slavery in the territory; regardless of the outcome, slavery would still be legal, since the only thing rejection would accomplish was prohibiting the further importation of slaves.[107] Thanks to the free-state boycott, the constitution won approval by an overwhelming majority, and with a cursory glance this may imply that the proslavery forces in Kansas were stronger than ever.[108]

However, the proslavery party lost control of the territorial legislature in that same year, and a second vote on the full Lecompton Constitution in 1858 soundly defeated its submission, making this document the last attempt on the part of slaveowners and their allies to write a proslavery constitution.[109] Its demise also signaled a serious break within the Democratic Party over popular sovereignty's implementation. The failure of the Lecompton Constitution did not banish slaveholders from the territory, but it certainly made them less sure of their property rights. Of course, the constitution's collapse did not directly affect the slaveholding class on the Missouri side of the line, although the potential pitfalls of being bounded by two free states and one free territory were not lost on slaveholders. They too went on the defensive. An article in the *Western Journal of Commerce*, published in Kansas City, Missouri, boldly asserted that slaveholders "intend to buy and hold all the niggers we need, and sell them when we desire so to do, and we also expect to protect our rights when invaded."[110] In 1858, Democratic president James Buchanan attempted to reenergize the flagging proslavery cause when he stated in his annual address to Congress that "it has been solemnly adjudged by the highest judicial tribunal that slavery exists in Kansas by virtue of the constitution of the United States. Kansas is, therefore, at this moment as much a slave state as South Carolina or Georgia."[111] In practice, of course, this characterization was undoubtedly hyperbole, and while it may have served a purpose on the national stage, such posturing would not change the reality on the border.

By 1858 and 1859, the majority of Kansans and Missourians recognized that Kansas Territory was going to enter the Union as a free state, even before the drafting of the Wyandotte Constitution (which became the state constitution when Kansas entered the Union in 1861). This constitution expressly prohibited slavery, though its final incarnation did not grant suffrage to African Americans. That said, slaves still lived and worked in the territory right up to statehood, though their numbers grew smaller, due both to escape and to slaveholders' out-migration. By 1860, only two were recorded in the census. According to an 1859 article in the *Western Journal of Commerce*, "Kansas is a non-slaveholding country, and all the Dred Scott decisions in the world, or all the congressional enactments that could be piled upon her, would not be able to make her otherwise."[112] Interestingly, the author attributed this to "soil, climate, and latitude" and not to increased Northern emigration, perhaps as a way to elide the proslavery party's failures in this regard. Still, the fact remained that Kansas was no longer a feasible target for those who encouraged slavery's expansion. By approximately 1857 and early 1858, the border region, which had once seemed continuous, distinguished only by an "invisible boundary," was redefined as a line dividing slave-holding communities in Missouri from free communities in the territory.[113] At this point, the fates of Kansas and Missouri began to diverge.

James Montgomery, a white abolitionist living near Mound City in Linn County, Kansas, penned a letter to his comrade George Luther Stearns in the fall of 1860, detailing the movement of fugitive slaves into the territory. "We have several fugitives on hand, and more are expected. Some of them are from Missouri, and some from Arkansas," he wrote. "When a keen, shrewd fellow comes to us, we send him back for more."[1] This letter, one of many that Montgomery sent to friends and allies back East, foregrounds the importance of slave mobility to the demise of slavery in Kansas. Although this source comes from the white perspective, and Montgomery often privileged the assistance of white abolitionists over the work of enslaved people, it nevertheless attests to the system's fragility in the face of political and social instability. Southern political and demographic dominance in the territory decreased in 1857 and 1858, and cracks in the slave system became fissures. And, in Missouri, slaveholders wondered if slavery's end in Kansas indicated trouble for the institution in their state or a waning interest in expanding slavery westward.

In the later years of Bleeding Kansas, both local and national rhetoric shifted away from questions of slavery's viability in the territory and toward documenting and analyzing the system's breakdown. Although emigration from both the North and the South continued after 1857, the race to populate the territory in advance of the first elections was over, so for many Americans the process assumed less political urgency. Thus, while both Northerners and Southerners remained interested in territorial politics, more attention shifted toward those who were fleeing bondage, not whites seeking to create a slave society out west. The national dialogue that consumed the media, general public, and Congress—beginning with the Kansas-Nebraska Act in 1854, stretching into the worst year of violence in 1856—had already made this border the focus of national attention, giving slaves' movement in these later years a symbolic authority in addition to the tangible.

Slaves' knowledge of the social geography and access to the physical landscape were central to this unraveling. By 1860, the census noted only two enslaved individuals in Kansas, a decrease of approximately 99 percent.[2] This dramatic decrease cannot be attributed solely to slaveholders' own decision making, although slaveholders did voluntarily remove their households when slavery here seemed doomed to fail. Those bondspeople who remained on the border continued to travel the countryside and access public spaces—running errands, visiting loved ones, and conducting business—but now movement into Kansas was no casual act. Slave mobility had political implications.

Of course, the struggle for control of slave mobility was not new, but this region was uniquely situated both geographically and culturally. National dialogue over slavery's expansion played out via the local landscape, with the key players being enslaved men and women who were sometimes assisted by either white or black abolitionists in the region. Slaveholders grew increasingly concerned about their inability to curb slaves' movements. As historical geographer Allan Pred has argued, "place . . . always involves an appropriation and transformation of space."[3] In this case, the border region was defined and transformed by slaves' bold appropriation of these liminal boundaries and their knowledge of its social geography.

Slave mobility—a mobility shaped by their own dictates and desires, not merely a reactionary movement—had the potential to dramatically alter the balance of power. In the case of the Kansas-Missouri border, small-scale slaveholding made slave movement a more frequent component of everyday life. This was less common for African Americans on large plantations in the Deep South, which could primarily function as self-sufficient units staffed with blacksmiths, wheelwrights, and other craftsmen, with an on-site mill, orchard, or smokehouse. Because the average slaveholding in Kansas in 1855 was 2.3 slaves, and the average slaveholding in the Missouri border counties according to the 1860 census was 4.5, virtually no slaveholding farm or homestead was fully autonomous, making slaves' movement an integral component of any slaveholder's attempt to make a profit.[4] Although the border was a site where slaveholders sought to reproduce the social and cultural systems that had existed in their home states, and this included attempts to control the slave community by limiting access to the physical landscape, slaves' mobility in the years prior to 1854 had primed them for the work to come. "Space and the control of bodies in space were important to both slaveholders and enslaved people, and they were major points of conflict," as historian Stephanie Camp noted in her study of enslaved women in the South writ large.[5] Enslaved men and women capitalized on the instability of Bleeding Kansas to assert themselves more aggressively, foiling slaveholders' attempts to control the slave population. Especially beginning in 1857 and 1858, slavery in Kansas, and in western Missouri as well, was being undermined.

This unsettling of an established social system came in various ways. The voluntary removal of slave property became more common as the proslavery element in Kansas lost their edge, or as a Quaker abolitionist recalled later, when "things began to look quite critical here for the slavery interest."[6] According to Benjamin Harding, a free-state settler in Doniphan County, Carey Whitehead maintained that "'he had never lived in a free state and swore he never would,' so when the slavery question was settled in Kansas, in spite of the protests of his wife (a native of Mississippi), he traded his farm for a family of negroes and moved [back] to Missouri."[7] Whitehead, who had relocated from Saint Joseph, just across the river, already owned two slaves in 1855 when the territorial census was recorded. In 1859, Rush Elmore, an associate justice of the territorial Supreme Court, sent all of his and his wife's slaves to his brother Albert Elmore in Alabama, asking Albert to "sell them as early as possible. I would prefer them to be sold in families; but if they will sell better by separating the larger children only do so."[8] The slaves set out for Alabama at the end of that month under the authority of John Martin, a friend of the Elmore family who had power of attorney. Some were divided among Elmore's family members. He continued to write letters to his brother dictating how much each slave was worth and other details.[9] Other accounts suggest that removal from the territory was not an uncommon occurrence for enslaved Kansans. For bondspeople who had hoped to take advantage of their proximity to Nebraska and Iowa, removal to places in the South was surely a profound disappointment, as it severely limited their chances to escape. Removal to border counties in Missouri, though not ideal, may not have prevented future attempts but surely complicated them.

Another testament to this unsettling comes from some slaveholders' choices to manumit their slaves. Most of the documented cases occurred after 1857. Hiero T. Wilson, the former sutler of Fort Scott and founder of the town of the same name, voluntarily freed his slaves in 1859.[10] His motivations are unclear, but the historical record shows that he was ardently proslavery, though a Unionist during the war. At some point prior to 1861, Dorcas and her husband, property of Wyandot leader William Walker, gained their freedom, and historian Charles Cory maintains that several of the foremost Wyandot slaveholders also freed their slaves during this time.[11] Given the tribe's deep divisions over slavery, stemming from both cultural and religious disputes, it is possible that Walker and his fellow slaveholders sought to keep peace within the Wyandot. Or, perhaps Walker had developed antislavery feelings and chose to free them on moral grounds. In another case, Lizzie Allen's owner told her in the winter of 1859 that she should "go to Kansas. I can't keep you any longer. They'll kill me. Maybe you can come to us again."[12] It is not clear whether this was a legal manumission. Whatever the reasons, these enslaved individuals benefited tangibly from the political instability that enveloped the border.

Since slaves functioned in this economy as a form of capital, nervous slaveholders sometimes sought to transfer that capital from human property (increasingly seen as an unstable investment) into hard currency. This development was much less likely to work to a slave's advantage. For instance, Cynthia, part of the George Young household located in Topeka, was sent to Saint Louis sometime in 1860 or 1861, where she was sold.[13] Cynthia had only recently come into the possession of John Young (a relative of George Young), and likely Young decided that slavery was no longer profitable. This was especially true after the passage of the free-soil Wyandotte Constitution in 1859 and overwhelming evidence that Kansas would enter the Union as a free state. We know almost nothing about Cynthia's life, but no doubt she was apprehensive about her sale. In another case, an unidentified slaveholder in Jackson County posted an advertisement in 1857 selling an "elderly woman, a good cook and first rate house servant" since the owner was "intending to remove to the Territory."[14] Likely there were other instances that remain undocumented. In each case, slaveowners sought to retain some semblance of power and financial solvency. This was a preemptive strike, in one sense, but it also exemplifies the perceived inability of either law or government to protect slaveholders' interests.

Not surprisingly, local media sources voiced the slaveholding community's fears about what these incidents meant, and about what repercussions might come from voluntarily entering the nonslaveholding class. The *Weekly Free Democrat* of Saint Joseph published an article in August

1859 announcing Jackson County's reports from its assessor: "It appears that the number of negroes (slaves) in that county has decreased 500 in the past year, which is about 17 per cent," the author wrote. "This conclusively proves that the agitation of the slavery question on our frontiers is having the effect of inducing the owners of slaves to sell their negroes South. The decrease noticed above was produced mainly by negroes being sold out of the state."[15] Other articles highlighted this trend, such as one that concluded that "the movements of the Nigger is Southward."[16] The interstate slave trade was a convenient avenue for anxious slaveholders to relieve themselves of this burdensome property. From the enslaved perspective, being sold south was perhaps the worst-case scenario. This not only deprived them of familiar faces and loved ones, setting them on a forced emigration toward the unknown, but it physically removed them from a geographically ideal region for resistance. The prospect of freedom just across the line, or easy access to Nebraska and Iowa, likely had a reassuring effect to help mitigate the horrors of enslavement in this middle ground. Slaveholders' defensive measures illustrate how slavery was being undermined as they reversed course and encouraged out-migration as a protective measure.

These examples of slavery's unsteadiness, however, privilege the power of the slaveholding community and grant it top billing in this ongoing saga. The clearest example of the system's unweaving was slaves' own actions as they escaped bondage. Enslaved people in Kansas and Missouri were agents of their own independence. Escape might take varied forms, including temporarily "lying out" or running away without any assistance. The existence of a strong antislavery presence in the territory also encouraged slaves' movement on the Underground Railroad.[17] Of course, escape was not a new form of resistance, and Missouri's borders (including those with Iowa and Illinois) had always been porous. But, the later years of Bleeding Kansas saw both an increase in the number of fugitives and also an unmistakable visibility through both local and national media outlets, whose eyes were trained on the border, looking for the next big headline. Slave escapes into or through the territory occurred on a regular basis throughout the Bleeding Kansas period. Richard Sheridan proposes that between nine hundred and one thousand fugitives came through Douglas County alone, but accounts conflict, so the exact figure for the entire territory cannot be known with certainty.[18] Proportionally, this was a small percentage of Missouri's border slave population, but its rhetorical effects imbued these escapes with a symbolic power. The records are especially spotty, but the most active years of the Underground Railroad in the territory were from about 1857 to 1861. It was during those years that the white population had reached a critical mass of antislavery men and women, including those who were willing to serve as conductors, as well as free blacks who settled in the territory and established safe houses for their escaping brethren.[19]

Many general histories of fugitive slaves and the Underground Railroad have highlighted the kindness and courage of white stationmasters, often eliding the true nature of slaves' own work to liberate themselves. In recent decades, free blacks' and slaves' roles in organized "Railroad work" has also received significant attention, as our definition has broadened to view the Underground Railroad "not as a single entity but as an umbrella term for local groups that employed numerous methods to assist fugitives."[20] Scholarship of both an academic and popular nature centers on these networks' organization, the locations of routes and safe houses, and how these actions contributed to slavery's downfall. In this region, which has received less attention from scholars than areas in the Mid-Atlantic or Midwest, these local networks lacked significant organization, membership in the group known as "conductors" remained flexible, and both white and black abolitionists made in-the-moment decisions about what constituted a safe space. The political discord of Bleeding Kansas had created instability within border communities. The military was legally bound to enforce the territory's proslavery statutes, mobs of partisans roamed the countryside, and personal quarrels sometimes ended in violence. The Underground Railroad here was less a structured system than a flexible, grassroots movement that hinged on slaves' knowledge of the social geography as much as on the goodwill of kindly whites.

Conductors kept no records and rarely spoke about their activities until after the Civil War, because the Fugitive Slave Law of 1850 prohibited any action on the part of Northerners to assist fugitive slaves. This statute specified that new federal slave commissioners could, upon "satisfactory proof being made," sign warrants authorizing the return of any fugitive, regardless of how long that individual had been living as a functionally free person. The law clearly favored slaveholders, since incarcerated slaves could not testify on their own behalf, and slaveowners could marshal the power of the federal government to retrieve their property. Furthermore, commissioners collected a ten-dollar fee for each runaway returned to slavery, but they would only receive five dollars if that slave remained free. Average citizens were now required to aid in remanding fugitives, and anyone caught aiding a fugitive could face six months in prison and a $1,000 fine.[21] The Fugitive Slave Law remained a controversial piece of legislation throughout the North. Contrary to its intent, it did little to discourage abolitionist assistance, but it still hung over the Underground Railroad as a harbinger of potential complications for anyone caught aiding fugitives. Mary Abbott, who operated a safe house in Kansas with her husband, recalled later that "the less we knew about them, the easier it would be to answer the questions of the pursuers."[22] The cardinal rule of the Underground Railroad was secrecy.

Missouri laws regarding fugitives, stretching back to its territorial days, also remained on the books. A statute from 1804, which was copied almost verbatim from Virginia's slave code, authorized justices of the peace to issue warrants for runaways "lurking in swamps, woods, and other obscure places," and the local sheriff could detain these runaways in jail, with the jailing fee at the expense of the slaveholder.[23] Because the Missouri River was a particularly appealing escape route, this slave code also stated that any boat pilot who transported a slave without the slaveholder's express permission was liable to a fine.[24] As Missouri's population grew, additional statutes were added to further restrict slaves' movements. An 1817 statute passed by the Missouri territorial legislature stated that all slaves found traveling without a written pass were assumed to be fugitives and any person who found such a slave was obligated to bring them before the justice of the peace. If the owner could not be located, the person who recovered this fugitive was responsible for running a newspaper advertisement.[25] Furthermore, it was actually illegal for the state assembly to pass any emancipation law that did not compensate slaveholders, a mandate that complemented Missouri's harsh treatment of anyone accused of aiding or abetting a fugitive.[26] These laws remained in effect until the Civil War, and all of these exemplify the government's commitment to protecting slaveowners' interests by preventing escapes and limiting slave mobility.

Additionally, in the midst of Bleeding Kansas, there were other statewide attempts to restrict slave mobility. There were at least two bills submitted to the state legislature calling for extensive slave patrols along the border, although neither passed, perhaps because of the manpower involved in policing such a vast area. Still, as early-twentieth-century historian Harrison Trexler has described, the problem so consumed Missouri border counties that in 1857 the Missouri General Assembly appealed to the federal government for additional protection for property rights as outlined in the Constitution.[27] Individual towns also took escapes seriously. In November 1855, the City of Kansas (now Kansas City,

Missouri) passed an ordinance that severely limited free blacks' mobility within the town's confines, which was one way to curb slave escapes. By requiring all free blacks to have a pass when traveling between the hours of ten o'clock in the evening and four o'clock in the morning, any patroller or slave commissioner who found an African American without a pass might reasonably assume that that individual was a slave.[28] This ordinance hurt both the free black and enslaved communities.

The Kansas territorial legislature, which was a proslavery body in its earliest incarnations (due largely to the fraudulent 1855 election), passed a law in 1855 that offered severe punishments for anyone caught aiding escapees. According to section 4, "if any person shall entice, decoy, or carry away out of this Territory, any slave belonging to another, with intent to deprive the owner thereof of the services of such slave, or with intent to effect or procure the freedom of such slave, he shall be adjudged guilty of Grand Larceny, and, on conviction thereof, shall suffer death, or be imprisoned at hard labor for not less than ten years."[29] Even though the legislature's threats were ineffective, abolitionists had every reason to take such threats seriously. As long as this proslavery territorial legislature received official sanction from the federal government, all U.S. marshals, military officers, and other agents of the proslavery party could legally apprehend fugitives.[30] The United States government was now even more engaged in the business of limiting slaves' mobility and kowtowing to Southern pressure. This realization radicalized abolitionists and made them even more convinced that slavery enjoyed a far-reaching grasp.

These runaways came from a variety of situations. Some, like the slaves of Jabez Smith who escaped en route to California, lived on large plantations on the border, but most escaped from smaller households in Missouri and nearby states like Arkansas.[31] According to historian Harriet Frazier, if one goes solely on the basis of runaway advertisements in Missouri newspapers, most fugitives were men between the ages of eighteen and fifty, a statistic that is comparable to demographic data on runaways elsewhere in the Upper South.[32] Women did escape, although many historians (including Frazier and Stephanie Camp) often reference women's decreased mobility as the result of childbearing and childrearing responsibilities, which remained the primary domain of enslaved mothers.[33] The presence of children limited their opportunities to escape unless they could bring their offspring, which would depend on the children's ages and physical strength. However, it appears that women fugitives did pass through Kansas in some numbers, since within the surviving reminiscences left by white abolitionists (virtually no accounts from the African American perspective are available), women appear with some regularity. For instance, when John Brown assisted in the escape of eleven slaves from Vernon County in late 1858, that group contained several women, including one who was pregnant and gave birth on their journey northward.[34]

Fugitives' rationales for running away varied greatly, and unfortunately most of their stories have not survived, or they have only been kept alive in the reminiscences of white abolitionists who aided their escapes. As a result, tales of those who escaped without white assistance are incredibly rare, and scholars therefore rely on evidence from more organized, white networks. Even through white accounts (which are often self-congratulatory), it is still possible to uncover some feelings and motivations of the enslaved men and women who embarked on these hazardous journeys. One white Kansas abolitionist, James Abbott, spoke later about some fugitives' reasons for escaping. If a Missouri slaveowner truly believed that his property was being threatened, and determined to move farther south, the bondspeople within that household would often "make an effort to secure [their] freedom before the difficulties were increased and the opportunities were gone."[35] Other fugitives took advantage of their owner's absence. An enslaved man named George escaped with his wife, Fanny, and their three children in 1858. Lewis Bodwell, a Congregational minister living in Topeka, assisted them in their escape to Nebraska. According to his later reminiscence, George and Fanny chose to flee Leavenworth after George's owner, a military officer, was relocated to a different assignment and Fanny's owner, a woman from Alabama, returned south. It appears that George worked as a house servant while Fanny was a laundress. Bodwell wrote that, "the master far west, the mistress far south, some good friends near, and their only responsible keeper having her cares and duties taking precedence of this, truly 'the cat was away and the mice might play.'"[36] In this case, the entire family made it safely to freedom.

In some cases, education and the ensuing ability to read and write inspired Missouri bondspeople to break free from slavery (much as Frederick Douglass did in Maryland). An unidentified slave of Peter Abell who lived in Weston learned how to read, write, and interpret a compass to navigate the countryside. Having access to this gave him greater control over his own movements and a greater chance of making it north, so much so that he took two companions (slaves of Jack Vineyard) with him. The exact particulars of this case are unclear, but in the words of one local abolitionist, Abell was convinced that "slavery [was] the best thing that ever either spontaneously grew, or was ingeniously contrived and made," which made voluntary manumission unlikely. Escape became these men's best chance.[37] Like most escaped slaves, their ultimate fate remains unknown to us today.

The potential of separation by sale posed another common motivation for escape. In 1858, Jim Daniels of Vernon County discovered that he; his wife, Narcissa; and his children were soon going to be sold or hired out as part of an estate sale. Often, in sales and hiring agreements such as these, families were separated. For the Daniels family, escape would have to happen quickly if they were to stay together, so Daniels contacted John Brown's nearby camp to seek assistance.[38] This was also the case with Napoleon Simpson, a fugitive from Jackson County, who spent some time at the Joseph Gardner home near Lawrence. According to a later reminiscence left by Gardner's son, Simpson had been sold to a slave trader who took slaves south, but he escaped to Iowa and then returned to the border, hoping to liberate his wife and children.[39] Charles Carr decided to flee his Missouri owner when a slave trader came to his home and Carr feared he would be sold south.[40] Duff Green, a slaveholder in Atchison County, sold a mixed-race woman and her one-year-old child to a slave trader in October 1859, and while awaiting their removal by steamboat, they escaped with the assistance of an unidentified African American and John Byrd, a local minister. Byrd ushered the two to the house of Andrew Evans before dawn the next morning, where they remained for about three days as arrangements were made for them to continue to the next station, a nearby Quaker settlement. Green printed and circulated a handbill, offered a reward, and sought help from neighbors, though it does not appear he had any success.[41] The circumstances surrounding this incident are unclear, but this woman may have had various motivations for escaping—perhaps she wanted to remain with the child's father, or she had other family nearby, or she simply did not want to leave the territory. Clearly there was a network of communication, perhaps headed by the local black community, which allowed her to alert sympathetic parties to her wishes.

In order to ensure the secrecy (and thus the efficacy) of these passages to freedom, the travel routes varied, both depending upon the starting location on the Kansas-Missouri border and on contingencies that often remained outside slaves' and abolitionists' control. Some accounts describe escapes across the Missouri River in the vicinity of Leavenworth or Atchison, although this was riskier because of the river's unpredictability; still, some fugitives escaped by building or stealing a raft, swimming, or crossing on the ice during the winter. Generally fugitives traveled on foot, sometimes covering many miles, but sometimes they acquired some form of transportation.[42] Although it is likely that at least some white Missourians were sympathetic to fugitives, the historical records show little evidence that escapees received assistance on the Missouri side of the line. That was, consequently, the most difficult stretch of the journey for many enslaved people.

Historian Richard Sheridan maintains that most Missouri slaves crossed overland in the counties south of the Kansas City area.[43] According to later accounts of the more organized networks, there were two routes that might be modified when necessary. The first, or "northern," route began in Quindaro, a short-lived abolitionist town in Wyandotte County. It then proceeded to Lawrence, Oskaloosa or Topeka, Holton, and then up to Nebraska. Within Douglas County, several sites existed, including the homes of James Lane and James Abbott in Lawrence, and other spots that saw less action, like the home of Richard Cordley, minister of the Plymouth Congregational Church. Annie Soule Prentiss, whose father, Amasa Soule, operated a station near Palmyra just south of Lawrence, later wrote that her father "would always take in all the Negroes he could."[44] Joel Grover's barn, completed sometime in 1858, was another key hiding place, and many conductors, including John Brown, spent time on the Grover farm.[45] This route was only roughly laid out and depended very much on political circumstances (Douglas County also included active proslavery bases, such as that in Lecompton). Lawrence was notorious for its abolitionist bent, which made it a prominent target for fugitives; Northern folk often reveled in its politically charged beginnings, while Southerners despised it for those same reasons. Yet, clearly strategic locations like Lawrence served not only to anchor the free-soil landscape but also to shape the contours of slave resistance. Although slaves sometimes lacked knowledge of the official Underground Railroad, they did have familiarity with the border's geography, which translated into an awareness of freedom just beyond their reach. News of towns like Lawrence was not hard to come by in Missouri border communities.

The second, or "southern," route often began in Mound City (in Linn County) and then went northward to Topeka and Holton.[46] In southern Kansas, several abolitionists, including Zeke Downing, James Montgomery, and John Brown, were active in aiding slave escapes. Once fugitives made their way farther north and deeper into the territory, "Topeka was the rallying point of the line."[47] In 1856, during the most violent years of Bleeding Kansas, Missourians attempted to curb further Northern emigration by preventing free-state emigrants or their materiel from entering the territory via Missouri. During this blockade, James Lane pioneered a route that allowed eastern travelers to avoid Missouri altogether by journeying through Tabor, Iowa, then westward into Nebraska and down to Kansas, effectively avoiding potential pitfalls on the Kansas-Missouri line.[48] This route, known as the Lane Trail, went in both directions and became a major route on the Underground Railroad.

Besides Lawrence, Topeka was perhaps the most active hub of Railroad activity, thanks to its key location as the ending point on the Lane Trail, its sizeable population, and the town's proximity to the Kansas River. Three prominent places of refuge were the homes of John Armstrong, Daniel Sheridan, and John Ritchie. John Armstrong constructed a two-story stone house (with a basement) sometime in 1856, located on what is now the northwest corner of Quincy Street and Fifth Street in downtown Topeka; he shared this with the Scales family, who operated a boarding house. Because his home was located near the Kansas River, which must be traversed if one was using the Lane Trail, he ferried fugitives and their white guides over the river.[49] Daniel Sheridan operated a safe house in the present-day Highland Park neighborhood on a farm owned by Mrs. Curry; at the time, this site was approximately two and a half miles south of town.[50] Both of these abolitionists gained a reputation throughout the community as persons willing to aid fugitives and other conductors. John Ritchie's house still stands at 1116 N. Madison in downtown Topeka; it was another spot where slaves sequestered themselves before passage farther north. John and his wife, Mary, were well known in the surrounding community for their abolitionist beliefs and for their friendship with John Brown, making their home a target for proslavery military operations intended to capture fugitives. It is fitting that Topeka played such a significant role, as it was a strategic spot for the free-state movement, serving as home of the unsanctioned free-soil legislature and later as the state capital.

Although slaves' experiences while traveling on the Underground Railroad have primarily survived within later reminiscences of white abolitionists, historians can still get some sense of what these bondspeople encountered while traveling. Fugitives dealt with various hardships along their journey. A mother and her two children ended up at Harrison Hannah's station in Shawnee County. In order to get past any prying eyes, the young boy hid underneath the wagon seat, where his head repeatedly bumped against the wagon's floor as they drove along the rough roads.

Even though the journey was painfully unpleasant, he managed to keep quiet. The woman hid her face behind a veil and disguised her daughter's appearance, but no doubt all three were apprehensive.[51] The family of five (George, Fanny, and their children) who had Lewis Bodwell as their escort encountered heavy rain. Although on one night, Fanny and her children found shelter inside a small log cabin, George, Lewis, and another guide named Emerson had to bunk in the wagon bed. Two days later, on the banks of the Nemaha River, they found that the river was too high and they were forced to go well out of their way to seek a shallower crossing. The entire party needed to disembark from the wagon, but with witnesses on the riverbank (who had the same idea) this had to be done discreetly. As Bodwell recorded, "George was advised to slip out at the front of the wagon and team and take to the brush, which he did. Then to Fanny, with sunbonnet tied close, and baby under her shawl, the preacher [Bodwell] said, 'Come mother, you'll have to get out,' which she did in plain sight of the provoking curious crowd. The others followed." Trouble continued, since this unexpected detour caused them to run out of provisions.[52] The rest of their journey presented similar difficulties; the escapees were stressed and constantly fearful that these setbacks might result in their capture. The party eventually reached Iowa, much to everyone's relief.

Bill Riley and his wife were fugitives from Missouri who had settled in Lawrence sometime in 1858, but they were caught by "human blood hounds" while attempting to head out of state in early 1859 with John Doy's party of abolitionists and other escaped slaves. His wife was presumably returned to her owner in Lexington, Missouri. Riley was taken to Platte County and jailed with Doy and nearly a dozen other slaves being sold south (including, perhaps, other fugitives). He was able to remove the bars from his cell window and escape on foot, crossing the Missouri on "floating cakes of ice." He then hid on a sandbar among cottonwood trees, before walking thirty-five or forty miles to the home of Ephraim Nute, in Lawrence. Nute was a Unitarian minister, friend to John Brown, and active conductor on the Railroad. He organized Riley's move to another "depot" about a month later and also preserved Riley's story for posterity.[53] Such perseverance in the face of adversity signals Riley's commitment to freedom and also demonstrates his knowledge of the countryside, as he traversed great distances independent of white aid.

Charles Carr, born in Kentucky and brought to Missouri as a slave sometime in the 1850s, detailed his harrowing flight to Luther Chapin Bailey sometime at the turn of the twentieth century. Although Bailey's account is particularly florid and likely embellishes many details, it is clear that Carr also understood the region's geography (even as a relatively recent transplant). Carr feared being sold to a slave trader who was canvassing the area, so he planned his escape in great detail. Bailey writes that Carr snuck out to the Missouri River, where "he carefully investigated the feasibility of crossing over into Kansas, determined to proceed northward when once across." He also found a fisherman's boat that could be used during the escape. After saying goodbye to his wife and children, he inspired two other enslaved men to join him when he escaped late that night. Despite a violent altercation with a posse, he was able to reach freedom in Nebraska. He and his family later relocated to Topeka, having been reunited some time later in Leavenworth.[54]

Perhaps the most famous example of a daring escape fraught with challenges is that of John Brown's 1858 raid into western Missouri, where he helped free eleven slaves who lived on farms in Vernon County. Jim Daniels had sought out Brown's help, having traveled across the border under other pretexts. On December 20, Brown and the main element of his force went to the farm of James Lawrence (who had died and willed the estate to his son-in-law, Harvey Hicklan) on the north side of the Little Osage River, where Jim Daniels, his wife and children, and Sam Harper were held in bondage. Meanwhile, Aaron D. Stevens, a member of Brown's band (who would later join Brown's raid on Harpers Ferry, Virginia), took a smaller party to farms located south of the river.[55] The slaves' perspective has not survived, but for those such as the Daniels family (who expected Brown's arrival), the few days prior to the raid were conceivably full of both anticipation and fear that these white abolitionists may not keep their promises. In this instance, Daniels's knowledge of Brown's location in the territory illustrates his willingness to exploit his unsupervised access to the landscape. Even a published history that was unsympathetic to the slaves' plight noted that "the negro men [on these farms] frequently went unattended into the territory, mounted on good horses, hunting for stock."[56] Such freedom signaled these men and women's knowledge of the border's social and physical geographies.

Once Brown and his posse arrived to aid the slaves on the former Lawrence farm, Daniels began separating out all the personal property belonging to the estate so the fugitives could collect essentials. According to George Gill, a member of Brown's party, both Brown and these bondspeople considered this property "as being owned by the slaves, having surely been bought with their labor. . . . They, the slaves, were the creators of the whole, and were entitled to it, not only as their own, but from necessity."[57] Sam Harper joined Daniels, his wife, and their two children, although it is not clear whether Harper knew about the raid in advance or decided spontaneously to make his escape.[58] In any case, they came out of slavery with more possessions than the average fugitive, including two horses, a wagon, cattle, bedding, clothes, and other miscellaneous belongings and foodstuffs.[59] After finishing at Lawrence's place, the group headed to Isaac LaRue's farm. The slaves on this farm did not have advance notice. Nevertheless, five more enslaved persons gained their freedom, and as before, they took with them much-needed possessions like horses, clothing, and food.[60]

In the interim, Stevens's party liberated a woman named Jane (later Jane Harper), but in the process they killed her owner, David Cruise. According to early historian Wilbur Siebert, Jane stated that "her master would certainly have fired upon the intruders had not Whipple [Stevens] used his revolver first, with deadly effect."[61] This is the only time that Jane's perspective is available, if the story is true, and it illustrates how enslaved individuals fully understood that slaveowners were willing to resist abolitionists with force when necessary, making violence a natural response. Stevens's actions on the Cruise farm infuriated slaveholders in surrounding areas, and the governor of Missouri put out a $3,000 bounty on Brown's head that encouraged proslavery vigilantes to track the group's movement north.[62] Brown, his men, and the eleven fugitives made their way deeper into Kansas and, after spending time in Osawatomie (at the home of Brown's brother-in-law Samuel Adair), they moved northward and spent the night at Joel Grover's barn in Douglas County. From there they bunked down in a makeshift barricade known as Bain's fort before going to Topeka and hopping on the Lane Trail.

One white reminiscence described the fugitives' frame of mind during the ordeal. Cyrus Packard's daughter Olive Owen, who witnessed her father's abolitionist work, recalled that "they were quite a jolly set."[63] This was even the case after they had slept outside in wagons hidden behind some thick brush near the Packard home (at Kansapolis, now known as Rochester). The group set out again before daylight. Both the U.S. military and independent bounty hunters were hot on their heels, and after a lengthy pursuit the two parties met in a brief, bloodless skirmish near Holton that became known as the "Battle of the Spurs."[64] The escapees made it safely to Nebraska and Iowa before being escorted to Canada. One woman gave birth during the journey, bringing their number to twelve. All told, the journey took almost three months, and the fugitives traveled approximately twenty-five hundred miles.[65] According to James Redpath, this incident

FIGURE 5. Samuel and Jane Harper. Samuel and Jane Harper were freed during John Brown's raid in Vernon County, Missouri, in 1858. They eventually settled in Windsor, Ontario. Courtesy of kansasmemory.org, Kansas Historical Society.

spurred an increase in escapes, since in Missouri border counties news of the "raid" inspired mass panic. While slaveholders planned to sell their property or move it elsewhere, African Americans took advantage of the chaos and escaped in large numbers.[66] If true, Jim Daniels's desperate plea for help precipitated an impressive chain of events. Though Brown is often considered the hero of the story, none of this would have transpired if Daniels had not taken the initiative—thanks to his testing of these liminal boundaries, at least twelve bondspeople gained their freedom.

As those fleeing Vernon County well knew, the most frightening prospect for any fugitive was being captured and returned to slavery. Between Missouri's established slave patrols, impromptu posses, the U.S. military, and local residents with unknown sympathies, dangers abounded. This made it absolutely imperative that white allies and escapees collaborate to find effective (and sometimes ingenious ways) to hide fugitives. Many of these techniques were similar to those used in other Northern states on different "lines" of the Railroad. The unnamed woman and child who were formerly property of Duff Green hid at George Evans's house by huddling on a platform that was balanced on the cross beams of his cabin's roof. They stayed there for at least two or three days.[67] In Shawnee County, John Armstrong's stone house, built in 1856, had an immense hogshead in the cellar, which could fit more than one fugitive comfortably. Fugitives hid there until Armstrong thought it was safe enough to row them across the Kansas River.[68] Similarly, in Quindaro, Clarina Nichols hid a woman named Carolina in her cistern, with a chair, pillow, and comforter to keep her warm.[69] In a thicket on Shunganunga Creek, near the Ritchie house in Topeka, fugitives could safely hide. Mary Ritchie brought them food in her water bucket and then filled her bucket with water to carry back to the house. In 1856, John Ritchie narrowly missed being arrested by a contingent of U.S. soldiers who came to his house seeking a fugitive who, unbeknownst to them, had just left for Holton.[70]

Slaves' movements in the border region had always been under close watch from the proslavery communities in both Kansas and Missouri, but with increased activity on the Underground Railroad, slavery's supporters intensified their efforts to recapture fugitives. Slaveowners sometimes came to Kansas (or sent a representative in their stead) to retrieve what they considered their chattel. Isaiah Brown, a slaveowner who lived just a few miles across the border in Missouri, came to abolitionist Zeke Downing's house near Ottawa (in Franklin County) seeking news about any runaway slaves in the area. Downing had a well-fortified second level with portholes in his house; this house was the first house on the road when coming from Missouri. Sometime in 1857 or 1858, an enslaved man from just a few miles across the border, Brown's slave in fact, came through the area and hid in this part of the house, called "the fort." Downing denied seeing anyone, but Brown did not take him at his word, and they looked around the property thoroughly before returning to Missouri.[71] Rain Hutchison came all the way from Kentucky to recapture Charley Fisher, who had made a life as a free man in Leavenworth. Hutchison filed civil suits against the abolitionists who aided Fisher's escape.[72] Under the terms of the Fugitive Slave Law, no escaped slave was safe within the United States' borders. Slaveowners who could marshal the funds to mount a pursuit would receive full support from the military (and regular citizenry were also legally obligated to help).

Slaveholders sometimes enlisted aid from slave catchers. The quickest and perhaps most effective method of retrieving slave property was to post a notice in the local newspaper, especially if it offered a monetary reward. Either a posse or an individual might then apprehend the fugitive; this exemplified the significant role mobility played in shaping slaves' opportunities for resistance but also how whites' own mobility curtailed such movement. At the Abbott home, near Lawrence, one male fugitive had a very close call with a group of slave catchers. Two men had come to the home while James Abbott was away, and although his wife attempted to dissuade them, they searched the grounds with a bloodhound. She sent this young man out into the woods with an axe and instructed him to kill the dog if his hiding place was discovered. A short while later she heard a yelp—then silence. The slave catchers left empty-handed and the escapee came back to the house. He had been so scared that he was trembling when he raised the axe, and it took two strokes to kill the dog.[73] In 1859, slave catchers tracked an enslaved man from Linn County to Lawrence. There, much to Ephraim Nute's embarrassment, the posse found willing helpers among the town's residents. These "hunters" came at the behest of this man's owner, spurred by a reward of $600.[74] Another fugitive was captured near Osawatomie by a "man stealer" named Day, but abolitionist James Montgomery formed a posse and proceeded to Day's house, where he conducted an impromptu trial. After Day's "conviction," they threatened him with lynching in an elaborate charade. According to a later account of the incident, Day "was sorry for what he had done, and if permitted to life would never be found again, restoring the poor panting fugitive to his former master."[75] They released him. This account fails to state how the fugitive responded to this, although it is presumed that Montgomery aided the man's escape. Although white participants recorded these episodes, they confirm the precarious and unpredictable nature of the Underground Railroad and slaves' apprehensions as they sought freedom.

In addition to fearing discovery from a slaveowner or their associates, fugitives also had to keep an eye out for opportunistic, unscrupulous individuals who kidnapped slaves or free blacks and sold them for profit. Such an incident occurred in 1860. A free black man, who had been in the Lawrence area for two years and was staying with abolitionist John E. Stewart, was accosted in a field and the kidnappers began beating him with a club to silence his cries for help as he was carried off. Stewart and a fellow conductor rushed to the man's aid. The account does not divulge whether or not Stewart was able to successfully fend off the kidnappers, but hopefully this young man was able to get away.[76] A similar event occurred near Topeka, where a proslavery man named Isaac Edwards captured a lone fugitive named Felix and headed toward the town of Tecumseh, just east of Topeka. When word of this spread to the local abolitionist community, several Railroad conductors, including John Ritchie and John Armstrong, moved to intercept the pair but were unsuccessful. Felix escaped successfully near Leavenworth and came back to Topeka, a story that illustrates not only slaves' determination in becoming free but also their ability to navigate the landscape and use that knowledge to their advantage.[77]

Because the federal government officially recognized slavery's existence in Kansas Territory, military officers and members of law enforcement were often involved in apprehending fugitives. As one free-state man recalled, "United States Government officials were working hand in glove to make Kansas a slave state. . . . The government officials at Leavenworth often sent United States soldiers out to hunt for and capture runaway slaves, that, all of us objected to."[78] An article in the *Kansas Herald of Freedom* described a group of soldiers who forcibly entered John Ritchie's home in Topeka without written permission (such as a warrant). Luckily no slaves were found within. The article asked "how long our citizens are to be harassed in this way, the sanctity of their dwellings outraged, themselves subjected to pillage and insult."[79] It was not unusual for railroad work to pit escaped slaves and abolitionists against government authorities. A free-state man named Benjamin Van Horn witnessed slaves being hidden at a boarding house in Topeka.[80] One morning while Van Horn and the other guests were eating breakfast, word came that the military was tracking fugitives. Everyone jumped up from the table and moved some floorboards to make a small hiding place for the escapees. While the soldiers searched the house, Van Horn recalled "we were very busy eating, not a man cracked a smile, and we ate an uncommonly hearty breakfast that morning and were a long time at it."[81] These guests were committed to abolitionist principles, even in cases where doing so challenged federal power. Slave catchers' freedom to pursue fugitives—and military cooperation—was particularly grating to those who strongly opposed the Fugitive Slave Law's enforcement and fought alongside African Americans to help them achieve their freedom.

The lingering presence of the Fugitive Slave Law of 1850 meant that even fugitives who traveled safely to a free state farther north, like Nebraska or Iowa, could still be remanded back into slavery. Sometimes in predominantly white communities, a growing free-black population was cause for concern. In a letter to Thaddeus Hyatt, John E. Stewart outlined his reservations, stating that "there is something wrong in Nebraska & Iowa I am fearfull that some have been captured there & sent back."[82] Even in towns that had a reputation for welcoming fugitives, such as Tabor, Iowa, fugitives and their abolitionist allies might encounter resistance. After Jim Daniels and the other Vernon County slaves in John Brown's party reached Iowa in the early months of 1859, the citizens of Tabor held several meetings to decry Brown's actions (partly because it resulted in the death of a Missouri slaveowner, David Cruise). Fortunately, according to George Gill's account of this journey, there were enough sympathetic souls in town to aid the hungry and tired group before they proceeded eastward to Illinois.[83] Many Northerners were hesitant to aid fugitives, condone violence, or question government authority on fugitives' behalf. Contrary to the comfortable mythology that exists in popular culture today, Northerners were not universally abolitionist.

Resistance to the Fugitive Slave Law, and legal challenges to slavery's very existence in the territory, combined in the case of Charley Fisher. In 1859, Frank Harrison, Frank Campbell, and T. I. Jeffords were charged with kidnapping Fisher, a twenty-seven-year-old mixed-race man and resident of Leavenworth. The territorial Supreme Court in previous years had pursued a proslavery line, but by 1859, the court had shifted course. In that year President James Buchanan replaced Samuel Lecompte, the territory's first chief justice (and a slaveholder himself), with John Pettit, a former congressman from Indiana.[84] The evidence presented in this case hinged largely on three issues: whether slavery legally existed in Kansas, whether the Fugitive Slave Law was legal and applicable, and whether Fisher was detained lawfully with a warrant. Although details of the Court's final decision are unclear, the indictment of these slave catchers exemplifies competing definitions of what constituted the legal boundaries of slavery. In this case, slaveholders and slave catchers had been confident in their legal authority, seemingly caught off guard by the indictment. The prosecution, meanwhile, took this opportunity to question slavery's status in the territory, arguing that it was a "free territory" and that the slave catchers had not followed the terms of the Fugitive Slave Law in their apprehension.[85] This tale also highlights the sometimes fraught position that enslaved people found themselves in—here Fisher's would-be captors were arrested and prosecuted for "rekidnapping a nigger," seemingly a positive development, but these court cases failed to materially impact his own experience or address the racial prejudices at play.

Incomplete transcripts of *Territory of Kansas v. Harrison et al.* have survived; as a black man, Fisher himself was not allowed to give testimony, if he was even present at the trial. Our evidence, then, comes solely from white testimony along with a few newspaper accounts and white reminiscences. Fisher had worked as a barber at the Planter's Hotel, a bustling hub that served both locals and military personnel from nearby Fort Leavenworth. It appears that Harrison, Campbell, and Jeffords learned of his presumed fugitive status from police in Saint Louis who worked with Rain C. Hutchison of Kentucky, father and guardian to Fisher's alleged owners, who were minors. Hutchison had offered a $200 reward for the return of this fugitive. Late at night on January 13, 1859, they went to the Planter's Hotel to arrest Fisher, where they apprehended him in the barbershop and handcuffed him in front of several witnesses. After making a couple of brief stops, the group traveled on a stolen boat across the river, and while his captors slept, Fisher somehow escaped on a skiff. He returned to the Kansas side, where a sympathetic friend sawed off the handcuffs.[86]

At this point, the local abolitionist community became involved and hid him from his pursuers; the focus in contemporary accounts then shifted from the particulars of Fisher's situation to the battle between proslavery and abolitionist ideologies in this liminal space. Fisher was now a symbol of the Slave Power's reach, not unlike what occurred in other more publicized fugitive cases back East, like those of Thomas Sims and Anthony Burns. Unfortunately, the story muddies here, but at some point his allies in Leavenworth refused to acquiesce when Hutchison demanded that Fisher be jailed until the federal slave commissioner could hear the case. Despite their protests, Fisher was put under guard at the Planter's Hotel. Later, during a court recess, Fisher escaped (thanks partly to several abolitionists who were later indicted under the Fugitive Slave Law). Hutchison left the territory empty-handed.[87] From Leavenworth he made his way to Reverend Hugh Dunn Fisher's home (no relation) before heading to Canada. On the way, he was reportedly captured farther north and sold in the New Orleans market, remaining in the Deep South until the Civil War. After the hostilities ended, Fisher made his way back to Lawrence.[88] The case may have brought local attention to the Fugitive Slave Law's relevance and implementation, but Fisher did not succeed in his quest for freedom until after the Civil War.

Fisher's apprehension explains the reach of the Fugitive Slave Law in practical terms, but more significantly it speaks to the role slave mobility played in shaping the boundaries of resistance. Fisher claimed to be a free man when he spoke at a public meeting in Leavenworth. Unfortunately, the details of his speech before that body have not survived. The only other knowledge we have of Fisher's background comes from the court testimony of Rain Hutchison, who had a financial and personal incentive to emphasize Fisher's legal status as chattel. Even within Hutchison's clearly biased account, though, it becomes clear that if Fisher had been enslaved at some point, he enjoyed significant mobility. According to Hutchison's testimony, he had purchased Fisher in Baton Rouge, Louisiana, and then allowed him to hire out on steamboats on both the Mississippi and Missouri Rivers. Unquestionably, his training as a barber gave him a marketable trade. Fisher—who at that time was known as Peter, not Charley—spoke not only English but also French, along with a little Spanish and Dutch, likely as the result of his time in Louisiana among a diverse slave population heavily influenced by Creole culture.[89] If any elements of Hutchison's testimony were true, Fisher's lifetime of mobility and access to steamboat travel could be partially responsible for his decision to settle in Kansas. Leavenworth was the largest town in the territory, had a well-established black community that could lend support, and its bustling downtown provided plenty of opportunities for Fisher to make money. His knowledge of geographies elsewhere primed him for life on this border.

In this case as in others, the dangerous nature of Underground Railroad work and slaveowners' dedication to recapturing fugitives meant that escaped slaves and their abolitionist allies sometimes used violence as a defensive measure. Based on surviving reminiscences, abolitionists who participated in Railroad activities embraced the more radical aspects of the abolition movement with few reservations. In the attempt to help Charley Fisher escape his captors, several friends were charged with aiding his flight. Lewis Weld, for instance, was charged with using a club, knife, pistol, and "other hurtful weapons," although the case never went to trial.[90] Fugitives who found refuge on John E. Stewart's farm in

Douglas County could expect to be armed. For example, in the summer of 1860, a group of slave catchers was pursuing some fugitives, and in anticipation of their arrival, "Stewart had armed the Negroes and he and the Negroes successfully withstood the kidnappers, who got but one slave."[91] Slavery here, as elsewhere in the South, was maintained by violence, and thus could be resisted only with commensurate use of force; as one conductor wrote, "it would only be eradicated by violence with blood and the clash of Arms!"[92]

Napoleon Simpson, who was living with the Gardner family in Douglas County, helped fend off his kidnappers in that same year. Simpson had made his way northward the year before, but he returned to retrieve his wife, who remained a slave in Missouri. She was, however, confined to bed so Simpson crossed the line back into Kansas and stayed there in the hopes that he could save her in a few weeks' time. He stayed with the Gardner family, where they "furnished him with a Sharps rifle and instructed him in its management." When a proslavery posse attacked the home, Simpson fought gallantly. When he was reloading his rifle, a member of the posse hit him with buckshot, shattering his shoulder and killing him. According to Theodore Gardner's later recollection, Simpson "fell upon his pallet, exclaiming, 'Oh! I'm shot.' Fifteen minutes later, when he was struggling for breath, father went to him and asked if there was anything he could do for him. He said, 'Fight! Fight hard!'"[93] It is unclear whether this last line was an embellishment added to the family lore. The escalating violence in this borderland came from more than one direction. While proslavery and antislavery settlers clashed over the ideological controversy regarding slavery's expansion, enslaved people used violence to liberate themselves, although in Simpson's case, he did not succeed.

The situation on the border was further complicated by the fact that passionately proslavery communities and free-state towns sprouted up in close proximity to each other, further testament to the complex demographic makeup and social geography of the borderland. In Platte County, which bordered Kansas along the Missouri River, proslavery citizens formed the Platte County Self-Defensive Association in 1854. Although antislavery men and women lived in the county—even within the rabidly proslavery town of Weston—this association sometimes failed to see the distinctions between antislavery and abolition, and they did much to intimidate both the enslaved and their white allies. In early 1854, they posted a notice in the *Platte Argus* newspaper advertising a public meeting to address subversive influences in the area. The notice read as follows: "Whereas several valuable slaves have recently been decoyed by abolitionists, and induced to run away; and whereas it is manifest that we have some negro stealers in our midst, therefore all good citizens are requested to meet at Weston on next Thursday afternoon, July 20th to make the necessary arrangements for the security of our property."[94] The same paper noted in 1856 that a black woman had been hiding in an abandoned house outside of town, having been "induced" to leave by an abolitionist, and "we think our citizens would do well to look for him."[95] Further north in Buchanan County, citizens of Saint Joseph held a meeting and decided to remove the abolitionist editor of the *Free Democrat*, since "there are several yankee abolitionists in Saint Joseph who have been stirring up mischief for some time."[96] The implication, of course, was that unrest in the black community must naturally come from outside agitators; slaveowners remained convinced that bondspeople were otherwise content. Each community (whether proslavery or free-state) looked out for their own interests even if it meant employing drastic measures against free whites.

Even around solidly abolitionist settlements like Lawrence, the proslavery supporters in the surrounding countryside and in Lecompton (which was the proslavery territorial capital from 1855 to 1861) were watchful for any activity they deemed suspicious. Jacob and Thomas McGee, who lived a few miles east of Lawrence, had a reputation for spying on abolitionists. They were closely allied with Jake Hurd, who was later described as "the most reckless and daring border ruffian that ever lived in Kansas."[97] This posse regularly assisted slaveholders who came into Kansas looking for their slave property. When John Doy, his son, and another man set out to escort some former slaves and free blacks northward in 1859, they were intercepted by Hurd's gang, who imprisoned Doy and his son in a Platte County jail and sent most of the African Americans into slavery.[98] In this case, white abolitionists' relative freedom of movement reinforced black mobility, complementing fugitives' individual work in getting across the state line.

Another vigilante named Charley Hart—better known by his given name, William Quantrill—painted himself as an abolitionist advocate even as he worked alongside the McGees and Hurd to sabotage free-state initiatives in the region. Sometime in 1860, Quantrill heard that a group of abolitionists were looking to raid Morgan Walker's plantation, and he signed on to help. This large farm, situated near Blue Springs in Jackson County, included twenty-six slaves in the household. Quantrill secretly notified Walker and his family, who were able to collect some neighbors to fend off the impending attack. When the abolitionists struck just after dark, they faced an ambush; Edwin Morrison died instantly, but Chalkey Lipsey was injured in the hip and crept into the timber with his friend, Charles Ball. An enslaved man in the Walker household chanced upon Ball and Lipsey's hiding place and led Walker and his neighbors to the spot, where they murdered both abolitionists. Later accounts stated that Walker shot Ball through the forehead with his shotgun, and Quantrill put his revolver into Lipsey's mouth and fired.[99]

The unidentified slave's motivations are unclear, but there are at least three possible explanations for his behavior, if the story is true. First, perhaps he was unsure of the abolitionists' intentions, since sometimes slave stealers kidnapped slaves and sold them for a profit, a frightening prospect. Second, it is possible he was attempting to curry favor with his owner by allying himself against abolitionists, perhaps as misdirection to gain further autonomy and opportunities for resistance at a later date. A third, but less likely option, is that he did not welcome their help; fugitives often had to leave loved ones behind in their pursuit of freedom, which sometimes gave these men and women valid reasons for staying at home. Of course, any combination of these three explanations is viable. Aside from this enslaved man's involvement, the brutality of the incident inflamed the already fired passions within free-state communities across the line in Kansas. It is a perfect example of how abolitionists and their opponents clashed over slavery. It also illustrates how dedicated pro-slavery partisans were to quenching all abolitionist action in the border region. Because of this, free-state communities had to maintain a continuous state of watchfulness.

When considering the Underground Railroad, instead of conceiving of it as moving bondspeople *through* the territory, it is also important to note that some fugitives settled in Kansas permanently. Black communities grew organically, but they were generally at geographically strategic places—these were urban environments (to provide greater opportunities for community building and employment), set close to Missouri, and were often places where there had been a black presence prior to 1854. The presence of sympathetic and unflinchingly discreet conductors willing to aid fugitives might also have helped some towns in the territory gain a reputation as friendly places for black settlement. One such town was Lawrence, where several safe houses existed both within the town limits and beyond. In the words of one former conductor, "Lawrence has been (from the first settlement of Kansas), known and cursed by all slave holders in and out of Mo. [Missouri] for being an abolition town."[100] The several individuals that John Doy hoped to assist out of the territory had all made new lives for themselves in Lawrence. By 1860, Joseph Gardner had felt that fugitives would be safe there, so he hired some escaped slaves from Jackson County to help him quarry rocks for building fence posts. These men were not safe, it turned out, since proslavery men in the vicinity formed a posse that came out and attacked Gardner's home.[101] Reverend Richard Cordley, minister of the Plymouth Congregational Church in Lawrence, helped a fugitive named Lizzie who stayed in the area for an extended period of time.[102] These men and women required a network of support should a slaveowner, or a vigilante seeking bounty, come looking for them.

Black communities also grew in towns directly on the Kansas-Missouri line. One safe haven for fugitives was Quindaro. Abelard Guthrie and Nancy Quindaro Brown (a Wyandot), along with some New England abolitionists, founded the town in 1856. They intended the site to be a safe docking point for free staters trying to enter the territory through hostile Missouri.[103] The town especially welcomed fugitives from Platte County, which lay just across the river.[104] Orrin Murray's grandfather escaped with his family on a skiff that he rowed across the water. The Murray family stayed in the area, and Orrin lived only a few blocks from Quindaro's ruins in what is now Kansas City, Kansas.[105] Even towns in Kansas that had a reputation for being proslavery settlements—like Leavenworth—had a significant free black community that could lend support for fugitives seeking a new life in the territory. According to the 1860 census, of the 625 free black persons residing in Kansas, 295 of those were in Leavenworth County.[106] The hustle and bustle surrounding the fort, along with the town's position on the Missouri River, made it a prime site for free black settlement. It remained a dangerous one, however, for free blacks and fugitives who could not blend into the population or forge free papers, as we saw in the case of Charley Fisher.

The political fervor during Bleeding Kansas contributed to a unique social and political context where ordinary actions, on either side of this tense fault line, carried larger implications. While abolitionist sentiment was unwelcome in the South, slaveowners on the border were generally confident in the system's ability to tolerate bumps and bruises. Now, increased abolitionist talk put slaveowners on edge. Despite its geographic proximity to the North, Missouri remained unfriendly to abolitionist or antislavery ideologies. As R. R. Boone, a resident of Buchanan County, noted in a letter dated 1858, "the Kansas excitement is great here. I am a great mind sometimes to gather my rifles and go and scalp some of these infernal thieving abolitionists. They certainly all ought to be scalped."[107] There had been a fledgling colonization movement in previous decades, and some half-hearted attempts at gradual abolition, but these ended in failure. In the 1850s, the influx of antislavery German settlers into Saint Louis and central Missouri counties also unsettled the proslavery faction. Those espousing antislavery views publicly were often under surveillance and immediately aroused suspicion, and while we do not know if Boone ever followed through on his threats, the rhetoric in both slaveholders' private correspondence and the proslavery media speak to the prevalence of such attitudes.

From the proslavery perspective, abolitionists did more than just incite heated discussions and debates over the issue; abolitionists worked in collusion with slaves and free blacks and could do real financial harm to slaveholders. The most rabidly proslavery newspaper in Kansas, the Atchison *Squatter Sovereign*, warned its readers about the effect of emigrants from "eastern cities" who spoke with slaves and encouraged their dissatisfaction. Slaveholders who did not heed this warning would find that their stubbornness could have powerful effects. The same newspaper argued that sometime in 1855 an enslaved woman in the area was "induced to believe that she 'was illegally held in bondage,' and that she was 'on an equality with her owners;' since which time she has been unruly, and shows evidences of discontent." As the *Squatter Sovereign* diligently informed its readers, "the existence of an organised band of abolitionists [is] in our midst. We counsel our friends, who have money in slave property, to keep a sharp look out."[108] Similarly Axalla Hoole, who lived in Douglas County, noted in a letter that "one of our neighbors has missed a Negro fellow and supposes he has been carried off by the Abolitionists. . . . They have tried to induce a good many to run away."[109] A Kansas abolitionist, Charles Leonhardt, related the story of Jack, who said there were "lots of stories about you Kansas men, that stole Niggers and helped them to Canada."[110] Publishing or otherwise sharing such fears could spur proslavery communities into action, serving both a practical and a rhetorical purpose. Talk of abolitionist threats also shows how intently slaveholders understood the national implications of western slavery—its failure to thrive here may foreshadow its eventual downfall elsewhere in the South.

Yet, what these white perspectives did not recognize was the possibility that abolitionists (who these sources categorically assumed to be white) had in fact done very little to encourage these specific slave escapes. It is just as possible that the enslaved woman in Atchison had already come to these conclusions herself, and that the "Negro fellow" Hoole references had previously considered running away. While white abolitionists might have had prior contact with both of these unnamed individuals—we do not know the details—the important role that blacks themselves played in their own liberation did not even occur to the proslavery contingent. It was easier for slaveholders and their allies to blame outside agitation and foreign philosophies than to recognize the very real discontent within the slave community. This refusal to recognize slaves' resistance as independent of abolitionist influence was, in one sense, a boon to the black community. If responsibility for escapes could be publicly shifted to white allies, thus deflecting attention from the escapees, blacks' opportunities to access public spaces might remain relatively open. Provided, of course, that their movements did not visibly intersect with anyone who harbored abolitionist feelings. There was no doubt increased supervision over slaves and greater paranoia among the slaveholding class, but the interactions between enslaved people that occurred away from a master's prying eye remained fertile ground for talk of freedom.

Public discussion of abolition, aside from directing slaveholders' ire toward other whites, potentially helped enslaved men and women determine friend from foe. Slaveowners' fears that abolitionists exerted undue influence over bondspeople were not entirely unfounded. Sometimes former slaves told their conductors that "they never would have known anything about a land of freedom or that they had a friend in the world only from their master's continual abuse of the Lawrence abolit[ionist]s."[111] According to an article from the *Western Journal of Commerce*, "more slaves have been run off from Missouri by the intemperate discussion and excitement on this question in their presence, by those who do not own any, than from all other causes."[112] In the Bill Remington household in Platte County, "men came across the river and talked to the Negroes in secret. The slaves gathered at night around their cabins and talked about the great promises made them."[113] Some in that household crossed over into Kansas, including Lizzie Allen, whose memories were recorded (albeit second hand) in a *Leavenworth Times* article.[114] Kansas abolitionist John E. Stewart was particularly creative in his methods of conversing with Missouri slaves. He reportedly traveled among Missouri border communities with a peddler's pack, "but instead of selling goods, he soon begins talking of freedom and Canada."[115] For anyone who wished to join Stewart, he brought along a wagon and team that he hid in the woods until the group could depart under cover of darkness.

Bill Simms, a former slave from Osceola, Missouri, who ended up in Ottawa, Kansas, recalled later that "slaves were never allowed to talk to white people other than their masters or someone their master knew, as they were afraid the white man might have the slave run away."[116] These white-black relationships might lead to escape, but they also foreshadow the assistance enslaved people received during the Civil War, when white allies helped freedpeople materially and financially.

In some cases, these white abolitionists had prior experience with shepherding fugitives to safety in other regions of the United States, which equipped them for the challenges of "Railroad work" in Kansas. Quakers were some of the early conductors on Railroad routes elsewhere, and the Quaker community near Pardee reportedly came from Springdale, Iowa, known for its abolitionist leanings.[117] John Brown, who spent time in Osawatomie with his half-sister, Florella Adair, and her husband, Samuel, had participated in Underground Railroad activities while living in Ohio, as had Augustus Wattles, who maintained one of the few safe houses in Linn County.[118] Cyrus Flanders, who lived in Shawnee County, reportedly assisted in the attempted rescue of Anthony Burns in 1854, a free black man in Boston who was taken back into slavery under the terms of the Fugitive Slave Law.[119] Thus, while proslavery partisans brought their own views on slave mobility out to the Kansas-Missouri border, so too did white abolitionists who hoped to improve slaves' opportunity to reach freedom.

Of course, white abolitionists on the border were not the only ones to encourage slave escapes or resistance. An abolitionist named John Bowles noted that, of these fugitives, "none ever failed to be a successful missionary in the cause." One unidentified former slave helped at least twenty-five bondspeople to freedom, and the useful information he shared with other individuals no doubt allowed other slaves to follow in his stead.[120] A free black man from Kansas came to market in Jackson County in 1860 with two white companions to sell produce. He reportedly spoke privately to an unnamed slave from Clay County, who was also in town doing business, and induced him to run away. The slave returned to his owner, Mr. Knight, and told him of the conversation and they laid a trap. The two white men and the free African American were apprehended, jailed, and threatened with lynching but were eventually released.[121] The enslaved man's motivations are unclear, but it is possible he hoped to curry favor with his owner, or perhaps he felt pressured into an escape he was not yet equipped to make. The free black man in this case used his business dealings across the border in Missouri, and his own mobility, to make contact with the enslaved community in a context that frightened local whites. Examining the Underground Railroad from this perspective, despite the dearth of records, can be fruitful. As Cheryl LaRoche has noted, "concentrating on the landscape, Black communities, and Black churches emphasizes the self-determination of free Blacks."[122] Their dedication to assisting others to freedom came out of their own experiences with racial discrimination, whether they had been born free or born into bondage. It is no surprise, then, that they were active participants in the Railroad system (even if their own words have not survived the passage of time).

It was for this reason that proslavery supporters in both Kansas and Missouri were suspicious of free African Americans. In early 1855, the Platte County Self-Defensive Association, staunchly supportive of slaveowners' interests, notified the free blacks living in Weston that they must leave within the month or face a whipping. Some citizens of the town resisted this and, after rumors circulated that armed men were coming to forcibly expel these free men and free women, they formulated a plan for defense. The attack never occurred, but this incident points to the heated animosity between members of the Self Defensives and the average citizenry of the county.[123] This was the same group that had organized a night patrol in the fall of 1854 to limit slaves' mobility and keep an eye on abolitionists. In Frederick Starr's words, "this patrol was very quickly made up, many notorious nigger whoremasters volunteering their services in order to get the pay and the better to prowl around any of the negro cabins and enter them at their option for their own purposes."[124] The not-so-subtle implication here was that these patrollers were seeking more opportunities to assault enslaved women. The Self Defensives promoted themselves as agents of law and order, but in reality, they preyed on both free black and enslaved people in the county.

Among the white population there was no consensus on the issue of how slaves' and free blacks' movements should be restricted and who was responsible for enforcing those limits. But, among the slaveholding class, there was a rote argument that circulated in various mediums throughout the Upper South. One example is an 1858 letter to the editor of the *St. Louis Republican*, reprinted in the *Western Journal of Commerce*, that listed various justifications for removing free blacks from the state altogether. "They, together with the unprincipled abolitionists that sometimes come among us, succeed in decoying a great many from us," he wrote. "Why should we tolerate their presence when we see that they do the slaves and their owners an injury?"[125] This question, which concluded his letter, neatly encapsulates the very prescient fears of the slaveholding population throughout Missouri.

Public interactions between white and black residents of the border also came under increased scrutiny during Bleeding Kansas, indicating slaveholders' fear of an impending breakdown of social mores. The prominent case of Frederick Starr, a Presbyterian minister in Weston, illuminates the way abolitionism challenged slaveholders' attempts to control the enslaved population and exclude them from contested spaces. Starr, a native of Rochester, New York, was already suspect due to his Northern heritage.[126] In 1854, he was put before the community in a mock trial where he faced three principal charges. First, even though he secured permission from their owners, he held an informal school for slaves where he taught them how to read and write in an effort to help them grow in their Christian faith. This behavior threatened slavery's future by giving slaves access to an educated space, putting them on a more even plane with local whites and providing them with another language of resistance. Second, Starr had at least one conversation with a parishioner about freeing his slaves. Although he claimed to be a free soiler and a colonizationist, not an abolitionist, this form of dissent was intolerable in a zealously proslavery community like Weston. Last, and most shockingly, Starr once rode in a buggy next to an enslaved woman, sitting side by side in a way that connoted equality and aroused a great deal of speculation. While he had not broken any laws or preached against slavery from the pulpit, Starr was an easy target in a community already on edge, having violated the social mores and questioned the boundaries of order. He was run out of Platte County in 1855 and did not return to Missouri.[127]

Abolitionism on the border challenged the functioning of established social spaces, defied the authority of slaveholders in their homes and communities, and undermined the border economy. Yet another alarming example of its negative effects, at least in the eyes of whites, was when proslavery families in Kansas faced physical harassment from antislavery agitators. In 1856, two families living near Hickory Point (in Jefferson County) were driven away. According to the newspaper article that described these families' plights, "they were not permitted to take with them any of their stock (about 200 head) of cattle or negroes. The negroes, though, afterwards made their escape and followed their masters to this place, and crossed with them into Clay county."[128] The newspaper editor—knowing full well that stories such as this could strike fear in the hearts of any slaveowner—highlighted what he considered the positive element of the story: the slaves refused to cooperate with the abolitionists. The slaves' perspective on the encounter is more difficult to uncover. The article notes that an enslaved man and woman both agreed to remain in the territory (although apparently they rethought this decision later), but "a young negro girl refused to remain with them [the abolitionists], and was, after great irritation, permitted to accompany her master."[129] In these cases, abolitionists and free soilers could potentially affect slaves' daily experiences in a profound way. Being driven away from one's home by so-called allies—however new that home may be— could be a traumatizing experience and no doubt had repercussions that could either mitigate or complicate the horrors of the slave system. And of great concern to Missouri whites was abolitionists' role in ejecting slavery from a territory where it was legal.

Of course, such harassment extended in both directions. In addition to the case of Frederick Starr, there are other notable incidents of anti-abolitionist violence in border communities. In 1855, at least two hundred residents of Platte County formed a mob in Parkville that attacked the offices of a free-state paper called the *Parkville Luminary*, throwing furniture and the printing press into the Missouri River. They issued an ultimatum to the proprietors, George Park and William Patterson, threatening forcible expulsion or death if they did not leave voluntarily.[130] According to eyewitness accounts, the mob was riled up and they originally intended to tar and feather both men. Luckily, Park had allies who warned him in advance. He fled town, while Patterson's wife reportedly intervened to save his life.[131] A public meeting in neighboring Clay County, headed by slaveholder and former Indian agent John Dougherty (now a resident of Liberty), supported the mob's actions. They issued a statement maintaining that "to speak or publish in a slaveholding community sentiments calculated to render slaves discontented, to irritate them to escape or rebel, is not an exercise of the 'liberty of speech,' but is an act of positive crime of the highest grade, and should receive summary and exemplary punishment." Abolitionists were, by these standards, "traitors harbored in our midst."[132] As John R. Kelso, a minister and former resident of Platte County, noted in his memoirs, "everybody on our side of the river was suspected and ostracized who was not wont to loudly hurrah for slavery, and to just as loudly curse the abolitionists and the 'Black Republican.'"[133] Given the continued violence across the border in Kansas, such outrage was not surprising. This incident illustrates how slavery's compromised situation throughout the border region promised to unsettle slaveholders' control.

The later years of Bleeding Kansas did not go well for slaveholders. Slaveholders throughout the border region had dedicated time and effort to maintaining a firm hold on their slave property, controlling slaves through legal restrictions, slave patrols, and posses following the trail of fugitives. Because the federal government continued to uphold the Fugitive Slave Law, even in areas where it was unpopular, slaveholders could marshal significant power in their defense. But, enslaved African Americans consistently pushed back against these regulations and carved out various opportunities for resistance. Slaves and abolitionists upended power relations by appropriating border spaces and putting them to their own uses. Even in the midst of partisan discord, slaves on the border sometimes enjoyed a remarkable degree of mobility that was sanctioned (or even welcomed) by white heads of the households; small-scale slaveholding sometimes demanded such concessions. However, the very concession that had made slavery viable out west now threatened to tear it asunder.

This contradiction testifies to a stark disconnect. Whites at the pinnacle of the racial hierarchy, particularly those who embraced paternalistic attitudes about the inferior intelligence of African Americans, could not fathom why an enslaved individual might disregard their owner's wishes in favor of willful confrontation or escape. Yet, at other times, slaveowners feared that their slave property would no longer be safe as long as political tensions continued to plague the border. This was not an irrational conclusion, since slaves continued to escape in numbers that demonstrate their overwhelming desire for freedom. The tide toward freedom was rising in Kansas. Both individual escapes and abolitionist assistance via the Underground Railroad worked to uproot a slave system that had previously been a stable component of border society. Official records show that only two slaves remained in Kansas by 1860. This was a continually evolving social landscape that exhibited the tensions between clashing definitions of freedom and individual autonomy. This story illustrates how the political strife over slavery's expansion promised local, specific consequences in this middle ground.

5 / Entering the Promised Land: The Black Experience in the Civil War Years, 1861–1865

In the late nineteenth century, Maria Seals, a former slave living in Kansas City, Missouri, applied for a pension based on the Civil War service of her late son, Sam Denny. While enslaved, Seals had worked as a wet nurse and house servant for the Marsh family in Liberty. Sometime around 1830 she met and married her husband, Jackson, in an abroad marriage. She bore twelve children; four died during the war, and several others were "taken away by the white people." She was separated from her son, Sam, and daughter, Melinda, in 1844. They were gifted to her owner's daughter, Harriet, as a wedding gift, although they remained in the same neighborhood.[1] Sam enlisted in the Sixty-Seventh United States Colored Infantry (USCI) in January 1864, at the age of twenty-two.[2] Around that same time, Seals's owner moved to Clinton County and "left me and my youngest boy Slaughter all alone, but allowed me to live in and use the kitchen room in the house, but said I would have to do for myself now as I was free and I could not depend on her." Seals and her husband formalized their marriage and struggled to make ends meet during these difficult years, made more difficult by Sam's death in Morganza, Louisiana, in November 1864 of disease.[3] The rich depositions in this pension file highlight the struggles that African Americans in Missouri and Kansas faced not only during slavery but also in the tumultuous years of the Civil War. For Seals, as for other black residents in the region, the breakdown of social and political institutions bore special meaning for their futures as free men and women, caught in a whirlwind of events that promised them freedom but also brought untold challenges.

Kansas entered the Union as a free state on January 29, 1861, shortly before Abraham Lincoln's inauguration, a month after South Carolina seceded from the Union, and a mere ten weeks before the surrender of Fort Sumter. Residents of the state enthusiastically supported Lincoln during the secession crisis and the ensuing war; most were not "reluctant Unionists," to paraphrase historian Daniel Crofts.[4] Just over twenty thousand Kansans served in the Union army, from a population of close to thirty-three thousand men of military age, and Kansas had the highest mortality rate of any Union state.[5] Public rhetoric emphasized preservation of the Union, not slavery, as the primary cause of the conflict. Yet, Kansans embraced their reputation as the freest of the free states, even if many Kansas whites still harbored noticeable racial prejudices and discouraged black emigration. If any Southern sympathizers remained in Kansas, they were a small (and likely quiet) minority.

Missouri remained a Union slave state, though a state deeply divided. As in other border slave states, a pro-Union government did not equate to a populace supportive of antislavery views. White border Southerners were connected to slavery economically, politically, and culturally, seeing federal safeguards as crucial to the system's continuance.[6] Union militias, pro-Southern paramilitary organizations, and outright criminals all played a role here, often capitalizing on citizens' divided loyalties. In addition to fighting a war against the Confederacy in the South, and a political battle against the Copperhead peace movement in the North, the Union faced an internal rebellion that existed "in nearly all the slave States of the Union, and has assumed the dignity of a belligerent power."[7]

Missouri's Northern, Western, and Southern identities grappled for control during secession winter, as Unionist, secessionist, and moderate factions all fought to determine the state's future.[8] This made for a complicated initial meeting of the Missouri State Convention in February 1861, a body tasked with considering the relationship between the federal and state governments, and consequently, debating the merits of secession. Working separately from the state legislature, called the General Assembly, this convention met periodically throughout the conflict and existed as a bridge between the federal government's policies and Missouri citizens. Most delegates were Southern born, but they were also primarily pro-Union and generally moderate.[9] Former governor Claiborne Jackson, General Sterling Price, and other pro-Confederate officials fled the capital of Jefferson City on June 14, 1861, remaining in exile for the next four years. Jackson quickly spearheaded a pro-Confederate shadow government headquartered in Neosho in southwestern Missouri, which passed their own ordinance of secession on October 28, 1861. Jefferson Davis gladly accepted, and Missouri earned a star on the Confederate flag. By this point, the officially recognized state government had placed a moderate judge named Hamilton R. Gamble as the state's provisional governor. Gamble was a Unionist who opposed abolition (calling abolitionists "black hearted" and "insane").[10] He did his best to limit guerrilla violence and support Lincoln's policies, but he struggled to maintain order during these tumultuous years.

On the Kansas-Missouri border, a place well acquainted by this point with competing political allegiances and social instability, unassuming and ordinary people brought about a restructuring of American society. Like their counterparts elsewhere, bondspeople were the primary force behind the mass migration of fugitive slaves and contrabands both prior to and during the war years.[11] Emancipation here, as in the South, was a process.[12] This process played out differently depending on the local context, but in general, enslaved people first challenged the borders of contested spaces, whether this meant movement to Kansas, flight to nearby Union lines, or remaining at home and utilizing other means of resistance. After they took this first step, they could use local power dynamics to their advantage. And use these dynamics they did. The border's geographic distance from power centers in Saint Louis and the East, when combined with the relative inattention of many Union military officials, dictated that this movement for freedom came not as the result of national policy but through complicated relationships between the white and black communities, and between soldiers and civilians.

Of course, as Ira Berlin has noted, all the parties involved, including President Lincoln, "played their parts in the drama of emancipation. . . . Emphasizing that emancipation was not the work of one hand underscores the force of contingency, the crooked course by which universal freedom arrived."[13] Freedpeople took these first steps toward freedom, and then the legal process of determining their status could take center stage. Former slaves did not have the means to defend their freedom in every context, so the federal government played a role in challenging Southern white supremacy to "make their freedom meaningful."[14] What mattered on this border, as elsewhere, was timing. Well before President Lincoln and Congress had come to terms with the concept of emancipation as a war aim, enslaved individuals comprehended and internalized the broader implications of the Civil War. For them, any war against the South would invariably have consequences for the peculiar institution.

Emancipation was central to African Americans' priorities. Current scholarship on slavery's unraveling emphasizes the key role that enslaved people played in their own freedom; as Martha S. Jones noted in her introduction to a recent special issue of *The Journal of the Civil War Era*, "enslaved people were agents of their own liberation."[15] The Second Confiscation Act of 1862 and Lincoln's Emancipation Proclamation in 1863 provided for slaves' new legal status, but in the messy, boots-on-the-ground world of partisan warfare in Kansas and Missouri, slaves were unwilling to wait for higher ups. As Barbara Fields argued in her landmark study of Maryland, another Upper South state that remained in the Union, "as soon as federal troops appeared in the vicinity the slaves took the first step, absconding from their owners and seeking refuge with the army."[16] The situation on this border was no different, as former slaves ignored the Union's misgivings and inconsistencies by continuing the same kinds of resistance they had carried on while enslaved. Nineteenth-century white contemporaries sometimes noted as much; Richard Cordley, a minister in Lawrence, wrote later that "slaves on the border took advantage of it to make sure of their own freedom, whatever might be the result of the conflict. They did not wait for any proclamation, nor did they ask whether their liberation was a war measure or a civil process."[17] Enslaved individuals implemented their own goals on their own terms, exerting their newfound independence by escaping to Union lines as "contrabands," settling independently in Kansas, or enlisting in the U.S. Army.[18] In doing so, they challenged established notions of blacks' fitness for life in free society, including dispelling stereotypes about African Americans' ability to carry out their duties within the military. They also challenged restrictions on their mobility by reclaiming access to social spaces and forging new paths to freedom.

The story of the Kansas-Missouri line illustrates that creating an artificial hierarchy—wherein contrabands encouraged military commanders to consider emancipation, and then those military officers convinced government officials of its necessity—oversimplifies this process, and in so doing, trivializes the work of the enslaved community. While earlier scholarship in this vein encouraged historians to seek out African American voices, this rigid chain of contact places former slaves' political agitation at the lowest rung, privileging the actions of whites in the "real" work of emancipation. Contact with refugee slaves affected some Union soldiers' views on slavery, especially those who had never been exposed to its horrors, but on this border many Union soldiers had already witnessed slavery's workings firsthand. Obviously Missouri was a slave state, and for Kansans, their proximity to Missouri meant that they had likely traveled in Missouri or other slave states enough to witness slavery's workings to at least some degree. Slavery's long history in this region, stretching back to the early French fur trade fifty years prior, meant that many native Kansans and Missourians had already formulated clear opinions on the matter. Whites cannot be removed from the story of emancipation and black enlistment, but neither can they take center stage.

Geographic distinctions mattered too, since this mass migration was possible in large part because in Missouri, the only slaveholding border state to be surrounded by free states on three sides, the war brought significant chaos. This posed challenges for Lincoln's antislavery administration. One of President Lincoln's greatest concerns during the opening months of the war was how to keep the border slave states within the Union, and correspondence by Union officials reflects their identical concerns for how to maintain control over Missouri specifically. In reference to his western border with Kansas, Governor Gamble drew a connection between previous border "troubles" and this conflict. Gamble was particularly struck by how Kansas troops took advantage of the war to inflict retribution on their Missouri neighbors, even going so far as to ask President Lincoln to prevent Kansas troops from entering Missouri.[19] Union officers also lamented the state of affairs in Missouri, albeit from a different perspective. John Brown Jr., the eldest son of John Brown and a radical abolitionist himself, remarked that the Missouri public's allegiance to the Union was transitory at best; some Union supporters would "take the oath of allegiance in the forenoon and in the afternoon shoot you from behind a thicket of brush."[20] This tense situation affected all Missourians, black and white, serving as a reminder that the days of Bleeding Kansas were not yet in the distant past.

John C. Frémont, commander of the Western Department in 1861, bemoaned the instability in Missouri, especially "its disorganized condition, the helplessness of the civil authority, the total insecurity of life, and the devastation of property by bands of murderers and marauders."[21] As a result of the dire situation, he declared martial law on August 30, 1861, and included a clause that specifically freed any slaves whose owner "shall take up arms against the United States, or who shall be directly proven to have taken active part with their enemies in the field."[22] Lincoln overturned Frémont's emancipation edict and removed him as commander of the Western Department, but Frémont's willingness to call for emancipation as a war aim speaks to the conflict's seriousness.

Some accounts of guerrilla activity were perhaps exaggerated out of fear or out of a belief that such horror stories would bolster the Union cause. Regardless, Missouri's status as both a slave state and a Union state led to chaos unlike the situation in border states like Delaware, which had overwhelmingly sided with the Union.[23]

Plus, the trans-Mississippi West was, despite its importance to the Union cause, often considered peripheral. Aside from two battles in Lexington, the Battle of Mine Creek (in Kansas), the Battle of Carthage, and several battles in the vicinity of Westport and Independence, there were few large engagements on this border and none rivaling those of the eastern theater. However, infantry, cavalry, and artillery units were stationed in the region, and there were a number of smaller battles and skirmishes. These were in addition, of course, to widespread guerrilla warfare. As historian Mark Geiger concluded, despite its place on a geographic periphery, "Missouri ranked third among the states in the amount of military activity within its borders."[24] This intense guerrilla warfare, coupled with the breakdown of what little political cohesion existed, provided an outlet for enslaved men and women to make exodus a tangible reality. Between the movements of the organized military (including the Union's Missouri State Militia and Sterling Price's Missouri State Guard), the unauthorized actions of Confederate guerrillas and bushwhackers, and jayhawking raids into the state, Missouri slaves found ample opportunity to escape. Although sympathetic whites sometimes assisted them, most of these escaped slaves liberated themselves, taking advantage of sudden opportunities to control their own mobility and obtain their freedom. Union soldiers' cooperation had a practical usefulness, but there is little evidence that African Americans universally embraced the army as a force for liberation, though often they did see the military as a source of protection and employment. This "self-liberation" may not have been emancipation in the legal sense, but as one border newspaper termed it, it was a "virtual" freedom.[25]

As enslaved men and women latched onto the opportunities that arose amid this disorder, and slave escapes increased, more and more slaveholders on the state line sought to protect their property. Many accounts, ranging from reminiscences to pension file affidavits, mention slaves being taken to Texas. Larry Lapsley recalled in his reminiscence that his owner, Samuel Lapsley, took all of his slaves to Texas during the first year of the war. While in Texas, he was hired out to various neighbors before a harrowing escape through Indian country that finally led him to Fort Gibson, which was under the control of Union forces.

At Fort Gibson, a Kansan named Luke Parsons hired Lapsley and took him north to Salina, Kansas.[26] A slaveholding woman in Jackson County named Margaret Hays, left to tend to affairs while her husband, Upton Hays, fought with the (Confederate) Missouri State Guard, wrote frequent letters describing slavery's precariousness. As early as June of 1861, she commented to her mother that "people is taken their negros off in drooves to Texas."[27] She had adopted a different approach and attempted to prevent one of her slaves, Andy, from escaping by sending him "off with my mules" so he was not around when Union forces ransacked their property. He would eventually escape.[28] As a woman now tasked with slave management, Hays's letters attest to her difficulties in adapting to the new social order on top of the destruction of her other property by Union militias.

Occasionally, and for a variety of reasons, slaveowners helped their slaves relocate to Kansas. B. W. Lewis of Glasgow, Missouri, wrote to the governor of Kansas in August 1863, lamenting that almost every night there were at least a handful of slaves who fled from their owners. "In view of these facts," Lewis wrote, "we propose on or about the 1st day of November next to set all our negroes free, who may desire it. . . . From present indications most of them will go to your state at any rate before the close of the year."[29] In this case the chaos of civil war, by Lewis's estimation, made voluntary manumission a less troublesome option for the slaveowner. According to recruitment lists for Missouri, he was the owner of Spotswood Rice, who would later enlist without an owner's permission in Glasgow.[30] It is unclear if Lewis had freed other slaves already, or if Rice remained enslaved. The letter does illustrate how slaveholders, who saw enslaved people as property of some value (even this late in the war), sought to remain proactive. Rather than wait for the inevitable, Lewis chose to make the decision on his own terms.

Civil insurrection could, then, lead to stricter oversight of slaves in the hopes that slaveowners could keep their property safe, but it was just as likely that this chaos benefited slaves seeking to escape. Many Missourians on the border lived in near constant fear of marauding Jayhawkers, Kansas soldiers who were nominally connected to the regular Union army. With a distracted master or mistress, and the potential of assistance in the form of Jayhawkers or the U.S. military, some slaves capitalized on their owner's preoccupied state. One slave on the farm of Jacob Hall, in Jackson County, took advantage of his owner's absence to negotiate with Jacob's wife, Mary, who had been left alone to tend the farm. According to a letter that Mary wrote in 1863, this slave named

George received an offer of thirty dollars per month to work at Pike's Peak, Colorado Territory, presumably in the gold fields. George then informed Mary "he would go unless I paid him $15 per month. I thought I would have to do it, as I could not get a long without some one. . . . He has changed very much, I do not like [him] half as well as I used to, he is spoiled, were you here he would do much better."[31] George understood that his mistress was under unusual stress and desperately needed labor, and he took advantage of this situation to better his own lot. During the war, white slaveholding women were often left alone to manage farms and plantations, and they regularly lacked the ability to fully manage the increasingly rebellious slave population. This allowed the enslaved population an opening.

Yet, the two-faced nature of life on the border—where many Missourians were Union by day and Confederate by night—could also thwart escape attempts. For slaves who lived within a few miles of the Kansas-Missouri line, escape could be swift, since previous knowledge of local geography was probable. But for those slaves living farther into the Missouri interior, locating a safe place to hide during an extended journey often proved difficult. How could one know whether a person was truly antislavery or whether those antislavery professions were just an act played out for the benefit of Union soldiers? Who could be trusted when allegiances shifted nearly as fast as the brisk western wind? Sometimes knowledge of local communities did not translate to a clear understanding of this new wartime context.

Even encounters with federal soldiers did not grant assurance of safety, which meant that, for slaves in secessionist households, collusion with the Union sometimes backfired. An interesting anecdote from a Jackson County woman attests to this. Nellie Barrett, who had three brothers-in-law serving in the Confederate army, remained at home during the war with her children and wounded husband (a former Confederate soldier). In her reminiscence, she described the terror she felt when Union soldiers invaded the home of her in-laws, located within sight of her own log cabin. A Union corporal questioned Barrett's mother-in-law about her family's allegiance, and she swore that none of her sons were presently engaged in fighting. The corporal responded by saying, "'Madam, this Negro woman,' the corporal indicated Nan, the elder Barrett's Negro house slave, 'said you were rebels, therefore you lie!'" Nan, the accusing slave, pleaded with her mistress and said, "I never said that, honey, you know I never!"[32] In Nan's case a supposed ally—a Union soldier—was more concerned with locating a Confederate combatant than in ensuring Nan's safety.

There are two interesting components to this story. First, as Barbara Fields concluded, when the secessionists' attempts in Maryland failed, slaveowners were in the awkward position of defending their property rights while publicly proclaiming their loyalty to the Union. From that point on, the power dynamic shifted and "the slaves quietly occupied high ground."[33] Missouri slaveholders found themselves similarly situated, struggling to maintain a slave labor system while living in a Union state, albeit a divided one. Second, although it is difficult to determine Nan's motivations from a pro-Southern reminiscence, it is certainly possible that she did provide the Union soldiers with information, but when her mistress and her mistress's family learned of this, Nan felt it wisest to plead ignorance. This story illustrates the shaky middle ground that slaves navigated, trying to discern friend from foe. Union soldiers' devotion to the Union did not necessarily equate with devotion to emancipation, since some were proslavery or were even slaveholders themselves.

Enslaved people had to remain ever vigilant in deciphering the true intentions of soldiers, but some units came to be known for their antislavery proclivities. Part of James Lane's Kansas Brigade, known colloquially as Jayhawkers, canvassed the border region and gained a reputation for supporting black emancipation. Even before the U.S. government established procedures for dealing with black refugees, Jayhawkers and other pro-emancipation Union units sometimes took it upon themselves to aid slaves' escape; as John Brown Jr. put it, "more than two thousand slaves were by us restored to the possession of themselves, were 'Jayhawked' into freedom." His company, part of the Seventh Kansas Volunteer Cavalry, "proceeded to deprive the rebels of every means by which they had successfully carried on the war against the United States"—including slave labor.[34] Many accounts, from both Confederate and white Union perspectives, speak to the army's role in "stealing" or "liberating" enslaved people, although this terminology appears less frequently in the few black accounts that have survived from this region.[35] This sort of behavior on the part of Union soldiers stirred mixed reactions in Kansas, although there is evidence that Kansans supported the Jayhawkers more generally, since any action that could deprive Missourians of their property was at least tacitly condoned.[36]

In addition to encounters with jayhawking units, slaves had contact with Confederate guerrillas. For slaveholding Missourians, guerrillas could be useful for the defense of their property. When a group of several hundred slaves attempted to follow the Fourth Missouri, the commanding officer warned them that traveling with the army would attract the guerrillas' attention. Most turned away, but the next day a group of bushwhackers attacked the refugees and killed all but one.[37] Peter Lee had a similarly frightful encounter. One day, some of William Quantrill's raiders stopped by his owner's mill near Weston and offered him passage to Kansas. Lee politely declined, upon which Quantrill replied that Lee was "a 'good smart nigger,' ... for they intended to put a bullet in his head when they got him to the [Missouri] river."[38] Armilda Williams later recalled that bushwhackers "told the slaves that the Yankees had horns. . . . They told us the woods were full of men so we would be afraid to run away."[39] Their threats did not dissuade her father from creeping across the border and eventually bringing his family to join him in Kansas. Slaveholders had few resources at their disposal, so sometimes Confederate guerrillas donned the mantel of slave patrols and functionally reasserted the former racial order.

Some slaves even lived in guerrilla households, where being surrounded by active Southern sympathizers likely limited opportunities for resistance. Susan Younger, a slave on Bursheba Younger's farm, remained with the family during the war. Bursheba's son Cole Younger, a legendary guerrilla, remembered in his memoir that "Suse" once saved him from being captured by Union soldiers who came to the door late one night. He recalled that "she threw up her hands and pushed aside the guns. Her frantic screams, when they demanded that she deliver me up to them, caused a momentary confusion which enabled me to gain her side and together we made for the gate."[40] This story is one example of how the relationship between enslaved people and white family members was complicated. Although Cole interpreted this as a sign of her loyalty, Susan's motivations are unclear. She might have been concerned with his welfare, or frightened for her own safety, but it is also possible she used this opportunity to gain the family's trust, in the hopes that her heroic actions would pay later dividends.

One strategy that guerrillas utilized, intended primarily to strike out at Union sympathizers, included killing or kidnapping slaves or free blacks on either side of the line. In 1863, two men came through Atchison and stated that they were part of Charles Jennison's Union regiment, although they refused to give their names. Late one night, they ran into Joseph Gilbert's house and grabbed an African American man who was working on Gilbert's farm. According to the Atchison *Freedom's Champion*, "it is highly probable ... that some of the neighbors, who are known to be pro-slavery, secesh sympathizers, had given information concerning the whereabouts of the negro, and in this way aided in his capture."[41]

During Quantrill's raid on Lawrence in 1863, George Ellis was working on his family's farm outside town. The raiders came through and killed some Union scouts and George's father. Luckily George, his brother Ben, and his mother, Jane, managed to survive. George had hidden in the thicket near the Kansas River, and as the raiders burned the house Jane managed to drag Ben out of the flames by concealing him underneath a feather bed.[42] Quantrill's raid, which resulted in nearly two hundred deaths, was the most gruesome act of violence against civilians during the Civil War. Quantrill—like Bloody Bill Anderson and other notorious guerrillas—left a path of destruction in his wake.

Despite guerrillas' reign of terror over the countryside, though, the mass movement of enslaved people continued unabated. The greatest force in bringing freedom came from the actions of slaves themselves, who undertook a mass migration that built upon prior knowledge of the region's social geography, simply reframing it for the wartime context. Earlier control over their own mobility, engendered by the small-scale system on the border, now expanded to encompass more of the enslaved population. Historian Earl Nelson examined auditors' reports from Missouri (which record taxes) and concluded that in the first four years of the war some Missouri counties lost as much as one quarter to one half of their slave populations. Some slaves joined the army or fled to free states like Iowa and Illinois, but by his calculation, Platte County lost 23 percent of its slave population, and likely the majority of those refugees made their way to Kansas.[43]

Comparison between the federal census of 1860 and that of 1870 also illustrates the changes that occurred during and shortly after the war; in the western Missouri counties included in this study, the black population decreased by about 25 percent.[44] These demographic shifts come as no surprise, given that many black families throughout the South took to the roads to locate employment, reunite with family members in other areas, or escape escalating violence. Nationwide, somewhere between 500,000 and 700,000 enslaved people entered Union lines, and their movement ushered in a profound upheaval that dramatically affected the contours of Southern communities.[45] Enslaved Missourians were, however, already situated in a geographic space where slave mobility was central to the workings of the peculiar institution, and where earlier experience with the geographic and social landscapes could help inform their future decisions. This was the case for slaves elsewhere, to some extent, but the long history of slave mobility on the Kansas-Missouri line had laid a firm foundation for these wartime movements.

Some enslaved people, instead of seeking freedom independently, flocked to Union lines. This began early in 1861, even before Missouri's status in the Union was fully realized. Most Missouri slaves took the initiative without any prompting from Union forces, although unfortunately there are few surviving African American accounts of their individual motivations. These individuals did not enjoy legal freedom immediately, but this de facto freedom served as an intermediary position until they could be fully emancipated. Joseph Trego, an officer in Lane's Brigade, wrote home to his wife from Montevallo, Missouri, in October 1861, stating that "we send off niggers by the hundreds. Two hundred left for Kansas under the care of Capt. Baine the day we left Osceola."[46] Likewise, Chaplain Henry Moore of the Third Kansas marveled that in western Missouri "scarcely a day or a night passed that did not witness the arrival of colored refugees in camp. . . . Sometimes whole families, at other times parts of many families, would come together, making an addition of from ten to sixty to our camp in a night."[47] Not only were Kansas units overwhelmed with escaped slaves from Missouri, but Kansas troops in Arkansas and other reaches of the South had attracted refugees as well. George Titcomb of the Ninth Kansas Cavalry wrote from Arkansas that "the negroes are flocking from every direction and falling in with the column. All along the road as we march they are standing grinning from ear to ear, and waiting as they have been all the morning for the train to come along."[48]

Many white soldiers' accounts expressed surprise and dismay at the number of refugees entering camp. The sheer volume of refugees arriving at all hours of the day and night often concerned military officials, who struggled with the practicalities of dealing with this influx of needy people.[49] This mass movement of African Americans signaled not only their conviction that this war was indeed about slavery, but it also pointed to the larger implications for American society. Every region, whether North, South, or West, would see the upending of established cultural mores and the incorporation of African Americans into free society, at least in theory if not in practice. This revolution would not have been possible without bondspeople's labors and risk-taking.

This mass migration had nationwide implications as well. Former slaves' presence in military camps helped the U.S. government acknowledge the issue of slavery and its relationship to the Civil War, particularly the value of emancipation in aiding the Union's war aims. Of primary concern for many Union officials and military leaders was these refugees' legal status. In May 1861, Union General Benjamin Butler, commander of the Department of Virginia, argued that Confederate slaveholders no longer enjoyed the property rights granted by the U.S. Constitution and the Fugitive Slave Law of 1850. Thus, any slaves who entered his lines would consequently be designated contraband of war and would not be released to white ownership. As Kate Masur asserts, the term "contraband" was "a placeholder whose appeal would fade once it became clear that the war would secure permanent emancipation. Because 'contraband' had long been used to describe property, the term also implied the transitional status of the people to whom it referred. They were neither property with a clear owner (as in slavery) nor free people, but something in between."[50] This "transitional status," as she terms it, exemplifies how white military officers and politicians saw freedom as a linear process moving directly from coercive labor, to "contraband" status, to free labor.

Despite the ideological tidiness of Butler's contraband policy, the reality was much more complex. When it came to states clearly in rebellion such approaches might be clear cut, but four slaveholding states—Maryland, Missouri, Delaware, and Kentucky—remained in the Union. Secretary of War Simon Cameron suggested in an 1861 letter to Butler that the sensible course of action would be to accept slaves of loyal masters "into the service of the United States" in the same way as those of disloyal slaveowners, although loyal masters would be compensated for their slaves' labor. However, a few sentences later he explained that Union forces could not interfere "with the servants of peaceful citizens in house or field, nor will you in any way encourage such servants to leave the lawful service of their masters."[51] Loyal citizens' property rights must still be protected under the Constitution. Of course, the Fugitive Slave Law of 1850 further complicated the situation. While most slaveholding states had seceded, the law was still on the books and therefore applied to slaveholding states that remained in the Union. In response to this dilemma, the House of Representatives adopted a resolution on December 20, 1861, that stated that the Fugitive Slave Law would only allow for the recapture of a slave when his or her owner proved they were loyal.[52]

Out west, the situation was even murkier. If leading officials and military commanders could not get a handle on Missouri's political landscape, with a prosecession shadow government in Neosho and divided loyalties across the state, there would be no agreement on how to implement a coherent policy regarding escaped slaves. After Frémont was relieved of command on November 2, 1861, the remaining military commanders who were acquainted with the situation on the border in turn adopted—and attempted to enforce—a twofold policy. First, all decisions must go through legal channels. This circumvented the whims of individual army officers with their own personal agendas. Second, the law dictated that military personnel must return slaves to the appropriate owner if that slaveowner inquired about their human property. Slaveholders shouldered the burden of proof and "must establish the rights of property to the negroes as best they may."[53] General Henry Halleck, who took command of the Department of Missouri in November 1861 as Frémont's successor, attempted to clarify the matter by issuing General Order No. 3, which stated that fugitive slaves should not be welcomed behind Union lines.[54] All stolen property, including contraband property and fugitive slaves, should be returned to the Missouri populace. Thus the military could "be freed from these vexatious questions."[55] If there was one point where all leading officials could agree, it was this: soldiers' primary duty was to wage war, not to assist slaveholders in hunting down escapees.

Yet, answers that seemed clear in the abstract were more muddied on the front lines. When the general population seemingly shifted their allegiance on a whim, how might a military officer distinguish a legitimate, hired black worker from a fugitive, or a loyal slaveowner from a disloyal one? Nearly a year after Halleck's General Order No. 3, there was still disagreement within the ranks. Arthur Reeve, a fierce emancipationist, was enraged when his commanding officer, General Robert B. Mitchell, followed the dictates of Order No. 3 while the Second Kansas was in Tennessee. "General Mitchell (our Kansas Brigadier General) seems to have a fixed determination to compel the Brigade to kneel to his idol, slavery," Reeve wrote. After Mitchell ordered one of his captains to "find the slaves and put them 'outside of the lines,'" abolitionist Colonel Daniel Anthony (of the Seventh Kansas) instructed the camp guards to shoot anyone who attempted to eject contrabands.[56] Mitchell initially gave up on the matter, but after pressure came down from his superior—General J. F. Quinby—he arrested both Anthony and Captain J. L. Merrick. Even with two leading abolitionists under arrest, those who supported the refugees' quest for freedom effectively disobeyed the order, with only one exception.[57] Others like Odon Guitar, commander of the Enrolled Missouri Militia, continually refused to aid any fugitives seeking refuge.[58] The question came down to personal convictions and interpretation. As Jonathan White has noted in his recent study of Union soldiers' political values, the army's role in "liberating" slaves did not necessarily equate to a universally pro-emancipation sentiment in the ranks.[59] Halleck enforced Order No. 3 to the best of his ability. However, this order opened the floodgates to a debate about who constituted a legitimate worker, leaving it up to individual commanders to determine the distinction between a forbidden fugitive and a much-needed laborer who could bolster the Union's war effort.

This confusion and inconsistency on the part of the U.S. military made it imperative that slaves who successfully escaped behind Union lines remain vigilant. Shortly after Halleck issued Order No. 3, George Waring attempted to implement Halleck's wishes and ordered all unauthorized slaves out of the camp. Waring's regiment of Hussars had former slaves working as teamsters, personal servants, and nurses. When his subordinates went to carry out his orders, all the slaves "stoutly asserted that they were free. . . . Some of them I have no question are so; others I have as little doubt have been slaves but no one is here to prove it and I hesitate to take so serious a responsibility as to decide arbitrarily in the absence of any direct evidence."[60] This is a clear instance of slaves taking the initiative to establish their free status even in the face of opposition from Union officials. For the enslaved population, protection from former masters was prudent and necessary, but they already conceptualized their current status as freedmen and freedwomen, not as people who remained enslaved.

Slaveholders did not welcome or condone this determination that enslavement ended once bondspeople escaped their owners' physical and psychological control. On occasion, slaveowners appealed to military commanders in the hopes that they could retrieve escaped slaves.[61] Chaplain Henry Moore noted that loyal slaveowners were sometimes permitted within the military camp "to reclaim all his property, slaves as well as the rest, provided he could persuade them to return with him. This was frequently attempted, but in no instance with success that I know of."[62] In another instance, Lieutenant Colonel John Phelps, a slaveholder himself, had contact with concerned citizens from the area around Rolla, Missouri, who had brought slaves to his camp "for safe-keeping in order to be restored to their owners." Phelps knew some of these owners personally, and some of his own slaves had entered the camp "when the people fled from Springfield and vicinity with a wagon and team, clothing and supplies for their support. They feared they might be stolen by persons in the army and they fled to me for protection."[63] Slaveholding officers like Phelps would not have endorsed slaves' informal claims to personal freedom.

The influx of refugees sometimes necessitated the construction of separate contraband camps located near Union lines, although unlike camps in other parts of the South, the military did not specifically construct most of these camps. A resident of Vermont who traveled to Kansas in 1863, Charles Chase, visited a refugee camp located near Fort Scott. According to Chase, the camp was located in a timbered ravine with a stream of water nearby, and the refugees lived in "bowers and tents . . . in squads or families, accompanied generally by a span of good mules and a lumber wagon with what ever portables they can seize upon."[64] This particular campsite appeared well suited to the needs of the refugee community. Camps were intended to be temporary, however. Many of the slaves who entered these lines, if located close to the border, passed into Kansas and began a new life within the growing African American communities of the border counties.[65] Although some places in the South received assistance from organizations like the American Freedmen's Inquiry Commission, camps on this border had little aid, making resettlement in established communities the best means for addressing the refugee community's needs.

Although few contemporary accounts from the Kansas-Missouri border reference camp conditions, historians do know that freedmen and freedwomen often acquired a few possessions, which helped mitigate the challenging process of transitioning to freedom. John Brown Jr.'s regiment of Jayhawkers, for example, confiscated the physical property of those who were disloyal and loaded slaveowners' wagons "with such household stuff as would be especially needed to set their slaves up in housekeeping in Kansas."[66] Most refugees' possessions were, however, acquired by the refugees themselves with little aid from Union sources. Of course, not all the refugees were so lucky. Mrs. Byron Judd recalled that many of the refugees coming through Wyandotte were "carrying all of their earthly possessions in little bags or bundles, sometimes in red bandana handkerchiefs."[67] According to Chaplain Moore, the belongings that usually came alongside refugees consisted primarily of housewares, clothing, horses, and wagons. If slaves' former owners had left their home in haste, these men and women rounded up as much personal property as they could carry before heading out.[68] An unintended consequence of this influx of supplies was that it created additional headaches for the U.S. military, which sometimes put freedpeople and soldiers at odds. The added presence of refugees' property, particularly animals like horses and cattle, imposed a further burden on the military camp or contraband camp's infrastructure. These supplies were essential to freedpeoples' survival, but they could also impede the army's movements and pose other risks. This tension exposes the military's lack of preparedness for administering humanitarian aid, which was the natural result of an organization intended to wage war, not conduct relief efforts.

Contrabands' convenient geographic location near army encampments had one significant benefit: both men and women could find employment by working as cooks, servants, grooms, laundresses, and teamsters. Several refugees from near Springfield, Missouri, worked for Andrew Jackson Huntoon, the assistant surgeon in the Fifth Kansas Cavalry, managing the hospital's laundry. Huntoon spoke with one man who sought employment on Huntoon's farm once spring arrived.[69] A young boy worked for Colonel Horace Ladd Moore of the Second Kansas Cavalry as his personal servant.[70] James Montgomery and several other officers lived in Fort Scott; one of these officers, Joseph Trego, wrote a letter to his wife describing his living arrangements and noting that they had "a contraband wench for cook."[71] Seeking employment was generally the first step to gaining autonomy over one's affairs and access to public spaces, so a crucial step in the process of claiming freedom was becoming financially independent. Welfare efforts that existed elsewhere in the United States did not exist on this border, so this was particularly vital on the Kansas-Missouri line.

Along with opportunities for employment came challenges, though, as sickness and disease ran rampant in both army and contraband camps. Black refugees suffered from a variety of afflictions. Water pollution due to poor placement of latrines, close living quarters, a lack of sturdy shelter or weather-appropriate clothing, and various other unsanitary circumstances, all led to a proliferation of disease pathogens and death due to exposure. Medical professionals, who did not yet have knowledge of germ theory, were not up to the task. Also, racist feelings that sometimes ran deep within the army corps meant that African Americans failed to receive adequate treatment. As Jim Downs has argued, "the distress and medical crises that freed slaves experienced were a hidden cost of war and an unintended outcome of emancipation."[72] In regions where the physical environment exhibited severe stress—like the "Burnt District" of southwestern Missouri that was evacuated after Order No. 11—former slaves struggled with bodily consequences of this social and structural breakdown.[73] This was especially true for women and children, who were more likely to be confined to camp instead of leaving to perform farm labor. F. R. Newell, superintendent of contrabands and a colleague of Chaplain Hugh Dunn Fisher's, lamented that in his camp there was so much sickness that he desired to send more refugees to Leavenworth as a way to relieve the pressure. Out of 226 fugitives, 96 were children and there were "not over 20 capable men."[74] In some respects, however, the situation on the border was unlike that in other regions, since freedpeople more consistently resettled in established communities on the border; this stability, as opposed to lengthy stays in unhealthy, makeshift camps, mitigated some of the medical challenges that freedom posed.

Slaves' presence in camp literally signaled the continuing collapse of the peculiar institution, but many whites' racial attitudes toward African Americans did not change, foreshadowing the lengthy struggle for black suffrage and civil rights in the postwar period. Some military officers believed these former slaves were duplicitous and untrustworthy, and they questioned their presence in camp. They feared that slaves could— and would—transmit strategic information about troop numbers and movements to Confederate forces.[75] Despite some commanders' fears of subterfuge, enslaved men and women were more likely to share useful intelligence with Union forces. As Chaplain Moore wrote, "most of them brought us valuable information in regard to the enemy, or the condition of affairs in the neighborhood they left." Their usefulness came not only from their labor, but also from their knowledge of social geography and previous use of local landscapes. Contrabands provided timely intelligence about troop movements, guerrilla hideouts, civilian sympathizers, and the location of war materiel. His account also provides insight into the mindset of these refugees. Contrary to other white Kansans' perceptions, he firmly believed that "in almost every instance the slaves had a clear understanding . . . and were ready to cooperate with the army in its war policy."[76] Former slaves fully comprehended how their escape benefited the Union cause, but they still faced hurdles as they transitioned into free society.

Throughout the western theater, military chaplains took an active role in shepherding contrabands to safety, since Union camps could not contain all the needy refugees. For units stationed relatively near the Kansas-Missouri border, Kansas often became freedpeople's ultimate destination. In 1861, Chaplain Hugh Dunn Fisher of the Fifth Kansas Cavalry and a resident of Lawrence, along with Chaplain Henry Moore (Third Kansas) and Chaplain Reeder Fish (Fourth Kansas), had the distinction of taking the first group of contrabands into the state. They formed their company, nicknamed "The Black Brigade," in Lamar, Missouri, encompassing a wagon train close to a mile long. Their destination was Fort Scott, and in their journey the company would have to travel through forty miles of territory controlled by bushwhackers and Confederate regulars. According to Moore's account, "Col. Nugent was forwarding to Fort Scott a small wagonload of condemned muskets, and that the maddened lookers-on might not be tempted too strongly to pursue us, an order was issued that all the men should be armed before we advanced."[77] Even though the muskets would not fire, the ruse worked and the company made it safely to Kansas. The contrabands' reaction to entering the state was one of jubilation. Moore wrote that "when these pilgrims to a land of liberty were informed that they were in Kansas, that they were now treading on soil of freedom, their shouts and hurrahs rung out all along the line, in a way that one may not expect to hear twice in a lifetime."[78] This example perfectly encapsulates the divergent pathways to freedom, as it came in different ways at different times in different places, sometimes as an act of outright resistance, and at other times, through more peaceful means and deceptions. For these men and women, their freedom was contingent not merely on reaching Union lines but on successfully reaching the free state of Kansas.

While the U.S. military continued to hash out the intricacies of formal contraband policy, other freedpeople took control of their own mobility by making more permanent decisions about settlement. Kansas, the state that so many slaves considered a bastion of freedom, was an attractive option. Some enslaved men and women in Missouri were close enough geographically to cross over the line with no assistance from the military. Cities situated on the river—such as Wyandotte—witnessed the greatest numbers. Pension file affidavits regularly reference these larger border towns. According to a white resident of Wyandotte, "it was a sight to make one weep, those poor, frightened, half-starved negroes, coming over on the ferry, and the people of the village down at the levee to receive them."[79] These men, women, and children came from Missouri but also from places as far away as Mississippi. Once within the state's boundaries, black refugees quickly sought out food and lodging (however temporary that shelter may be). Their next order of business was to locate employment and get connected with other African Americans who could provide support.

Other key geographic sites in Kansas, which had in many cases already boasted free black or white abolitionist populations, were particularly attractive to freedpeople. Lawrence, long known for its antislavery roots, became a central site for the growing African American community in Kansas. The 1865 Kansas state census listed more than two thousand African Americans in Douglas County, a dramatic increase from the four listed in the 1860 federal census, with nearly all living in Lawrence.[80] Richard Cordley testified to the town's reputation, writing "the colored people of Missouri looked to it as a sort of 'City of Refuge'. . . . Lawrence was on the direct line to the North pole, even if it did lie to the West."[81] George Ellis and his family, originally from Jackson County, escaped to the Eleventh Kansas, stationed near Olathe. George, his brother Ben, and his parents settled down and built a log house outside Lawrence on a farm they leased from James Lane.[82] In 1863, Rebecca Brooks Harvey fled to James Blunt's command as they traveled through Arkansas, eventually moving to Lawrence with her children.[83] While there, she reunited with her husband, David.[84] In fact, there were so many refugees entering Douglas County that the residents became overwhelmed. Lawrence resident John B. Wood marveled that "131 came into Lawrence in ten days, yesterday 27 had arrived by 4 P.M. . . . There is not an intelligent slave in Mo. but knows where Lawrence is; and we shall have them here by the thousands."[85] Notably, both Wood and Cordley understood that these men and women were taking their freedom into their own hands with little help from whites. Lawrence's reputation as a free-soil town during Bleeding Kansas was widespread, even among the enslaved population of Missouri. It may not have always been their permanent home, but Lawrence served as a clearinghouse for many emigrants seeking to settle in the state.

Ample military protection and diverse opportunities for employment, coupled with the existence of a well-established black community, made Leavenworth another prime destination. In 1861, it was the largest town in the state, with five thousand inhabitants. By 1870, thanks partly to black emigration, it boasted close to eighteen thousand.[86] In 1865, there were 2,455 African Americans in the city, composing 16 percent of the population. Furthermore, there was interracial cooperation between white leaders and the First Colored Baptist Church, including the formation of the Kansas Emancipation League in early 1862.[87] They aided refugees in acquiring basic needs and finding employment, and more broadly, would "assist all efforts to destroy slavery."[88] Their target audience was freedpeople like Robert Richardson of Platte County, whose owner, Achilles Perrin, allowed him to move to Leavenworth prior to emancipation (sometime after 1861). He then returned to retrieve his wife, Sarah Ann, and his son, Jefferson. In an interview with Sarah Ann in 1909, she said that her husband "secured a horse from a friend, and, placing Mrs. Richardson and her son, Jeff, on the animal's back, struck out in the dead hours of the night on their journey of escape." The ferryman near Leavenworth refused to transport Sarah Ann and Jefferson across the Missouri, so Robert reluctantly left them behind while he crossed the river alone and located a canoe to transport his family to safety. They escaped successfully and began a new life in Leavenworth before settling near Atchison.[89] In these as in other cases, African Americans' control over their own mobility was an essential asset to their survival during this tumultuous period, and free blacks in Leavenworth served as a bridge between black escapees and the local white community.

Fort Scott, like Leavenworth, possessed both geographic and cultural advantages. For freedpeople who crossed paths with the Union military, often those units were headquartered in Fort Scott. This fort was a bustling center during the war, with more than sixteen hundred troops stationed there in 1864.[90] By 1865, Fort Scott had just over 350 African American residents, making up 26 percent of the town's population. When the first group of freedpeople entered the town in 1861, they were met by townspeople eager to take in able-bodied men, women, and children who could help them around the house or the farm; this was due both to altruistic motives and labor shortages in the area. Whites' objectification of black bodies shaped the reception these black refugees received, as they were divvied up among the white population in ways not dissimilar to a slave auction. Such treatment points to the Civil War's devastating effects on the white population of the border, where there was a true crisis of labor, but more importantly, it illuminates how white Kansans often harbored the same racial prejudices as their Missouri neighbors.

Throughout the state, there was no shortage of work in the harvesting season for freedpeople fit enough for farm labor, so despite the fact that white Kansans' attitudes toward black labor were prone to selfish motivations, employment opportunities abounded. John B. Wood, a resident of Lawrence, wrote that "thus far they [refugees] have been taken care of; as the farmers need help and hundreds if not thousands are now employed in harvesting."[91] The drought of 1860 to 1861 was followed by plentiful harvests, and with so many white Kansas men actively fighting in the military, there was great demand for capable farm labor.[92] Once winter set in, however, it would be difficult for escaped slaves to find gainful employment in farming pursuits. Wood's same letter suggested that "no doubt a part of the farmers will provide for those now at work for them, during the winter, but all will not do it." He continued, writing that "unless our friends from the east assist, there will be starvation and death among them."[93] His letter was addressed to George Luther Stearns, a wealthy New England patron who had helped finance John Brown's raid on Harpers Ferry and had enough influence to raise aid for these newly freed people.

Although some white Kansans sympathized with black emigrants' plight, the fundamental racism that still prevailed in Kansas—regardless of its reputation as the "freest" of the free states—made others resent the fact that black emigrants sometimes refused to work. White residents imposed their own conception of labor and its value onto a population that had a drastically different experience with manual labor. After visiting the thriving town of Fort Scott, Charles Chase wrote about what he deemed an elevated sense of self-importance among the town's newest inhabitants. "The town offers them work, but they do not incline to accept," he wrote. "Some are glad to get work and prove their manhood and usefulness; others lounge in idleness, refusing good offers, preferring to live on the hospitality of those who have erected little shanties and are now earning a living. . . . A poor nigger is often made dizzy by his unexpected elevation."[94] Unfortunately there is no evidence on hand to determine whether local employers actually offered freedpeople a fair wage. Blacks' refusal to compromise their own principles and receive unfair wages did not sit well with many white Kansans. This example illustrates whites' belief that recently freed slaves had a responsibility to seek out gainful employment immediately, regardless of the pay. That assumption was rooted in a lack of awareness regarding working conditions under slavery and thus did not align with black perceptions of their priorities.

Some Kansans who did sympathize with the freedpeople's suffering took their support to the next level and actively worked to provide relief. Chaplains Hugh Dunn Fisher and Henry Moore were both active in aiding black refugees, even outside of their official military duties. Toward the end of 1863, Fisher received instructions from the Western Sanitary Commission and Major General Schofield to travel back east and raise support to alleviate the refugees' suffering. These freedpeople were "reduced to a situation of great misery, and are perishing in large numbers."[95] Of course, such compassion on the part of the Western Sanitary Commission was tempered with stereotypical language, much like that of Charles Chase and other members of the general public. In a letter to President Lincoln, the leaders of the commission referred to the "helplessness and improvidence of those who have always been slaves."[96] Samuel Curtis, at this point serving as commander of the Department of Missouri, made some attempts to help freedpeople get fair prices for their crops by directing them to certain buyers. He wrote in a letter to his brother that, thanks to his advice, "the negroes got means to get out of the country; and about three thousand have left, leaving rebel masters stripped and less able to make further effect in the working rebellions."[97] Despite accusations to the contrary, Curtis steadfastly maintained that this assistance was not about advancing his own business connections; it was about caring for destitute freedpeople, while also striking a blow to Confederate sympathizers.

A significant component of this aid work came from Kansas residents who helped found schools and provide religious instruction. In Wyandotte, R. D. Parker, pastor of the Congregational Church, held religious services and instituted a Sunday school.[98] Chaplain Moore noted in 1862 that Lawrence had established two black churches, and there was another large one in Osawatomie.[99] In these churches there were several African Americans who took on leadership roles. As Richard Cordley remembered, Anthony Oldham was active in the African American church in Lawrence. Oldham had "been sort of a preacher among his people—and was ready to conduct services for the new church.... Everybody believed in him, and they all listened to him with respect. He was one of the sturdy kind whose convictions were as firm as a rock." Cordley also recalled that a white church in Lawrence started a night school for adults. This school functioned much like a Sunday School, with a Bible devotional, singing, and scripture reading, in addition to time spent learning how to read and write.[100] The men, women, and children who had sought refuge in Kansas were dedicated to education and eager to gain the attendant benefits.

Some freedmen entering Kansas did more than settle peacefully in the state. Many embraced the opportunity to fight for the Union cause and thus prove both their manhood and their suitability for inclusion in the body politic. Military service was a step closer to freedom, since blacks' willingness to fight for their country, and to restore the Union while standing and dying alongside their white Union counterparts, called into question blacks' subordinate civil status.[101] Unlike other transitions to freedom, however, black enlistment only came with the cooperation of white military officials. In this region, African Americans' service was truly essential for Union victory, since waging war against an insurgent population with a relatively small supply of white troops meant that manpower was in high demand. As Dudley Cornish has pointed out, "although the movement to use Negroes made slow progress in the North and East during the first year and a half of war, matters moved more rapidly in the trans-Mississippi West."[102] Contemporaries often credited this to the region's forward-thinking views on race, but there were many factors that went into Kansas's lead role in black recruitment.

In Kansas it was James Lane, a famed antislavery zealot during Bleeding Kansas, who spearheaded the movement to put black troops on the front lines. He was one of the first to consider enlisting black troops in the war effort. As early as October 1861, Lane stated that "confiscation of slaves and other property which can be made useful to the army should follow treason as the thunder peal follows the lightning flash."[103] Though never a proponent of racial equality, his outspoken support for the militarization of black refugees was crucial to the formation of black regiments.[104] At the beginning of hostilities, Lincoln had attempted to appease slaveholders in the Union border states by making clear that emancipation and the use of black troops was not a facet of the Union war strategy.[105] Lane made no such assurances. After raising white regiments in 1862 under the War Department's authority as "commissioner of recruiting," Lane's Brigade gained an unfavorable reputation among white Missourians partly because of his commitment to emancipation.[106]

Lane seemed immune to criticism from the administration and found sufficient justification for black recruitment in the Second Confiscation Act and Militia Act of July 1862. While the First Confiscation Act of 1861 only allowed for the confiscation of property (including slaves) directly used in the Confederate war effort, this made confiscation of all Confederate property a universal policy. It also permitted black service, though only with authorization from the president.[107] Prior to that point, any former slaves attached to Lane's Brigade were not mustered in, but now Lane saw his chance, and he decided to recruit without authorization.[108] Several military administrators, including General Henry Halleck, protested Lane's open flouting of authority, to no avail. James Williams, a captain in the First Kansas Colored, affirmed that "the work of recruiting went forward with rapidity, the intelligent portion of the colored people entering heartily into the work and evincing by their actions a willing readiness to link their fate and share the perils with their white brethren in the war of the great rebellion."[109] Most recruits rose out of the growing refugee population in Kansas, and they enlisted earlier in the war than those in Missouri regiments. They included many enslaved men from Missouri, such as Henderson Davenport, who escaped his owner in Platte County and traveled across the river with a number of other willing recruits.[110] Enlistment in a black regiment could bring additional income, freedom from an overbearing or abusive owner, respect from the local community, and the added bonus of Confederate defeat. Not all male refugees sought to enlist, so some commanders resorted to abusive techniques, perhaps subconsciously reenacting the paternalism inherent in the slave system by asserting themselves over black bodies. Lane's own recruitment style was, at times, unconventional; historian Dudley Cornish went so far as to call these tactics "impressment," an accurate description.[111] Despite such heavy-handedness, many recruits were eager contributors to Union victory.

These first recruits in 1862 hailed from several states, with close to 40 percent citing Missouri as their home state, 34 percent from Kentucky, and the rest from thirteen other states and Indian Territory.[112] Their wide geographic origins attest to the important role mobility played in the recruitment process and how access to a broader geographic landscape was crucial for freedom. These were the first black troops raised in the North, and the first to see combat, as many had served with Lane's Brigade prior to this point. However, because he did not receive authorization, they were not officially mustered into the army (nor were they eligible for pay) until January 13, 1863, when they entered the service at Fort Scott, serving first as the First Kansas Colored and then as the Seventy-Ninth USCI.[113] Uneasy with the concept of having armed African Americans at the front lines, some military commanders in 1862 balked at attempts to enlist black volunteers. Such hesitance was not the norm for Union officers on the Kansas-Missouri border.

In addition to the First Kansas Colored, African Americans in the state formed two other units. The Second Kansas Colored was organized later, mostly between July 14 and November 1, 1863, at Fort Scott and Fort Leavenworth. Like the First Kansas Colored, they had been part of Lane's Brigade and some had already seen action prior to their official enlistment. The regiment was also redesignated the Eighty-Third USCI on December 13, 1864. The Second Kansas spent most of their time in Arkansas on garrison and escort duty in and around Fort Smith.[114]

Black Kansans also contributed one artillery battery, called the Independent (Douglas's) Colored Battery (Light Artillery), organized at Fort Leavenworth in 1864 and 1865. This unit was the only battery commanded entirely by black officers. In 1864, Samuel Curtis, head of the Department of Kansas, sought permission to organize the battery, relying on two African Americans with prior military experience—William D. Matthews and Patrick H. Minor—as recruiting officers. Both served as officers in the First Kansas Colored but resigned their commissions in 1863 after being denied officer positions in the reorganized regiment.[115] The men of Douglas's battery came from a variety of backgrounds and with disparate motivations for serving. Most called Leavenworth home, but some

FIGURE 6. Douglas's Independent Colored Battery, 1864. Carte de visite of the Independent (Douglas's) Colored Battery (Light Artillery) on the grounds of Fort Leavenworth. Courtesy of kansasmemory.org, Kansas Historical Society.

came from elsewhere on the border. A major draw was the fact that they were promised the same pay, bounty, and clothing allowance as white recruits, an unusual guarantee for the time.[116] The battery spent the war at Fort Sully, part of Fort Leavenworth, building fortifications and serving on garrison duty. Though they never saw combat, they were one of the few all-black batteries in the Civil War, a testament to the achievements of Matthews, Minor, and other freedmen who populated its ranks.

Because of Missouri's tenuous situation as a slaveholding Union state, most Missouri officers and department commanders toed a fine line when it came to promoting black enlistment. The recruitment process in Missouri did not begin in full force until 1863, after the state legislature passed a gradual emancipation law, since the Emancipation Proclamation that went into effect that year did not apply to loyal states. In the spring of 1863, Secretary of War Edwin Stanton tasked Adjutant General and Brigadier General Lorenzo Thomas with touring the Mississippi River valley to investigate the status of contrabands and their usefulness for the Union cause. In May, the Bureau of Colored Troops was created within the Adjutant General's Office.[117] Thomas supervised the organization of two Missouri regiments: the First Missouri Colored Infantry (later reclassified the Sixty-Second USCI) and the Third

Arkansas African Descent (Fifty-Sixth USCI).[118] Missouri governor Hamilton Gamble stipulated that not all of these volunteers could be "credited" to Missouri, hence the Arkansas designation. General John Schofield, the new commander in chief of the Department of Missouri, spearheaded these recruitment efforts. He ordered Colonel William Pile, of the Thirty-Third Missouri, to enlist slaves whose owners were disloyal (but not to encourage the slaves of loyal masters to join the military). By the end of September 1863, Schofield contemplated enlisting the slaves of loyal masters; unsurprisingly, slaveholders did not appreciate this policy and appealed to President Lincoln, who sided in their favor.[119] However, in November of that year, Lincoln finally sanctioned this change, and Schofield issued General Order No. 135. This stipulated that each loyal slaveholder "was to be compensated 'not to exceed $300' for each of his slaves that enlisted."[120] Thanks to such compensation, both slaveholders and the enslaved population understood that service would result in freedom.

Still, the system of recruitment in Missouri was haphazard, speaking once again to the chaotic environment in this border state. Some provost marshals sent black troops into the countryside to actively locate recruits; Margaret Hays noted in January 1864 that "the country is full of negro recruiting officers."[121] As in Kansas, these activities could border on harassment, since black enlistment contributed toward Missouri's quota. Sometimes when enslaved men learned that they would be required to leave their families for long periods, they refused to enlist. In the case of Henderson Davenport of Platte County, his wife, Lucy, was "opposed to it," although her specific concerns are unknown.[122] He was close enough to Leavenworth that he could join a Kansas unit (the Second Kansas Colored), but her reservations mirrored those of other enslaved men and women on the border. Soldiers' hesitations may have stemmed from a fear that their families would be sold, abused, or abandoned in their absence, a concern not without a basis in fact. In other areas, provost marshals would only accept recruits who came to the enlistment office of their own volition. These provost marshals likely worried that advertising Order No. 135 would make it even more difficult to control the slaveholding population, many who were already disloyal.

This also meant that most Missouri recruits found their way to recruitment centers on their own initiative. There were four stations on the border (at Liberty, Saint Joseph, Weston, and Kansas City), although slaves living in these border counties could enlist at any of the other forty-one stations in the state. Nearly two hundred men from across the state enlisted at these four sites between November 1863 and October 1864.[123] There were not, however, many potential recruits to draw from, as there were only about one thousand "able bodied slaves" remaining, according to William Pile, so recruiting in the state "remained lackluster."[124] Those who did sign enlistment papers went to Benton Barracks in Saint Louis to be mustered in and receive their assignments. Eventually, Missouri contributed three additional regiments to those Thomas recruited: the Second Missouri Colored (Sixty-Fifth USCI), Third Missouri Colored (Sixty-Seventh USCI), and Fourth Missouri Colored (Sixty-Eighth USCI), with most border recruits serving in either the Sixty-Fifth or Sixty-Seventh USCI.

Unsurprisingly, most Missouri slaveholders deeply resented any attempts to arm African Americans, signaling their worry at a dramatic reversal of fortune: former slaves now carried firearms and could strike (or shoot) a white Confederate with government sanction. Slaves in western Missouri of enlistment age sometimes faced intimidation, assault, and threats to their family's lives. They also waded through the misinformation that slaveholders used to discourage recruits. Some slaveholders maintained that Union officers would be cruel taskmasters and that they might even sell slaves down south to bring in extra income. Slaves did not always have the means to discern falsehoods from truths. Encountering Union troops face to face might change their opinion of white soldiers, but given prevalent racism in the North, it could also serve to reinforce lingering fears of intimidation and abuse. Slaveholders sometimes took more direct approaches, using local guerrillas to patrol and apprehend enslaved men who might be traveling to a recruitment station.[125] These tactics stemmed from a combination of concerns, including fear of retribution for past abuses toward slaves, loyalty to the Confederacy (in some cases), and even sometimes legitimate concerns about blacks' welfare. Underneath each of these factors, however, lay a desire for maintaining the racial status quo.

Most importantly, both slaves and slaveholders recognized how enlistment was a phase in the process of gaining freedom and civil rights. Despite the fact that Missouri slaveholders could "claim" a slave at the recruiting station, the passage of a gradual emancipation law in 1863 demonstrated that emancipation was inevitable. Margaret Hays, who was from Jackson County but now sought (relative) safety in Calloway County farther east, commented in 1863 that Andy, who had recently left, "was dressed in his uniform and had his gun to fight for his freedom."[126] This breakdown of racial norms was even more apparent in another letter, where she marveled that African Americans would enlist to gain their freedom, return home on furlough immediately, and when interacting with their former masters tell them "that they are as free as they are."[127] If her story is true, the simple act of enlistment—not actual service—was enough to signal a changed status. Interestingly, Hays seemed to support black enlistment; since Missouri's enlistment quota could be met with black recruits, fewer whites had to serve.[128] White Missouri women suffered greatly in the absence of husbands and other male relatives, so this conclusion probably gave her some comfort; it relieved her of the burden of slave management while also protecting the lives of Missouri whites.

Black soldiers fighting against white regiments were also a threat to the Southern racial order; therefore, black soldiers' combat experience tied into the reframing of border society. The First Kansas Colored was the first black unit to see combat during the Civil War. On October 27 and 28, 1862, they encountered Confederate bushwhackers near Island Mound, in Bates County. Most of the skirmishing occurred on the Enoch Toothman farm, where the Kansas troops built fortifications that they dubbed "Fort Africa." With a force of only 225 men, white officers and black soldiers fought side by side and managed to hold off a rebel force twice their size, with only nineteen casualties.[129] The significance of this skirmish was monumental. The unit gained national attention and helped promote the use of black troops throughout the United States.[130] Back when they were enslaved, members of the First Kansas Colored had challenged slaveowners' control over the border landscape. Now, only a short time later, they left a lasting imprint by reclaiming these spaces and challenging slaveholders' domination of the land. The use of black troops so unnerved Missouri's proslavery Unionist governor, Hamilton Gamble, that even before the skirmish at Island Mound—when there was merely the *threat* of black-on-white violence—he begged President Lincoln to intervene. With heated prose, Gamble stated his concern over both black troops and a potential invasion from Arkansas, writing, "I appeal to you to save me from the necessity of diverting a portion of my force from this necessary object to the slaying of negro invaders."[131] This borderland was still split along the state line, despite the fact that both states remained in the Union. The very premise of black troops threatened the social order more than did an *actual* Confederate invasion. The greater jeopardy lay to the west in Kansas, not to the south.

Although their first encounter with Confederate forces occurred on the border, the First Kansas Colored saw action in various places along the western frontier, including Indian Territory and Arkansas. This significantly broadened their geographic movements, but it also brought challenges that reinforced how their presence was unwelcome in slaveholding states and territories. For instance, in a skirmish in Jasper County, not far from their post near Baxter Springs in southeast Kansas, Confederate forces attacked a small scouting party of black and white soldiers from the First Kansas Colored. Colonel James Williams attempted a prisoner exchange, but the Confederate leader, Livingston, "utterly refused to exchange the colored prisoners." Shortly after this, Williams learned that Livingston had executed one of the black prisoners. The Union's use of black troops was a great offense to Confederate soldiers, who perceived black regiments as a harbinger of emancipation and even race war. Williams responded by executing one of the captured Confederates. Apparently Williams's rejoinder worked and "ended the barbarous practice of killing prisoners so far as Livingston was concerned."[132] The Southern attitude toward black troops, driven by a deep-seated fear of armed rebellion, convinced Williams to respond in ways that ran counter to the code of war. In addition to fighting prejudice at home, black troops and the white officers of the First Kansas faced even greater challenges on the battlefield.

A similar incident occurred at Poison Spring, Arkansas, on April 18, 1864. This battle was part of the Camden Expedition (in the Red River Campaign), a Union offensive to regain control of Texas. Union General Frederick Steele's Seventh Army Corps, after combining with the Army of the Frontier (including the First and Second Kansas Colored), would move south through Arkansas to join with Nathaniel Banks's forces coming north from Louisiana. Together they would take Texas, the last stronghold of the western Confederacy. The Camden Expedition was a strategic failure, although there were several pitched battles where black troops saw combat.[133] While guarding a large forage train of nearly two hundred wagons near Camden in southwestern Arkansas, the First Kansas Colored; Eighteenth Iowa; the Second, Sixth, and Fourteenth Kansas Cavalry; plus fifty-eight artillerymen encountered unexpected rebel forces at a place known locally as Poison Spring. Due to sheer exhaustion, high casualty rates, and overwhelming numbers, the Union army was forced to retreat and lost the battle. The First Kansas Colored had approximately 40 percent of its fighting force killed or wounded.[134] Colonel James Williams learned from witnesses that black prisoners "were murdered on the spot."[135] Both white and Choctaw Confederates refused to give quarter, and in some cases, they mutilated the bodies as they lay on the battlefield. Although Confederate officials claimed the massacre was retribution for Union looting in the Arkansas countryside, they only targeted African American troops.[136] To Southerners, this changing racial order was a living nightmare. At Poison Spring, the First Kansas Colored bore the brunt of this fear.

The Second Kansas Colored spent the majority of their service on escort duty and garrison duty at Fort Smith, Arkansas, on the border with Indian Territory. Their combat experience also came during the Camden Expedition, although they were not present at Poison Spring. After hearing of the depredations against black comrades from the First Kansas Colored, they vowed to take no Confederate prisoners. A few days later at the Battle of Jenkins' Ferry on April 30, 1864, members of the Second Kansas Colored shouted "Remember Poison Spring!" and, according to some accounts, they killed Confederate soldiers who were wounded or had surrendered.[137] Although Colonel Samuel Crawford, the regiment's commanding officer, insisted that his men behaved honorably, soldiers' own accounts detailed their retribution.[138] This strike against the Confederates speaks to the pent-up frustrations of black regiments. These men retaliated for past abuses during slavery, the continued disrespect of black troops, and the persistent denial of black men's manhood.

Back at home, African American men served in the Kansas militia in 1864, as the state readied itself for invasion. In the fall of 1864, Confederate general Sterling Price began marching about twelve thousand men into Missouri, eventually veering west toward cities and towns along the Kansas-Missouri line. Questions about African Americans' civic responsibilities, as new members of free society, coalesced when black men in border towns joined with white citizens and organized regiments to defend their homes. General Samuel Curtis, head of the Department of Kansas, gained permission from Kansas governor Thomas Carney to call up the Kansas State Militia. This militia was, according to Kansas's 1864 militia act, to be populated only with white men; General Curtis sidestepped this mandate and called up male residents between the ages of eighteen and sixty, including African Americans.[139] Because these were only militia units attached to more organized regiments, there were no formal muster rolls to describe the exact makeup of these units. However, some militia units did have black officers; at least five of the officers from Leavenworth were leaders in their black community and statewide.[140] Of the one thousand black militiamen in Kansas who served, many helped repel Price at the Battle of the Blue and the Battle of Westport, both in Jackson County. Some of Price's men were slaveholders themselves, and also residents of border counties, so this meeting of former slaves and former masters held a symbolic significance as well as a military one.

Black infantry regiments created in Missouri primarily saw action outside of the state or were stationed at Benton Barracks, a Union encampment and recruiting center just a few miles north of Saint Louis.[141] Most spent the majority of their time in Missouri marching, serving on picket duty, and performing other manual labor. In addition to racial prejudices that questioned blacks' courage, it also seems likely that military officials were reluctant to use black recruits from a slaveholding state in combat against white troops, unless absolutely necessary. For instance, the first real battlefield experience of the Sixty-Second USCI was not until Sterling Price's raid in 1864, when they clashed with Confederate forces near Glasgow. The regiment then moved to Port Hudson, Louisiana, as part of a contingent to hold that key site on the Mississippi River, before they headed farther south to Brazos Santiago, Texas. There, Union forces unsuccessfully assaulted a Confederate outpost at Palmito Ranch in what became known as the last battle of the Civil War (in May 1865, after Lee's surrender at Appomattox).[142] Overall, black troops in Missouri did not see as much action as Kansas regiments.

Because racial prejudice ran rampant throughout the military, black troops from both Kansas and Missouri regularly encountered stereotypes and discrimination on the basis of race.[143] One such stereotype was the belief that black troops would not perform adequately in the heat of battle because "the negro race did not possess necessary qualifications to make efficient soldiers."[144] This assumption rested on the premise that blacks' inferior social status limited their courage and intelligence, and consequently there should be no allowance for African American officers. Additionally, as historian Roger Cunningham has noted, many whites erroneously concluded that black soldiers themselves would prefer serving under the command of white officers, even though these white officers were not always up to the task.[145] Though he played an integral role in recruiting for the First Kansas Colored, William Matthews was denied an officer's commission on account of his race. Secretary of War Edwin Stanton did finally agree to authorize Matthew's commission, but Matthews was absent on the day that the commissions were decided so his place was given to a white man.[146] Patrick Minor was in a similar situation; he left the First Kansas Colored in 1863 when he found out he would not receive a commission.

These examples illustrate how deep-seated racial discrimination was within the armed forces. To some white officers in Kansas, however, the refusal to allow officer's commissions to talented soldiers like Matthews

FIGURE 7. William D. Matthews, c. 1864. William Dominick Matthews, First Lieutenant, served in the Independent (Douglas's) Colored Battery (Light Artillery). Courtesy of kansasmemory.org, Kansas Historical Society.

and Minor was ridiculous. Twenty-one white officers penned a letter to James Lane stating that Matthews was "among the most thorough and efficient officers in our organization; a soldier in every sense of the term, drilled, disciplined and capable." Matthews himself wrote to Lane and insisted that his contribution to the regiment's formation demanded that he receive a commission.[147] Eventually he went on to serve in Douglas's Battery at Fort Leavenworth, but his story highlights the inherently racist military policies of the nineteenth century.

These stereotyped assumptions about black men's capabilities had no basis in fact. Commanders on the frontier offered nothing but praise for the dedication of the black troops under their command. Even before the recruits around Fort Scott saw any real action, N. P. Chipman, the chief of staff for the Department of Missouri, noted during his inspection that the troops were proficient at drill and their skills already surpassed those of more experienced (and presumably white) regiments. Overall he deemed them "highly satisfactory."[148] This served as much-needed encouragement for the black soldiers as well as their white officers. They also performed valiantly in battle. In 1863, General James Blunt stated it best when he wrote about the Battle of Honey Springs, saying "they fought like veterans, with a coolness and valor that is unsurpassed. . . . Too much praise cannot be awarded for their gallantry. The question that negroes will fight is settled; besides, they make better soldiers in every respect than any troops I have ever had under my command."[149] This so-called "question" of African American valor speaks more to nineteenth-century white America's reservations about black manhood than it does to the capabilities of black regiments.

Another of the greatest concerns for African American enlistees was whether or not they would receive compensation equal to that of their white peers. Throughout the western theater, as in other reaches of the country, it appeared that black troops would not collect equal pay and benefits. During the first months of black recruitment in Kansas, those troops did not receive any pay since their enlistment was not officially sanctioned in the first place. One official complained, noting that many of these troops were "intelligent free negroes—some having a good business at home, others leaving their families without any support; they have been kept together without pay & under but a quasi organization. They are now two months in camp and no one can tell what is to be done with them."[150] These men were understandably frustrated, and that frustration manifested itself in a "growing restlessness and insubordination."[151] White officers of black regiments, like James Williams, wrote with great concern that the paymaster paid white troops but had not distributed any to his men. He placed the blame for these "long trials and sufferings" squarely on the government.[152] Although the black troops' perspective is only partially discernable within white officers' writings, they undoubtedly resented this disparate treatment and spoke about it candidly with officers like Williams. The military's strict pecking order, combined with a racial hierarchy that privileged the words of white officers, meant that black troops sometimes had to rely on advocates within the higher ranks to present their pleas to the appropriate authorities.

Once a pay schedule was finally set in 1863, black troops received ten dollars per month, with three dollars going toward their clothing allowance;

white soldiers received thirteen dollars. Black troops were understandably indignant at their disparate treatment. Some white military officials, like William Pile, sympathized with enlistees. Pile testified before the Freedmen's Inquiry Commission that the system "should be revised, beyond all question. . . . By increasing the pay of non-commissioned officers, an increased motive to application would be furnished the negro, not only to learn his duty as a soldier, but to . . . prepare himself for his duties as a citizen."[153] Pile accurately recognized that this was more than just a monetary issue. Troop morale depended on whether or not these soldiers felt that higher ups believed them essential to the war effort.

There were many additional hardships while in military service, all of which affected African American units from the border. Illness and disease were frequent visitors. Armstead Bradford of the Second Kansas Colored, like many others, suffered from exposure. He was hospitalized at both Fort Smith and Little Rock, Arkansas, after having waded through several creeks in the cold of winter.[154] Allen Claybrook, who enlisted at Liberty in 1864, contracted camp fever near Memphis, Tennessee, and also was hospitalized for smallpox in New Orleans.[155] Joseph Carras of the First Kansas Colored suffered from such severe scurvy at Fort Gibson, Indian Territory, that he lost all of his teeth.[156] This lack of nutritious rations likely affected both white and black soldiers, but the Union military generally distributed the best food to white units. Of course, the possibility of injury was an ever-present fear. Henry Phillips was run over by an artillery piece while serving in Port Hudson, Louisiana, and Shelby Bannon of the First Kansas Colored was shot in the abdomen at Island Mound, Missouri; numerous pension applications from the postwar period attest to similar injuries that led to lifelong disabilities.[157] Like their white counterparts, these soldiers shared in the trials of war.

Through all of these challenges, African American troops dealt with battle trauma, the monotony of camp life, and concerns about their loved ones who remained at home. White troops encountered these same difficulties, but many black soldiers had the added stress of worrying about loved ones who were still enslaved. With Missouri slaveholders unsure of the institution's future and angered by slaves' exodus into free states, there were serious repercussions for the families of those who enlisted in the Union cause. Violence, an element of the slave system crucial to securing whites' control over the enslaved population (which was increasingly dwindling) continued unabated throughout the war. In 1863, Martha Glover, whose husband, Richard, was serving with the Second Missouri Colored, wrote her husband, admonishing him for leaving his family behind. She had warned him before his departure that his absence would have powerful repercussions for the family. "You recollect what I told you how they would do after you was gone," she wrote. "They abuse me because you went & say they will not take care of our children & do nothing but quarrel with me all the time and beat me scandalously the day before yesterday."[158] Richard had only been absent for two or three weeks, and Martha was heavily pregnant and had six children to care for.

Superintendent Pile took interest in the situation and corresponded with General William Rosecrans on Glover's behalf. Only a few short weeks after Martha penned her letter, her owner, George Cardwell, attempted to take her and the children into Kentucky for sale. After hearing of this, Pile "went in person immediately to the Scobee House [where Martha and the children were being confined and] took possession of the woman and children."[159] Since Cardwell was believed to be a "rebel," the Second Confiscation Act dictated that the Glover family was free. Although none of the correspondence states that this did indeed come about, it is suggested that Martha and her children gained their freedom. Though they do not come directly from African Americans, Pile's letters and testimonies before the Freedmen's Inquiry Commission make clear that black soldiers had very legitimate fears about their families' safety. Enlistment in the army was even more of a sacrifice for these men than it was for white enlistees. In the end, approximately 2,083 black Kansans and 8,344 black Missourians served during the Civil War, and in sum, African American troops made up 10 percent of the Union army.

Much of the politics surrounding blacks' service derived from the ongoing conflict in Missouri over emancipation, which took place in 1863 and 1864. Few white Missourians, aside from radical abolitionists, called for immediate action to end slavery at the beginning of the war. Frémont's 1861 proclamation that freed slaves of disloyal citizens was wildly unpopular, so when Lincoln rescinded the order and removed Frémont from command, many white Missourians breathed a collective sigh of relief. Governor Hamilton Gamble, a conservative, pledged early in the conflict to protect slaveholders' property, a promise he would be unable to keep.[160] Enslaved Missourians, uninterested in the political consequences and debates on the floor of the General Assembly, had initiated a mass movement as more and more slaves escaped their masters' clutches. Missouri politicians could only play catch up. In December 1862, Gamble delivered a speech calling for gradual emancipation, citing the economic benefits that accompanied free labor.[161] By 1863, the state legislature had

split into three camps: the conservative camp, which preferred gradual-
ist policies; the radical abolitionist Republican camp (sometimes called
the "Charcoals"); and the Claybank camp, which supported immediate
emancipation but disagreed with Republicans on other issues. Despite
their disparate opinions, however, all parties knew by 1863 that slavery
would not survive, so the question that remained was merely the best
process for implementing a plan.

Unfortunately, the General Assembly was not able to reach a consensus,
so Gamble decided to reinstate the Missouri State Convention (the body
that had debated secession in 1861) in the hopes that they might broker
a compromise.[162] Though it displeased radical abolitionists, the convention issued an ordinance of gradual emancipation on July 1, 1863, which
stated that slavery in Missouri would be abolished by July 4, 1870. "An
Ordinance Abolishing Slavery in Missouri," which passed through a new
constitutional convention on January 11, 1865, replaced this law. This was
less than a year before the ratification of the Thirteenth Amendment.[163]
Slavery was now illegal on both sides of the border, and the continued
work for African American rights could begin. Slaves' increased mobility under small-scale slaveholding had played a central role in resistance
prior to the Civil War, and during the conflict the mass migration of
freedpeople saw that resistance come to fruition. This borderland, which
had been bifurcated by war, was now transitioning toward free labor.

From 1861 to 1865, the situation that existed along the Kansas-Missouri
line was unlike the situation on any other border between a free state and
a slave state. Kansans and Missourians were already well acquainted with
guerrilla warfare by 1861. The violence here had begun nearly seven years
before South Carolina militiamen launched the first shot at Fort Sumter.
Now, however, the violence was more than a battle over the extension
of slavery into the territories—it was a conflict that threatened the very
existence of the Union. The Missouri population was divided in loyalties.
Confederate sympathizers clashed with Union regiments composed of
the same men who had made Kansas a free state. Throughout this conflict
the local black population exploited their knowledge of the border's social
and physical geography, some finding new challenges and fresh opportunities in the "promised land" of Kansas. Freedpeople demonstrated their
hunger for freedom and their dedication to the Union war effort, and in
doing so, carved out a "functional emancipation" that rendered slaveholders' claims to their labor moot. Despite the fact that they sometimes
required cooperation from people of different races and creeds, African
Americans sculpted this process. The true measure of freedom (however

that might be defined) came not just from the "liberating" force of the U.S. Army, nor from sympathetic white abolitionists, nor solely from the official policies of the Lincoln administration. Although true legal emancipation came later with the Thirteenth Amendment, enslaved people worked within the power dynamics of white border society—using their mobility as a force for change—to bring about a reshaping of civic responsibility and encourage new definitions of freedom.

Epilogue

In 1879, the Topeka *Colored Citizen* reflected on the many black refugees seeking new lives in Kansas. They noted that "the fame of Kansas has gone abroad, and poor white men and poor black men by the thousand have been for years, pouring into the state, and will continue to pour in." But, not all was gold in the Sunflower State. The author continued with a blistering condemnation of the white establishment and white Republican newspapers' failure to support black rights. Despite these setbacks, though, the author reminded readers that "better to starve to death in Kansas than to be shot and killed in the South . . . comparatively speaking the colored citizens of the state are getting along as well as are the whites," and any emigrants will "prove a blessing to the state."[1] The article's balance between encouragement and censure perfectly captures the complexities of the postwar black experience on the Kansas-Missouri border. Here black mobility lay central to the region's identity, running concurrently with whites' often different vision for the region's future. In a geographic space torn by war, white residents, former slaveholders, former slaves, and other free people of color all faced an enormous undertaking in rebuilding social and political relations. Contrary to popular culture's impression of Kansas and the West as bastions of egalitarianism and individuality, many white Kansans harbored deep-seated racial biases; as historian James Leiker has noted, "Kansas is a paradox."[2] Across the border in Missouri, the white supremacist impulses that existed during slavery persisted in this postwar society. The years after 1865 were regenerative, but the battle for

African American rights remained fraught with lingering antagonisms and prejudice.

Border society saw many changes in the postwar period. Blacks on the border reunited with loved ones they had been separated from during enslavement and formalized marriages that were not previously recognized by law. Emancipation restructured existing relationships between former slaves and their former owners, creating a new standard of labor relations. In other parts of the South, the sharecropping system emerged out of this labor vacuum and continued into the twentieth century. On this border, social relations remained largely segregated, and whites sometimes used violence in their quest to protect the prevailing social order. But there was no committed scheme to keep black Kansans and Missourians financially dependent. In fact, for African American laborers, the postwar period engendered new balances of power, as labor demands and urban growth allowed former slaves more latitude in making and breaking work contracts. Although it affected different communities in distinct ways, this postwar period was a time of rapid change. The border region saw increased economic development, growing industrialization, additional emigration, newfound cooperation between Kansas and Missouri, and most importantly the development of a new, at least nominally free, society.

Since Missouri did not secede from the Union and was not subject to either presidential or congressional plans for Reconstruction, its reshaping took on a unique cast. There was no military occupation, no significant redistribution of land, and the Freedmen's Bureau had only a peripheral presence in relief efforts. The revised state constitution of 1865 did, however, allow for at least a limited restructuring of society. It provided for black education by requiring segregated schools under the jurisdiction of white school boards. The number of African American schools in the state rose from 34 in 1866, to 212 by 1871, serving an African American population of around 118,000, with nearly eleven thousand of those residing in border counties.[3] It also disenfranchised all former Confederates as well as Confederate sympathizers, which gave Republicans control of the legislature, at least briefly.[4] Republican dominance came from both Missouri blacks and some Missouri whites. These advances, though initiated at the state level and not through official Reconstruction policy, opened an avenue for increased black political participation. Missouri's political heritage was being remade.

Yet, those who witnessed the guerrilla warfare in western Missouri and were victims of depredations by the Union military had some difficulty moving forward. At the war's end, western Missouri, at least the counties south of the Kansas City area, was in ruins. As one Kansan noted in his travels, "as far as the eye could reach in every direction you could see lone chimneys standing singly and in pairs, all that was left at that time of what was called good homesteads."[5] Thanks to General Thomas Ewing's Order No. 11, issued on August 25, 1863, as a response to Quantrill's raid on Lawrence, virtually the entire population of Jackson, Cass, Bates, and Vernon counties had been expelled and forced to relocate. Frequently, when these people returned after the war, there was little left.[6] Other areas along the state line suffered similar fates. The process of rebuilding Missouri's infrastructure opened opportunities for white emigrants and some enterprising Kansas neighbors to become involved in Missouri politics and economic boosterism. Some of these Kansans had lived in Missouri, having relocated to a safer environment just across the line during the war. For the most part, western Missouri counties simply did not have the resources to help destitute emigrants, and old prejudices worked against refugees who were African American. Some black emigrants settled in Missouri, but for the most part they went to Kansas, which had a reputation (fair or not) for being a state welcoming to freedpeople.[7]

With emancipation in Missouri came the struggle to expand citizenship rights to African Americans, as well as to secure the franchise for black men—both of these initiatives asserted that freedpeople must be accorded their rightful place in civil society. In addition to their disenfranchisement, at this time African Americans were still excluded from office holding and jury duty.[8] Black Missourians began an organized suffrage campaign in 1865, when a group in Saint Louis formed a local branch of the National Equal Rights League. The franchise allowed black men to exercise their manhood and establish themselves as useful citizens of the republic, but it also paved the way for other rights. African Americans on the western border, while not in leadership positions, and being further removed geographically from centers of power like Saint Louis, participated in petition drives. As Aaron Astor has noted, Platte County activists collected 3,816 signatures supporting black suffrage, likely drawing from surrounding counties like Clay and Jackson.[9] Although the historical record sheds little light on how white border residents responded to such initiatives, by some accounts, conservative feeling was strong in western Missouri, making suffrage work that much more difficult.[10] Nevertheless, this statewide, grassroots campaign left no corner of Missouri untouched.[11]

Like freed slaves in other states, there was a direct connection for African Americans between military service and civil rights. Nearly eighty-four hundred black Missourians had served in Missouri units, not counting those who enlisted in other states, and these men had demonstrated their valor and loyalty to the Union cause. They proved themselves responsible members of society in both word and deed. The executive committee of the Missouri Equal Rights League, the local branch of the National Equal Rights League, stated in a public address that black men had paid the same price as white veterans, having "bared their breasts to the remorseless storm of treason."[12] That reason alone—even aside from arguments regarding birthright citizenship, loyalty to the Union, and so on—demonstrated black men's fitness for incorporation into the political sphere.

Despite such organized efforts, the revised 1865 state constitution did not include universal manhood suffrage, and black Missourians generally doubted whether the Radical Republicans who controlled the state government wielded the necessary power to protect African American interests. Their fears were confirmed when the referendum on black suffrage failed in 1868.[13] The ratification of the Fifteenth Amendment two years later, however, opened the polls to black men, which brought approximately twenty-one thousand new Missouri voters into the franchise. As was common elsewhere in the United States, these new black voters generally supported Republican candidates; although in Missouri the party had broken into Liberal and Radical factions by 1870, both drew support from the African American community.[14] Black suffrage attracted strong denunciations from former slaveholders and other conservatives, opening a path for Redeemers to assume control, but such losses could not neutralize the rising current of black political agitation.

Kansas, unlike Missouri, continued to capitalize on its positive reputation among freedpeople in the South. This reputation was a conscious construction of Radical Republicans' desire to promote black empowerment and limit white Democrats' influence, but it had powerful rhetorical repercussions. The black community in the state grew significantly in the postwar years, from 12,527 in 1865, to 17,108 in 1870, and to 43,107 in 1880.[15] African Americans who came during the war or shortly thereafter generally found themselves welcomed as a labor force. Although many emigrants worked in agriculture, others found positions as cooks, baggage carriers, and porters. Large black communities in Leavenworth, Atchison, Lawrence, and Topeka developed mechanisms for aiding newcomers, including the establishment of new churches, schools, and social organizations. Some who had spent most of their lives on the border also remained, like Ann Shatteo, who in 1880 lived on the same farm in Topeka where she and her husband, Clement, had raised their five children.[16] Community leaders like William Matthews (of Douglas's Independent Battery) and Charles Henry Langston (Langston Hughes's grandfather, an educator and social reformer) shaped the contours of this border society.

Not unlike Missouri, however, Kansas was slow to embrace black suffrage, with a white population that also questioned blacks' claims to civic equality. The state constitution limited the vote to white males only, and interracial efforts began to strike out the word "white" as early as 1864. Voting rights would ensure that African Americans could protect their property, affect the direction of local government, and employ other means to protect their civil rights. By 1866, activists had unsuccessfully sought support from the local Republican Party, which generally believed including black suffrage in their platform was untenable. This conclusion pleased some white Kansans who opposed suffrage by arguing that "the ignorant, immoral, dirty, filthy negro," if granted the right to vote, would bring "degradation and filth and dirt to a system already degraded and corrupt."[17] At times white resistance to suffrage came violently, with lynchings and riots in heavily Democratic towns like Wyandotte.[18] As was the case elsewhere in the United States, black suffrage was also put in artificial competition with women's suffrage.[19] Despite the work of groups like the State Executive Committee of Colored Men, and suffragists who supported both suffrage campaigns, black male suffrage failed in November 1867 with 10,483 votes in favor of striking the word "white" and almost double that number (19,421) opposed.[20] Women's suffrage failed as well. The ratification of the Fifteenth Amendment three years later vindicated blacks' cause, and while violence and intimidation existed, blacks were not systematically disenfranchised during Jim Crow.

The most significant development in this borderland, in regards to postwar race relations, was the Exoduster movement into the region, especially into Kansas. This was an extension and refashioning of blacks' mobility while enslaved.[21] In this great exodus from the South, approximately forty thousand former slaves entered Northern states like Kansas, many coming from as far away as Mississippi and Alabama.[22] This mass emigration began within a decade of the war's end, but with Reconstruction's collapse and the withdrawal of federal troops from the South, African American emigration took on a new urgency in the late 1870s and early 1880s. Kansas's black population grew rapidly between 1870 and 1880, from 17,108 to 43,107, with the majority settling in the eastern part of the state. Although some came from Northern states and would not have identified themselves as Exodusters, by Nell Irvin Painter's account, at least six thousand Southern blacks entered Kansas in 1879 alone.[23] Despite some white Southerners' attempts to coerce Exodusters into returning to the plantation, these men and women "know too much to return to the land of shot guns and bulldozers," as one black newspaper stated. "Liberty is too sweet to be thrown away."[24] Some stopped just across the state line in Kansas City, Missouri, where there were significant Exoduster settlements in the East Bottoms, West Bottoms, and along the southern edge of town. Kansas City's black population increased from 3,770 in 1870 to 7,914 in 1880, reflecting both emigration from the hinterland and from the Deep South.[25] This dramatic influx drew national attention, but for those living on the border, it also shifted focus away from established black communities (composed of those who had gained freedom before the Civil War) and toward these newcomers.

White accounts of this demographic and political shift often used language laced with racial stereotypes about blacks' inability to function in free society, but at least some white residents welcomed Exodusters as their new neighbors. According to one Topeka newspaper, these emigrants had valid reasons for coming north. "Having so long endured the woes and inhumanities of bondage," the author wrote, "he would not willingly flee from his native soil, when emancipated, unless treated with unparalleled brutality."[26] Whites who were sympathetic to refugees—who often entered the state with very few personal possessions and no money—formed aid organizations like the Kansas Freedmen's Relief Association (KFRA). This organization, in existence from 1879 to 1881, supplied medical care, clothing, food, bedding, schoolbooks, and other supplies to refugees. They also orchestrated settlements like the short-lived Dunlap Colony.[27] In the state capital of Topeka, there was a large barracks that housed many recent arrivals. This relief work was absolutely essential.

Despite white rhetoric to the contrary, refugees were eager to support themselves, but rising from destitution was no simple task. According to an agent for the Labette County Freedmen's Relief Association in Parsons, a local auxiliary of the state organization, many emigrants had very large families. They also had significant health concerns like pneumonia and mumps, and due to the "alternately cold and wet weather, out-door labor is nearly stopped, and many parents find it impossible to earn sufficient to procure the common necessaries of life."[28] The influx of refugees by 1881 became so vigorous that the KFRA and its affiliates began redirecting refugees to nearby states; they could not adequately provide for freedpeople's needs, and some white communities complained about the public burden of such relief work.[29]

This white relief work complemented the work of black organizations in the state, some of which had been in existence for at least a decade, founded originally to aid the wartime refugee population. Charles Henry Langston helped found the interracial Kansas Emancipation League, which encouraged education and stable employment among the black population, promoting the doctrine of racial uplift and respectability politics. A more recent addition was the Kansas State Colored Emigration Bureau. Black Baptists in Topeka, including the editor of the Topeka *Colored Citizen*, formed this organization in April 1879 to aid new arrivals.[30] Both public and local attention focused almost entirely on Exodusters by this point, eclipsing both the challenges and successes of the already-existing African American community, but black locals apparently tolerated the shift because they recognized the refugees' needs. The most famous Exoduster colony, in Nicodemus, situated near the lazy Solomon River far out in Graham County, was the brainchild of black Topekans (and a white ally named W. R. Hill), all recent emigrants to Kansas.[31] Although the hundreds of emigrants who settled at Nicodemus sometimes struggled out on the high plains, the colony flourished briefly and today has the distinction of being the only surviving all-black colony in the West.

Local relief efforts sometimes partnered with national organizations, and given Kansas's reputation, even influential African Americans who had no previous ties to the state found themselves out west. This included Benjamin "Pap" Singleton, who first visited in 1873, and Columbus Johnson, a delegate from Tennessee at the Republican National Convention in 1872.[32] They worked primarily at resettlement in all-black farming colonies, drawing from populations in Tennessee and Kentucky. Singleton was skilled at advertising, circulating broadsides and pamphlets throughout the Upper South. He was also a colonizationist and founder of the United Transatlantic Society (UTS), which supported emigration to West Africa as a way to "better the condition of the African race politically, socially and financially."[33] Although the UTS was not successful in its international endeavors, Singleton was responsible for several (albeit short-lived) black colonies in Kansas, including the Singleton Colony in Cherokee County (founded in 1873).[34] By devoting significant energy to promotion and cultivating self-reliance, Singleton gained the nickname "Father of the Exodus."

Although Exodusters sometimes found a bounty of opportunity in Kansas, all was not well, as racial discrimination and intense prejudice toward black residents persisted through Reconstruction and beyond. Despite pervasive contemporary claims that such racial violence only occurred in the South, African Americans in Kansas were not always safe. Whites sometimes embraced violence to subordinate the black community and exclude them from the protections of citizenship. Historian Brent M. S. Campney has found nineteen documented incidents of lynching between 1864 and 1874, with thirty-three male victims, although likely other acts of racist violence remain undocumented.[35] This does not include other common practices that proscribed blacks' movements and limited their opportunities.

Economic discrimination was widespread, and some black families struggled to find jobs that paid a living wage and could not save enough money to buy their own land. According to an 1886 case study of household earnings in Wyandotte County, an area that received many refugees, the average Exoduster household collected $262.75 in annual wages, while white workers made $333.09 per year.[36] Racism and economic inequality often stemmed from caricatures of African Americans in popular culture, leading some whites to conclude that black emigrants were "lazy" or "immoral," and true equality in the realm of civil rights remained a distant reality for many black Kansans.[37]

In the end, the Exodus was a continuation of African Americans' fight for control over their own mobility and for access to public spaces, another chapter in the story of black resistance on the Kansas-Missouri border. In the years prior to the Civil War, slavery was an integral component of the frontier experience for both enslaved and white slaveholding residents. For slaveholders, slavery's expansion into the West was central to their imaginings of progress and financial solvency. When comparing border slavery to the institution elsewhere in the Upper South, these slaveholders effectively replicated their small-scale formula in a new environment. The markers of a small-scale system, including close contact between slaveholder and slave, varied forms of employment, an active slave hiring market, and the prevalence of abroad marriages, were all found here.

Yet, these attempts at asserting control were only partly successful. For the enslaved, who entered the border region unwillingly, it was possible to carve out opportunities for increased autonomy. These men and women struck back by taking control of their own movements across the landscape. They formed abroad marriages and friendships with slaves on other farms, engaged in physical altercations with slaveholders, negotiated additional privileges, found ways to make their own money, and escaped on the Underground Railroad. These same conflicts inevitably occurred between slaves and slaveowners living elsewhere in the Upper South.

Still, the unique social geography of the Kansas-Missouri line—a region that was simultaneously Western, Northern, and Southern—sculpted the peculiar institution in unprecedented ways. These influences acted in concert to provide slaves with increased opportunities for resistance. While slavery was perpetuated through slaveholders' use of coercion and violence, slaves sometimes found ways to gain the upper hand.

White rhetoric over the expansion of slavery may have taken center stage during the sectional conflict—if one goes by the historiographical trends of the last century—but enslaved people were themselves a visible presence in this borderland. Bondspeople in this region were not an artificially constructed symbol, a tool of propaganda, created to rally antislavery proponents to the cause. These were real people, with real stories. Within this region's boundaries are tales of the physical, emotional, and psychological hardships that defined both the tragedies and triumphs of the African American experience. For former slaves and former slaveholders who remained on the border in the postwar period, their fortunes were once again linked, but this time, in the task of shaping this modern—and free—society.

ABBREVIATIONS

CARL	Combined Arms Research Library, Fort Leavenworth, Kansas
HL	The Huntington Library, San Marino, California
JCHS	Jackson County Historical Society, Independence, Missouri
KHS	Kansas Historical Society, Topeka, Kansas
MGC	Midwest Genealogy Center, Independence, Missouri
MHML	Missouri History Museum Library and Research Center, Saint Louis, Missouri
MVSC	Missouri Valley Special Collections, Kansas City Public Library, Kansas City, Missouri
NARA	National Archives and Records Administration, Main Branch, Washington, D.C.
NARA—KC	National Archives and Records Administration, Central Plains Branch, Kansas City, Missouri
SHSM	State Historical Society of Missouri, Columbia, Missouri
SRL	Kenneth Spencer Research Library, Lawrence, Kansas
WHMC—C	Western Historical Manuscript Collection, Columbia Branch
WHMC—KC	Western Historical Manuscript Collection, Kansas City Branch

Notes

Introduction

1. Zu Adams diary entry, June 30, 1892, in Zu Adams Papers, Diary No. 2, KHS. Throughout this book I use the terms "slaves" and "enslaved" interchangeably, and on occasion the term "bondspeople" will also appear. The advantage of using the term "enslaved" is that, as Daina Ramey Berry maintains, "it forces us to consider that bondpeople did not let anyone 'own' them. They were enslaved against their will" (Berry, *Swing the Sickle for the Harvest Is Ripe*," 167, note 4). I use the term "slave" as well because that is generally the precise descriptor used within historical sources. I also use the terms "African American" and "black" interchangeably.

2. Zu Adams, "Slaves in Kansas," September 28, 1895, in Slaves and Slavery Collection, KHS.

3. This definition of "frontier" is used throughout the book and is based loosely on Stephen Aron and Jeremy Adelman's definition of the frontier as "a meeting place of peoples in which geographic and cultural borders were not clearly defined" (Adelman and Aron, "From Borderlands to Borders," 815). My use of the term does not connote an adherence to Frederick Jackson Turner's well-known thesis on western settlement. The nineteen counties forming the central axis of my study are the western Missouri counties of Buchanan, Platte, Clay, Jackson, Cass, Bates, and Vernon, and the Kansas counties of Doniphan, Atchison, Leavenworth, Jefferson, Shawnee, Douglas, Wyandotte, Johnson, Franklin, Miami, Linn, and Bourbon. Miami County was originally named Lykins County, but it will be referred to as Miami County in the text.

4. I adopt a broad definition of "Southernness"; as Christopher Phillips has suggested, the South was defined by its strong religious and conservative roots, a recent frontier experience, white cultural uniformity, humid climate, reliance on cash crops cultivated with slave labor, a predominantly agrarian population, and the presence of large African American communities (Phillips, "The Crime Against Missouri," 61). Although, as Phillips correctly points out, Missouri cannot be neatly categorized as Southern since it was also a Western state. Here I will use the terms "West" and "Western" to reference geographic locations west of the Mississippi River.

5. United States Bureau of the Census, *Seventh Census of the United States*, 1850, Slave Schedules; Franklin and Schweninger, *Runaway Slaves*, 282.

6. I define the term mobility as movement across or within, as well as access to, the physical and social landscapes.

7. Geographer Allan Pred argues that "place is therefore a process whereby the reproduction of social and cultural forms, the formation of biographies, and the transformation of nature ceaselessly become one another at the same time that time-space specific activities and power relations ceaselessly become one another" (Pred, "Place as Historically Contingent Process," 282).

8. Hämäläinen and Truett, "On Borderlands," 338. For more on typical models of borderland interactions, see Baud and Van Schendel, "Comparative History of Borderlands," 220–221.

9. Everett, *Creating the American West*, 8.

10. As Matthew Salafia observed in his study of slavery on the Ohio River, borderlands are "complicated zones . . . where dichotomies could not apply." Salafia, *Slavery's Borderland*, 2.

11. As Jeremy Neely writes, "by the end of the border war, the Kansas-Missouri line was the most pronounced political, ideological, and cultural divide in the entire nation" (Neely, *The Border Between Them*, 3–4).

12. Etcheson, *Bleeding Kansas*, 5.

13. For comparison, the slave populations of Deep South states (except Florida) in 1850 were over 40 percent: Georgia (42.1 percent), Alabama (44.4 percent), Louisiana (47.3 percent), Mississippi (51.1 percent), and South Carolina (57.6 percent) (United States Bureau of the Census, *Seventh Census of the United States*, 1850, Slave Schedules).

14. Lepore, "Historians Who Love Too Much," 141.

15. As Nicole Etcheson has remarked, "African American history may be one of the last fields to receive a micro-historical treatment. . . . Scarce records, especially the lack of firsthand accounts for many aspects of black life, make microhistory's tight focus on the 'proudly small' difficult to achieve" (Etcheson, "Microhistory and Movement," 392). This manuscript makes a small attempt at enriching this literature.

16. I have identified fewer than fifteen reminiscences by former slaves available for the border region (not including Civil War pension file affidavits and depositions), with only a handful of those recorded with minimal white involvement.

17. United States Bureau of the Census, *Seventh Census of the United States*, 1850, Slave Schedules.

18. *1855 Territorial Kansas Census*; John Speer, editor of the *Kansas Tribune*, collaborated with a fellow Kansan to count at least four hundred. See Oertel, *Bleeding Borders*, 41. In 1860, the free black population in Kansas was 625, and there were two enslaved individuals, so the total African American population in the territory was 627. See United States Bureau of the Census, *Eighth Census of the United States*, 1860, Population Schedules and Slave Schedules. In 1860, the total population of the Missouri border counties covered in this study was 100,006, with 14,311 enslaved people.

19. Cory, "Slavery in Kansas," 236.

20. Berlin, *Generations of Captivity*, 8–9. A central theme through both this work and his earlier *Many Thousands Gone* is tracing slavery during its formative years in specific regions of the United States (what Berlin calls the "charter generation"). Missouri's status as a new state—plus the various designations of Indian Territory,

Kansas Territory, and the state of Kansas across the border—in many ways paralleled the establishment of slavery that Berlin addresses.

21. SenGupta, "Bleeding Kansas: A Review Essay," 340.

22. Aron, *American Confluence*, xviii.

23. Oertel, *Bleeding Borders*, 2–3.

24. Neely, *The Border Between Them*, 23.

1 / Westward Ho!

1. George Champlain Sibley to Archibald Dorsey, August 29, 1827, in George Champlain Sibley Papers, MHML.

2. George Champlain Sibley to Samuel Hopkins Sibley, September 25, 1813, in George Champlain Sibley Papers, MHML.

3. I use the term "household" in reference to both the free and enslaved individuals who lived on the farm or plantation, which follows Elizabeth Fox-Genovese's description of the household as "a basic social unit in which people, whether voluntarily or under compulsion, pool their income and resources" (Fox-Genovese, *Within the Plantation Household*, 31). See also McCurry, *Masters of Small Worlds*, 6. Although both of these historians emphasize its social and economic functions, Thavolia Glymph has emphasized the political functions of slaveholding households (Glymph, *Out of the House of Bondage*, 2–3).

4. Fischer and Kelly, *Bound Away*, 216.

5. Burke, *On Slavery's Border*, 19.

6. Peck, *Forty Years of Pioneer Life*, 146.

7. Oakes, *The Ruling Race*, 76.

8. Fischer and Kelly, *Bound Away*, 291.

9. Berlin, *Generations of Captivity*, 161–162.

10. Berlin, *Generations of Captivity*, 226.

11. Foley, *The Genesis of Missouri*, 300.

12. Burke, *On Slavery's Border*, 50.

13. Rothman, *Slave Country*, 4.

14. Berlin, *Generations of Captivity*, 8–9.

15. Greene, Kremer, and Holland, *Missouri's Black Heritage*, 8–9.

16. Aron, *American Confluence*, 47.

17. Greene, Kremer, and Holland, *Missouri's Black Heritage*, 10–12.

18. Foley, *Genesis of Missouri*, 114–115, 146.

19. Foley, *Genesis of Missouri*, 151. The bill that incorporated Louisiana Territory into the United States divided the territory along the thirty-third parallel, with the northern portion called Upper Louisiana (officially the "District of Louisiana") and the southern portion designated the Territory of Orleans. See Foley, *Genesis of Missouri*, 134–135, 149.

20. Burke, *On Slavery's Border*, 23–24.

21. Foley, *A History of Missouri*, 128–130.

22. Foley, *Genesis of Missouri*, 205.

23. Fausz, "Becoming a 'Nation of Quakers,'" 36–37.

24. Wilcox, *Jackson County Pioneers*, 38.

25. Foley, *History of Missouri*, 131–132, 156.

26. Holt, *Political Crisis of the 1850s*, 19–20.

27. Gitlin, *The Bourgeois Frontier*, 97–99.

28. Hyde, *Empires, Nations, and Families*, 29.

29. Marra, *Cher Oncle, Cher Papa*, 24.

30. The three slaves in 1830 included a male slave thirty-six to fifty-five, a female child under ten years, and a woman aged twenty-four to thirty-six (United States Bureau of the Census, *Fifth Census of the United States*, 1830, Population Schedules).

31. Marra, *Cher Oncle, Cher Papa*, 55–56.

32. Marra, *Cher Oncle, Cher Papa*, 19.

33. Marra, *Cher Oncle, Cher Papa*, 204.

34. United States Bureau of the Census, *Fifth Census of the United States*, 1830, Population Schedules; Marra, *Cher Oncle, Cher Papa*, 144, 149.

35. Marra, *Cher Oncle, Cher Papa*, 161. Many of the Chouteau men (as well as other French traders) had extensive relationships with native women, and this also appears to have been the case with François, although it is unclear whether François formed a permanent relationship with the native woman who bore him a child. See Thorne, *Many Hands of My Relations*, 160–165.

36. Glymph, *Out of the House of Bondage*, 4.

37. Marra, *Cher Oncle, Cher Papa*, 203.

38. Marra, *Cher Oncle, Cher Papa*, 117.

39. Phyllis Edwards Kite, "History of Westport Methodist Church," 1964, in Monograph Collection, JCHS.

40. Porter, "Negroes and the Fur Trade," 424.

41. Marra, *Cher Oncle, Cher Papa*, 175–177. Bérénice had both an uncle and a cousin named Hippolyte; from the context it is probable she was referencing her cousin.

42. Marra, *Cher Oncle, Cher Papa*, 173.

43. Astor, *Rebels on the Border*, 21.

44. Hurt, *Agriculture and Slavery*, 51.

45. Woodson, *History of Clay County*, 76.

46. United States Bureau of the Census, *Fifth Census of the United States*, 1830, Population Schedules.

47. United States Bureau of the Census, *Seventh Census of the United States*, 1850, Population Schedules. I narrowed the data to adults of both sexes of at least eighteen years because a high percentage of those under the age of majority were born in Missouri. This computation also excludes those over the age of eighteen who listed their birthplace as Missouri and the three individuals who were born outside the United States (Scotland and Ireland specifically). The percentages were rounded to the nearest tenth of a percent.

48. Combs, "The Platte Purchase and Native American Removal," 265–266, 272.

49. Aron, *American Confluence*, 230–231.

50. An early historian notes that as soon as the Platte Purchase opened, a company of almost one hundred emigrants arrived from Kentucky. Paxton, *Annals of Platte County*, 8. In some respects this functions as a memoir, since Paxton was a longtime resident of the county and a former slaveholder.

51. Combs, "The South's Slave Culture," 365.

52. Paxton, *Annals of Platte County*, 10.

53. Paxton, *Annals of Platte County*, 35, 60.

54. George Remsburg, "Old Weston," *Globe*, April 18, 1908.

55. Paxton, *Annals of Platte County*, 34. There were 8,913 residents of Platte County according to the 1840 federal census. See United States Bureau of the Census, *Sixth Census of the United States*, 1840, Population Schedules.

56. Willoughby, *The Brothers Robidoux*, 101–103, 107.

57. Willoughby, *The Brothers Robidoux*, 41–42.

58. Lewis, *Robidoux Chronicles*, 49.

59. Willoughby, *The Brothers Robidoux*, 34, 101.

60. *History of Buchanan County*, 396.

61. *Jeffrie, a mulatto boy v. Robidoux, Joseph*, October 1822, Case No. 39, Circuit Court Case Files, Office of the Circuit Clerk, City of Saint Louis, Missouri, available online at the Saint Louis Circuit Court Historical Records Project, http://stlcourtre-cords.wustl.edu/display-case-data.php?caseid=1186 (accessed January 25, 2015). Some are in French.

62. Willoughby, *The Brothers Robidoux*, 114–117.

63. Combs, "South's Slave Culture," 365.

64. Lamb, *Magazine of American History*, 111–112; Whitney, *Kansas City, Missouri: Its History and Its People*, 101.

65. Hewitt and Jarrell, *Journal of Rudolph Friederich Kurz*, 29.

66. Missouri River Heritage Association, *Heritage of Buchanan County*, 8.

67. *History of Buchanan County*, 286.

68. *History of Buchanan County*, 392–393.

69. Lewis, *Robidoux Chronicles*, 55.

70. United States Bureau of the Census, *Fifth Census of the United States*, 1830, Population Schedules.

71. Wilcox, *Jackson County Pioneers*, 121–122.

72. Wilcox, *Jackson County Pioneers*, 129–130, 36–37. According to lore, Fristoe had chosen the name Jackson County in honor of Andrew Jackson, who Fristoe served with during the War of 1812 and whose daughter married Fristoe's younger brother, Thomas.

73. Harris, "Memories of Old Westport," 465.

74. Wilcox, *Jackson County Pioneers*, 171. According to the 1830 census, James Aull owned five slaves, and Robert Aull acquired slaves sometime between 1840 and 1850, when he appears in the slave schedule as owning five slaves himself. See United States Bureau of the Census, *Fifth Census of the United States*, 1830, Population Schedules.

75. Mildred Cox, "James Hyatt McGee," MVSC.

76. Wilcox, *Jackson County Pioneers*, 44–46; *Illustrated Historical Atlas Map, Jackson County*, 31.

77. Aron, *American Confluence*, 201–202.

78. McCandless, *A History of Missouri*, 130.

79. Harris, "Memories of Old Westport," 472.

80. McCandless, *A History of Missouri*, 131.

81. Wetmore, *Gazetteer of the State of Missouri*, 97.

82. Wilcox, *Jackson County Pioneers*, 255–259.

83. William Fairholme, "Journal of an Expedition to the Grand Prairies of the Missouri, 1840," HL.

84. United States Bureau of the Census, *Sixth Census of the United States*, 1840, Population Schedules.

85. For more on the Osage, see Edwards, "Disruption and Disease," 223.

86. Tathwell, *Old Settlers' History of Bates County*, 20, 35.

87. Aron, *American Confluence*, 207.

88. Hughes, *Fort Leavenworth*, 1–5.

89. E. B. Bateman to Newton Bateman, May 2, 1848, in Newton Bateman Correspondence, HL.

90. Hughes, *Fort Leavenworth*, 1–4, 16–17.

91. P. J. Lowe to Zu Adams, May 20, 1895, in Slaves and Slavery Collection, KHS; Delo, *Peddlers and Post Traders*, 96–97.

92. Henry Schindler, "A Post Trader, A King Here in the Early Days," *Leavenworth Times*, November 19, 1911, in History of Fort Leavenworth Clippings, KHS.

93. Henry Schindler, "When Slaves Were Owned in Kansas by Army Officers," *Leavenworth Times*, October 13, 1912, in History of Fort Leavenworth Clippings, KHS; Blackmar, *Kansas: A Cyclopedia of State History*, 765.

94. Schindler, "A Post Trader, A King Here in the Early Days," *Leavenworth Times*, November 19, 1911, in History of Fort Leavenworth Clippings, KHS; L. Candy Ruff, "Musettes Homes Tour Has Stories to Tell, Sutler Is Rich to Remember," *Leavenworth Times*, April 9, 1989, in Fort Leavenworth—Topical—Buildings—Sutler's House Vertical File, CARL.

95. Mullis, *Peacekeeping on the Plains*, 130–139; Schindler, "When Slaves Were Owned in Kansas by Army Officers," *Leavenworth Times*, October 13, 1912, in History of Fort Leavenworth Clippings, KHS.

96. "United States Congress, Indian Removal Act, May 28, 1830," in Purdue and Green, *The Cherokee Removal*, 123.

97. Isaac McCoy, "Names and Numbers of Indian Tribes Which Must Have Possessions in the Indian Territory," November 1, 1832, in Isaac McCoy Papers, KHS; Unrau, *Indians of Kansas*, 56.

98. Unrau, *Indians of Kansas*, 58.

99. Hickman, "The Reeder Administration," 425, 425 note 3. This calculation was achieved when the number of Kansa, Kansa "half breeds" (as it calls them), and Osage (6,576) were deducted from the total.

100. Unrau, *Indians of Kansas*, 51–53. James Oakes argues that, in the case of Native American slaveholders, "the ownership of slaves was a reliable indicator that the master had accepted many of the values of white society" (Oakes, *The Ruling Race*, 46).

101. Abing, "Before Bleeding Kansas," 57.

102. Caldwell, *Annals of the Shawnee Methodist Mission*, 17.

103. Unrau, *Indians of Kansas*, 58.

104. Warren, *Shawnees and Their Neighbors*, 80.

105. Caldwell, *Annals of the Shawnee Methodist Mission*, 58; Bowes, *Exiles and Pioneers*, 115.

106. Abing, "Before Bleeding Kansas," 58; Bowes, *Exiles and Pioneers*, 114.

107. Christopher, "Captain Joseph Parks," 14.

108. Warren, *Shawnees and Their Neighbors*, 103, 117, 131–132; Spencer, "The Shawnee Indians," 400–401.

109. Warren, *Shawnees and Their Neighbors*, 130–131.

110. Spencer, "The Shawnee Indians," 401.

111. Bowes, *Exiles and Pioneers*, 160–161, 164.

112. Walsh, "Methodist Observation of the Ohio Wyandot," 198.

113. Cutler, *History of the State of Kansas*, vol. 1, 82.

114. *1855 Territorial Kansas Census.*

115. Statement of Benjamin Harding, October 13, 1881, in Benjamin Harding Miscellaneous Collection, KHS; *1855 Territorial Kansas Census.* In the census, his name was listed as Samuel McIrvin, which appears to be a corruption of his full name, Samuel M. Irvin.

116. Alexander S. Johnson, "Slaves in Kansas Territory," April 20, 1895, in Alexander and Thomas Johnson Miscellaneous Collection, KHS; Oertel, *Bleeding Borders*, 39.

117. W. R. Bernard to George W. Martin, July 24, 1905, in W. R. Bernard Miscellaneous Collection, KHS.

118. Caldwell, *Annals of the Shawnee Methodist Mission*, 12, 25–26. The term "Five Civilized Tribes" refers to the Cherokee, Creek, Chickasaw, Choctaw, and Seminole, who settled in southern Indian Territory (now Oklahoma) after removal.

119. Warren, *Shawnees and Their Neighbors*, 142.

120. Lewis B. Dougherty, "Biographical Sketch of John Dougherty," in John Dougherty Papers, KHS.

2 / Becoming Little Dixie

1. Most scholars employ the term "Little Dixie" in reference to centers of slaveholding and Southern influence at the heart of Missouri along the Missouri River, although each definition varies in terms of which counties are included. My definition expands the definition a bit farther west. See Marshall, *Folk Architecture in Little Dixie*, 1; Crisler, "Missouri's 'Little Dixie,'" 131–132, 137; Hurt, *Agriculture and Slavery*, xi–xiii; Burke, *On Slavery's Border*, 12.

2. "History of Larry Lapsley," undated, in Cecil Howe Papers, KHS. This reminiscence was published (with a few annotations) as Alberta Pantle, ed., "The Story of a Kansas Freedman" *Kansas Historical Quarterly* 11, no. 4 (November 1942): 341–369.

3. "History of Larry Lapsley," undated, in Cecil Howe Papers, KHS.

4. This signaled a shift away from a "charter generation" toward a society founded by those of the "migration generation." Berlin, *Generations of Captivity*, 6–7.

5. Dorsett, "Slaveholding in Jackson County, Missouri" in Miller and Genovese, *Plantation, Town, and Country*, 152–153.

6. My use of the term "plantation complex" is based on Phillip Curtin, who defined a "mature" plantation complex as a capitalist endeavor and site of specialized agricultural production where the main labor force was the enslaved population; slaveholders controlled bondspeople by adopting "feudal" tactics that gave them legal jurisdiction. See Curtin, *Rise and Fall*, 11–13.

7. Burke, *On Slavery's Border*, 4.

8. Hickman, "The Reeder Administration," 425, 425 note 3.

9. Burke, *On Slavery's Border*, 4–5.

10. Hurt, *Agriculture and Slavery*, 101.

11. "The Great Depression," *Liberty Tribune*, September 19, 1846.

12. Merchant, *The Columbia Guide*, 48–49.

13. Hurt, *Agriculture and Slavery*, 99–100.

14. Hurt, *Agriculture and Slavery*, 80, 86.

15. "To the Planters of Missouri," *Liberty Tribune*, February 18, 1848.

16. Hurt, *Agriculture and Slavery*, 80.

17. Eaton, "Development and Later Decline," 346–347, 352; Hurt, *Agriculture and Slavery*, 120–121.

18. Hurt, *Agriculture and Slavery*, 109–111; Chiarelli, "A Look at Slavery in Missouri," 13–14.

19. Stone, *Slavery, Southern Culture, and Education*, 26.

20. "Negroes! Negroes! Twenty-Five Likely Negroes for Sale," *Liberty Tribune*, February 16, 1849.

21. Eaton, "Development and Later Decline," 349.

22. "Hemp and Produce Commission House," *Liberty Tribune*, March 20, 1847.

23. Hurt, *Agriculture and Slavery*, 105, 121.

24. Gray, "Ex Slave Story," in *Slave Narratives*, vol. 6, *Kansas Narratives*, 8.

25. Paxton, *Annals of Platte County*, 10.

26. Wilcox, *Jackson County Pioneers*, 283.

27. "Fine Farm for Sale," *Liberty Weekly Tribune*, June 20, 1851.

28. Glenn, *History of Cass County*, 154.

29. Hurt, *Agriculture and Slavery*, 125.

30. Untitled, *Liberty Weekly Tribune*, September 10, 1847.

31. Hurt, *Agriculture and Slavery*, 126–127, 129–131.

32. Paxton, *Annals of Platte County*, 10–11.

33. United States Bureau of the Census, *Sixth Census of the United States*, 1840, Population Schedules; Hurt, *Agriculture and Slavery*, 137.

34. Chiarelli, "A Look at Slavery in Missouri," 15.

35. Christopher, "Captain Joseph Parks," 16.

36. "Mag Preaches Thrift," in Rawick, ed., *American Slave*, vol. 11, pt. 7, 263.

37. Glymph, *Out of the House of Bondage*, 2–3.

38. Septimus Scholl to Catharine Hinde, June 1847, in Scholl et al., *A Collection of Letters*, 23. According to the 1840 census from Clark County, Kentucky, Septimus Scholl's household included one enslaved boy under ten years and one male slave between the ages of ten and twenty-four (United States Bureau of the Census, *Sixth Census of the United States*, 1840, Population Schedules).

39. "Negro Woman and Child for Sale," *St. Joseph Gazette*, January 14, 1848.

40. "Negroes Wanted," *St. Joseph Gazette*, March 10, 1848.

41. Burke, *On Slavery's Border*, 133.

42. Gray, "Ex Slave Story," in *Slave Narratives*, vol. 6, *Kansas Narratives*, 8–9.

43. Glymph, *Out of the House of Bondage*, 51.

44. Oakes, *The Ruling Race*, 130.

45. Unruh, Jr., *The Plains Across*, 119–120.

46. Wilcox, *Jackson County Pioneers*, 142–144.

47. Unruh, Jr., *The Plains Across*, 68.

48. Missouri River Heritage Association, *Heritage of Buchanan County*, vol. 1, 12.

49. Wilcox, *Jackson County Pioneers*, 154.

50. "The Negro Race in History Hereabouts," *Kansas City Star*, July 11, 1912, in Negroes Clippings, vol. 6, KHS.

51. Missouri Mormon Frontier Foundation, "Jones H. Flournoy House," 1.

52. Wilcox, *Jackson County Pioneers*, 179.

53. O'Brien, "Hiram Young: Pioneering Black Wagonmaker," 56–67.

54. Greene, Kremer, and Holland, *Missouri's Black Heritage*, 70.

55. Warren, *Shawnees and Their Neighbors*, 122, 128.

56. Chick, "A Journey to Missouri in 1822," 100.

57. Ellis, "Uniontown and Plowboy," 215, 219.

58. Oliva, *Fort Scott*, 1.

59. Hiero Tennant Wilson Daybook, vol. 1, 1844–1845, KHS.

60. *1855 Territorial Kansas Census*.

61. Rothman, "Domestication of the Slave Trade," in Johnson, *The Chattel Principle*, 46.

62. Tadman, *Speculators and Slaves*, 31.

63. Johnson, *Soul by Soul*, 17, 19.

64. Trexler, "Value and the Sale of the Missouri Slave," 69.

65. Eakin, "Richard Fristoe," 22.

66. Eakin, "Richard Fristoe," 25–27. This note also mentions Ann, who appears to have been a slave (but was not in either inventory), and "Izara," which is likely a corruption of the name Isora, who was listed in the 1849 inventory as being about two years old. Fristoe's eldest daughter, Bursheba Fristoe Younger, owned an enslaved woman named Susan Younger, who is pictured on the cover of this book. However Bursheba does not appear to have received any slaves from her father's estate, and it is unlikely that this Susan is the same person mentioned in the inventory. See Brant, *The Outlaw Youngers*, 66, 318.

67. Permelia Jackson and Nat Coffman (guardian), to Lafayette Jackson, Isaac Jackson, and Sue Ann Jackson et al., November 22, 1852, in Jackson County Court Records, JCHS.

68. *Permelia Jackson v. Lafayette Jackson and others*, Petition for Sale of Slaves, in Jackson County Court Records, JCHS.

69. Nelson Scholl to Rodney Hinde, February 3, 1850, in Scholl et al., *A Collection of Letters*, 38–39.

70. Gray, "Ex Slave Story," in *Slave Narratives*, vol. 6, *Kansas Narratives*, 8.

71. "Negro Woman and Child for Sale," *St. Joseph Gazette*, January 14, 1848.

72. "Sheriff's Sale," *St. Joseph Gazette*, November 12, 1847. In a court of chancery, decisions are handed down based on the principles of fairness and equity, not according to legal precedent.

73. Lucy Crowbarger (Widow) Pension Application (A#506419), Service of Henderson (alias Crowbarger) Davenport, Eighty-Third USCI, Record Group 15, NARA.

74. "Sale of Negroes," *St. Joseph Gazette*, March 5, 1847. This administrator was a resident of Buchanan County, which is why slaves from Clay County appeared for sale in Saint Joseph (United States Bureau of the Census, *Sixth Census of the United States*, 1840, Population Schedules).

75. For one example, see "Negro Woman and Child for Sale," *St. Joseph Gazette*, January 14, 1848.

76. Rell, "Once Offered $800 for Me, Says Negro Corn Grower," *Topeka Capital*, September 1940, in Negroes Clippings, vol. 7, KHS.

77. Salafia, *Slavery's Borderland*, 179.

78. Missouri River Heritage Association, *Heritage of Buchanan County*, vol. 1, 20; Wilcox, *Jackson County Pioneers*, 193; "Negroes! Negroes!! Twenty-Five Likely Negroes for Sale," *Liberty Tribune*, February 16, 1849.

79. Doy, *Narrative*, 60.

80. Overdyke, "Southern Family on the Missouri Frontier," 223.

81. "Negroes! Negroes!! Twenty-Five Likely Negroes for Sale," *Liberty Tribune*, February 16, 1849.

82. Hiring or "renting out" a slave generally refers to cases where slaveowners hired out their slaves and kept all (or most) of the slave's profits. Some slaves were allowed to "hire out" their own time in order to earn their freedom, although this was less common.

83. Hughes, "Slaves for Hire," 282–283; Eaton, "Slave-Hiring in the Upper South," 663.

84. Burke, *On Slavery's Border*, 168.

85. Martin, *Divided Mastery*, 8. Robert Fogel and Stanley Engerman have argued that probably 15 percent or more of slaves in the South were hired out at some point, although this number fluctuated and depended on the region and health of the economy (Fogel and Engerman, *Time on the Cross*, 56). It is difficult to establish concrete percentages, since census records and slave schedules do not distinguish between hired slaves and those owned by the slaveholder. See Hurt, *Agriculture and Slavery*, 238.

86. Samuel Reed, Last Will and Testament, March 23, 1850, in Bates County Probate Court Records, Will Book A, MGC.

87. McKettigan, Jr., "Boone County Slaves, Part II," 278.

88. "The Negro Race in History Hereabouts," *Kansas City Star*, July 11, 1912.

89. Ann Archbold to Julia Anne McBride, May 6, 1848, in Indians History Collection, KHS.

90. "Negroes Wanted," *St. Joseph Gazette*, March 10, 1848.

91. "Aunt Ann's Story, More than Thirty Years in Kansas," May 12, 1875, in George Allen Root Collection, KHS.

92. "Aunt Ann's Story, More than Thirty Years in Kansas," May 12, 1875, in George Allen Root Collection, KHS. It appears that Crisp sold her to Lewis on December 29, 1847, who then declared his intention to free her and her children a few months later, on June 1, 1848. The official manumission of Shatteo and her children was signed on March 14, 1849. Also, I suspect that Chattilon and Shatteo might be a corruption of Chouteau, but this is only speculation based on the fact that her husband was "born to French parents in St. Louis" and was an employee of the American Fur Company. There is also some evidence from genealogical research to support this linguistic confusion. See Miller, "Chanteau—Chatillon—Chouteau: Genealogical Chaos," 1–4.

93. Alexander S. Johnson, "Slaves in Kansas Territory," April 20, 1895, in Alexander and Thomas Johnson Miscellaneous Collection, KHS.

94. McCandless, *A History of Missouri*, 57.

95. Boman, "The Dred Scott Case Reconsidered," 406.

96. Frazier, *Slavery and Crime in Missouri*, 87.

97. Trexler, *Slavery in Missouri*, 67–70.

98. Overdyke, "Southern Family on the Missouri Frontier," 223.

99. "Expenditures," *Liberty Weekly Tribune*, July 4, 1851; "Expenditures," *Liberty Weekly Tribune*, July 23, 1852.

100. Woodson, *History of Clay County*, 88.

101. *State of Missouri v. Anderson, A Slave*, Circuit Court Records, Clay County, Missouri, vols. 3–5, 1836–1852, MGC; *History of Clay and Platte Counties*, 140.

102. Frazier, *Slavery and Crime in Missouri*, 115.

103. *State of Missouri v. Frank, a Slave*, Circuit Court Records, Clay County, Missouri, vols. 3–5, 1836–1852, MGC.

104. Frazier, *Slavery and Crime in Missouri*, 239.

105. The owner is identified only as Mrs. Hughes. There is one female slaveholder with the last name Hughes listed in the 1850 slave schedule for Platte County, a Sarah Hughes. It is possible it was some other person. See United States Bureau of the Census, *Seventh Census of the United States*, 1850, Slave Schedules.

106. Although the record does not list first names, it is likely that this was Phineas Skinner, a slaveholder who operated a mill and store in Platte County before moving to Kansas in the 1850s. See U.S. House of Representatives, *Reports of Committees Made during the Second Session of the Thirty-Sixth Congress*, 1643; Paxton, *Annals of Platte County*, 56, 220.

107. *Skinner et al. v. Hughes* (1850), in Robards, *Reports of Cases*, vol. XIII, 441–444.

108. Roy Davis (Father) Pension Application (A#212439, C#184319), Service of Henry Cushenberry, Eighty-Third USCI, Record Group 15, NARA.

109. Matilda Norman (Mother) Pension Application (A#404061), Service of Edward Cockerell, Seventy-Ninth USCI, Record Group 15, NARA.

110. Kaye, *Joining Places*, 5.

111. Curtis, *Jackson County in Black and White*, vol. 2, 1.

112. Wilcox, *Jackson County Pioneers*, 191.

113. Paxton, *Annals of Platte County*, 10.

114. Genovese, *Roll, Jordan, Roll*, 9.

115. Marshall, *Folk Architecture in Little Dixie*, 11.

116. Burke, *On Slavery's Border*, 10–11.

117. Burke, *On Slavery's Border*, 201.

118. Maria Seals (Mother) Pension Application (A#335550), Service of Sam Denny, Sixty-Seventh USCI, Record Group 15, NARA.

119. Louisa Bowler (Widow) Pension Application (A#193388, C#870205), Service of James Bowler, Seventy-Ninth USCI, Record Group 15, NARA.

120. Lucy Crowbarger (Widow) Pension Application (A#506419), Service of Henderson (alias Crowbarger) Davenport, Eighty-Third USCI, Record Group 15, NARA.

121. The absence of legal documents in slave marriages complicated divorce. Laura Pigeon gave a deposition in the pension application of her mother, Mary Leggate, stating that Mary had never obtained a divorce from Laura's father (David Ross) before she met and married former soldier Dempsey Leggate; "our family thought that as it was only a slave marriage mother did not have to get a divorce from father." See Mary Leggate (Widow) Pension Application (A#569481, C#407434), Service of Dempsey Leggate, Seventy-Ninth USCI, Record Group 15, NARA.

122. Robert S. Withers, "'Doctor Wood's Skeleton,' Old Folks Tales," undated, in Withers Family Vertical File, SHSM.

123. Withers, "'Doctor Wood's Skeleton,' Old Folks Tales," undated, in Withers Family Vertical File, SHSM.

124. Withers, "'Doctor Wood's Skeleton,' Old Folks Tales," undated, in Withers Family Vertical File, SHSM.

125. Withers, "'Doctor Wood's Skeleton,' Old Folks Tales," undated, in Withers Family Vertical File, SHSM.

126. Greene, "Life at Shawnee Mission," 457.

127. Caldwell, *Annals of the Shawnee Methodist Mission*, 50, 65.

128. Harris, "Memories of Old Westport," 469.

129. "An Act Respecting Slaves, Free Negroes, and Mulattoes," February 16, 1847, in *Laws of the State of Missouri* (1847), in Blacks in Missouri History (pre-1866) Vertical File, SHSM.

130. Harris, "A Brief History of Old Westport," 116.

131. Cochran, "Wilhelm Kroll's Narrative," 1967, in Robert M. Snyder Jr. Collection, WHMC—KC.

132. Cochran, "Wilhelm Kroll's Narrative," 1967, in Robert M. Snyder Jr. Collection, WHMC—KC.

133. Wilcox, *Jackson County Pioneers*, 188.

134. William H. Stratton, Last Will and Testament, May 7, 1843, in Bates County Probate Court Records, Will Book A, MGC.

135. William Williams, Last Will and Testament, August 18, 1846, in Buchanan County Probate Court Records, Wills and Administrations, 1839–1857, MGC.

136. Maria Seals (Mother) Pension Application (A#335550), Service of Sam Denny, Sixty-Seventh USCI, Record Group 15, NARA.

137. Septimus Scholl to Rodney Hinde, January 1, 1849, in Scholl et al., *A Collection of Letters*, 29.

138. "Mag Preaches Thrift," in Rawick, ed., *The American Slave*, vol. 11, pt. 7, 263.

139. Harris, "A Brief History of Old Westport," 117.

140. Curtis, *Jackson County in Black and White*, 1.

141. Septimus Scholl to Rodney Hinde, October 19, 1847, in Scholl et al., *A Collection of Letters*, 24.

142. Septimus Scholl to Rodney Hinde, January 1, 1849, in Scholl et al., *A Collection of Letters*, 28.

143. Septimus Scholl to Rodney Hinde, April 8, 1849, in Scholl et al., *A Collection of Letters*, 30.

144. Camp, *Closer to Freedom*, 2–3.

145. Overdyke, "Southern Family on the Missouri Frontier," 223.

146. "$150 Reward," *Liberty Tribune*, June 2, 1848.

147. "An Act Respecting Fugitive Slaves," *Liberty Tribune*, March 9, 1849.

148. Wilcox, *Jackson County Pioneers*, 189.

149. Gray, "Ex Slave Story," in *Slave Narratives*, vol. 6, *Kansas Narratives*, 9.

150. Finnie, "Antislavery Movement in the Upper South," 336–337.

151. Greene, Kremer, and Holland, *Missouri's Black Heritage*, 64.

152. United States Bureau of the Census, *Seventh Census of the United States*, 1850, Population Schedules.

153. George J. Remsburg, "An Old-Timer of Missouri and Kansas," *Atchison Daily Globe*, April 11, 1911.

154. Overdyke, "Southern Family on the Missouri Frontier," 224.

155. "Daring Attempt to Murder," *Liberty Weekly Tribune*, April 5, 1850.

156. Woodson, *History of Clay County*, 94–96.

157. "Family Poisoned," *Liberty Weekly Tribune*, May 3, 1850.

3 / Contested Ground

1. Butler, *Personal Recollections*, 62–64. According to Butler's account, her owner was "dangerous" when intoxicated. The Atchison *Squatter Sovereign* also recorded

this in the July 31, 1855, issue. The first territorial census showed that there were three slaves in the Thomasson household: Malinda (age forty), Robert (age twenty-one), and Susan (a minor). It is probable that Lucinda and Malinda were the same person. See *1855 Territorial Kansas Census.*

2. George P. Remsburg, "Scraps of Local History," *Atchison Daily Globe*, August 9, 1907, in George Remsburg, *Historical and Other Sketches*, vol. 1, KHS; C. W. Rust to George Martin, June 14, 1909, in Atchison County History Collection, KHS. In Rust's account, this woman's suicide was the event that precipitated the abuse of a different abolitionist, Pardee Butler, but in Butler's own reminiscences he never states that his abuse at the hands of a proslavery mob was tied to Lucinda's death. It would appear that Rust conflated two different occurrences that took place in Atchison around the same time.

3. Butler, *Personal Recollections*, 63–64; Oertel, *Bleeding Borders*, 47.

4. Henderson, *A Glorious Defeat*, 177.

5. Holt, *The Fate of Their Country*, 32–34, 69–71, 86–87.

6. Etcheson, *Bleeding Kansas*, 14.

7. Childers, *The Failure of Popular Sovereignty*, 235.

8. "Value of Slaves in Kansas," undated, in General Pamphlets Collection, KHS; Wood, Wisely, and Sharp, *Proceedings of the Pro-Slavery Convention*, 23.

9. Phillips, "The Crime Against Missouri," 63, 72. Phillips also ties Missourians' interest in Kansas to a larger political progress, writing that "by allowing popular sovereignty to dictate the settlement of territories, Western agrarian settlers would forward their idea of democratic promise and thus triumph over a distant, urban, industrial, and thoroughly inferior Northeast" (72).

10. "From the West—Affairs at Fort Leavenworth—Slavery in Kansas, &c.," *New York Times*, July 15, 1854, in Kansas Territorial Clippings, vol. 3, KHS.

11. Kansas Territorial Legislature, "Report of Minority on Bill entitled 'An Act to exempt Slaves from execution,'" August 7, 1855, in Port Vault, KHS.

12. *1855 Territorial Kansas Census.* This source can only provide information on a very limited window of time, and with new emigrants arriving on a daily basis, it is not accurate. Other censuses taken in Kansas during the territorial period (for the years 1856, 1857, 1858, and 1859) do not provide information on slaveholdings, functioning more as voter lists.

13. *1855 Territorial Kansas Census.* Most historians, including Kristen Oertel and Nicole Etcheson, adopt either 192 or 193 slaves as the most accurate number. Gunja SenGupta offers a different calculation of 186 enslaved individuals, or 2.2 percent of the total territorial population. See SenGupta, *For God and Mammon*, 120. The census included the following information: name of each member of the household, their occupation, their age, their sex, where they emigrated from, and if they were a native-born citizen, naturalized citizen, declarant, or voter. It also had a column for "negro" and another column for "slave," but the census takers were inconsistent in how they filled in these columns. Some listed the name of the slave in the first column (except for their surname), their age, sex, and where they emigrated from, and then put a check mark in the "negro" and "slave" columns to signify that this individual was enslaved. Other census takers put the number of slaves in that household in these two columns, which meant that other demographic data on those enslaved individuals was not recorded. The 1855 census also failed to include slaves owned by non-whites, which would put the official tally closer to 200 or 210. It is difficult to ascertain how

many native people owned human property, but based on reminiscences a conservative estimate would be fifteen to twenty.

14. *1855 Territorial Kansas Census*. By my calculation there were seventy-eight slaveholders recorded in the census.

15. SenGupta, *For God and Mammon*, 41, 119–122; Shortridge, "People of the New Frontier," in Dean, *Kansas Territorial Reader*, 103. According to another source, there were 4,618 emigrants from slaveholding states (including 4,481 from Upper South states), out of 7,634 total emigrants. See Hickman, "The Reeder Administration," 453–454.

16. "Kansas to Be a Slave State," *The Kansas Herald of Freedom*, April 21, 1855.

17. Napton et al., *Address to the People of the United States*, 3.

18. "Slavery in Kansas," Atchison *Squatter Sovereign*, July 31, 1855.

19. Cutler, *History of the State of Kansas*, vol. 1, 98.

20. Overdyke, "Southern Family on the Missouri Frontier," 230–231, 235.

21. "A Relic of the Past," *The Kansas Chief*, August 16, 1883, in Doniphan County Clippings, vols. 1–2, KHS. The article describes a record book that contained the minutes of this association's meeting on June 24, 1854.

22. "Kansas—Slavery, Letter from B. F. Stringfellow," *New York Tribune*, January 27, 1855. One of the letter's recipients was Preston Brooks of South Carolina.

23. Baltimore, "Benjamin F. Stringfellow," 16–17.

24. National Kansas Committee, "Residents on Big Sugar Creek," c. 1857, in Thaddeus Hyatt Papers, KHS. The two slaveowners mentioned in this source were Phineas Meanes and William Overstreet. Neither appeared as a slaveowner in the 1855 census.

25. Cecil-Fronsman, "'Death to All Yankees,'" 27.

26. Zu Adams, "Slaves in Kansas," September 28, 1895, in Slaves and Slavery Collection, KHS.

27. Caldwell, *Annals of the Shawnee Methodist Mission*, 85.

28. Eldridge, "Major John Dougherty," 14.

29. Craik, "Southern Interest in Territorial Kansas," 347–353; "Southern Emigration to Kansas, Its Necessity and Objects," *Kansas City Enterprise*, May 31, 1856.

30. "The Jackson County Pro-Slavery Pioneer Association," *Kansas City Enterprise*, February 9, 1856.

31. "Pro-Slavery Aid Society of Platte," *Kansas City Enterprise*, March 15, 1856.

32. Craik, "Southern Interest in Territorial Kansas," 343–344, 347.

33. Craik, "Southern Interest in Territorial Kansas," 351, 497.

34. Peter T. Abell to L. M. Appelgate, 1855, in Peter T. Abell Miscellaneous Collection, KHS.

35. Foner, *Free Soil, Free Labor, Free Men*, 309.

36. George A. Moore, "Reminiscence of Early Days in Kansas and the Formation of the Pacific Mutual Life Insurance Company of California," HL.

37. Etcheson, *Bleeding Kansas*, 4–7.

38. Etcheson, *Bleeding Kansas*, 29; Malin, "The Proslavery Background of the Kansas Struggle," 289. While some historians (like Malin) have emphasized how the NEEAC was essentially a business geared toward financial profit, this organization and others like it did provide emigrants with supplies, transportation, and other necessities, in addition to initiating an onslaught of promotional literature, press notices, and other materials. These publications were successful as propaganda, since

slaveholders in Missouri and elsewhere in the South firmly believed that the NEEAC had been very successful in settling emigrants in the territory. Historians place the estimate of NEEAC-sponsored emigrants at around three thousand people (see Craik, "Southern Interest in Territorial Kansas," 345).

39. According to SenGupta, in District 17 slaves made up 15 percent of the total population. SenGupta, *For God and Mammon*, 119.

40. Etcheson, *Bleeding Kansas*, 67.

41. Robley, *History of Bourbon County*, 48. Robley was Hiero T. Wilson's son-in-law, having married Wilson's daughter Fannie Webster Wilson. See also H. T. Wilson, "History of Fort Scott," *Fort Scott Pioneer*, July 5, 1877, in Bourbon County Clippings, KHS.

42. Robley, *History of Bourbon County*, 48.

43. Caldwell, *Annals of the Shawnee Methodist Mission*, 85.

44. Robley, *History of Bourbon County*, 61, 79. See also Benjamin Harding to Zu Adams, September 9, 1895, in Slaves and Slavery Collection, KHS.

45. Kansas Territorial Legislature, "An Act to Punish Offences Against Slave Property, Passed by the Legislative Assembly of the Territory of Kansas, August 14, 1855," in General Pamphlets Collection, KHS.

46. Mullis, *Peacekeeping on the Plains*, 119.

47. Atchison Rangers, "Notice," August 23, 1856, in Atchison County History Collection, KHS.

48. Robley, *History of Bourbon County*, 88.

49. Appanoose Vigilance Committee, Statement of Purpose, undated, in Franklin County History Collection, KHS.

50. *History of Clay and Platte Counties*, 634–635. In another published county history, the author asserts that the PCSDA formed an internal vigilance committee called the Kansas League to carry out their dirty work. See Paxton, *Annals of Platte County*, 184.

51. "Kansas City," *Kansas City Enterprise*, December 20, 1856.

52. "Negroes and Mulattoes," *Kansas City Enterprise*, November 24, 1855.

53. *1855 Territorial Kansas Census*.

54. *1855 Territorial Kansas Census*; Zu Adams, "Slaves in Kansas," September 28, 1895, in Slaves and Slavery Collection, KHS.

55. Oertel, *Bleeding Borders*, 41.

56. Slave bill of sale between David Burge and Thomas Johnson, May 24, 1856, in Alexander and Thomas Johnson Miscellaneous Collection, KHS.

57. Slave bill of sale between C. A. Thornton and William Patton, September 9, 1856, in William Patton Papers, Kansas Collection, SRL.

58. Pryor Plank, handwritten notation regarding slave sale, undated, in William Patton Papers, Kansas Collection, SRL.

59. Johnson, *Soul by Soul*, 29.

60. Zu Adams, "Slaves in Kansas," September 28, 1895, in Slaves and Slavery Collection, KHS.

61. Franklin Adams and William L. Smith, Interview about slaves in Lecompton, in Slaves and Slavery Collection, KHS; William Learner to Franklin Adams, July 13, 1895, in Slaves and Slavery Collection, KHS.

62. W. H. Mackey to George, March 26, 1902, in Slaves and Slavery Collection, KHS.

63. John Speer, "Reminiscences of James Skaggs," July 13, 1895, in Slaves and Slavery Collection, KHS.

64. Marcus Lindsay Freeman, "Reminiscence of Marcus Lindsay Freeman, A Former Slave," c. 1895, in Slaves and Slavery Collection, KHS.

65. "Kansas—Slavery, Letter from B. F. Stringfellow," *New York Tribune*, January 27, 1855; SenGupta, *For God and Mammon*, 120, 123.

66. Zu Adams, "Slaves in Kansas," September 28, 1895, in Slaves and Slavery Collection, KHS. Charles Cory listed a Nathan Hawley as having six slaves on Crooked Creek (in similar wording to Adams's speech), but it is unclear if this is the same person. Neither Cory nor Adams included citations. See Cory, "Slavery in Kansas," 240. George Remsburg, an amateur historian, also stated that a Nathan Hawley owned six slaves, but it is likely that he drew that number from Cory's work. See Remsburg, "Early Atchison Negro History," c. 1932, in *Historical and Other Sketches*, vol. 2, KHS.

67. Overdyke, "Southern Family on the Missouri Frontier," 236.

68. Rush Elmore to Albert Elmore, January 13, 1859, in Rush Elmore Miscellaneous Collection, KHS.

69. Frederick Starr Jr. to unidentified recipient, December 29, 1854, in Frederick Starr Jr. Papers, WHMC—C.

70. "The Recoil," *Herald of Freedom*, January 10, 1857.

71. *History of Vernon County, Missouri*, 225.

72. Alexander Johnson reminiscence, April 20, 1895, in Alexander and Thomas Johnson Miscellaneous Collection, KHS.

73. Alexander Johnson reminiscence, April 20, 1895, in Alexander and Thomas Johnson Miscellaneous Collection, KHS.

74. "Negroes to Hire!" *Kansas City Enterprise*, December 20, 1856.

75. "Kansas—Slavery, Letter from B. F. Stringfellow," *New York Tribune*, January 27, 1855.

76. "'Tis Thirty Years Hence," *The Kansas Chief*, June 2, 1887, in Doniphan County Clippings, vols. 1–2, KHS. In the case of Solomon Miller's hired slave, the situation is unclear, although the article in *The Kansas Chief* assumes that the owner hired out this boy and kept the profits.

77. John Sedgwick Freeland, "The Slaves of Judge Rush Elmore," undated, in Slaves and Slavery Collection, KHS.

78. Zu Adams, "Slaves in Kansas," September 28, 1895, in Slaves and Slavery Collection, KHS.

79. Marcus Freeman, "Reminiscence of Marcus Lindsay Freeman, A Former Slave," c. 1895, in Slaves and Slavery Collection, KHS.

80. H. H. Johnson, "Early Kansas Days," *Farmer's Advocate*, March 21, 1879, in unnamed clippings volume, KHS.

81. Gray, "Ex Slave Story," in *Slave Narratives*, vol. 6, *Kansas Narratives*, 12.

82. Marcus Freeman, "Reminiscence of Marcus Lindsay Freeman, A Former Slave," c. 1895, in Slaves and Slavery Collection, KHS.

83. White, *Ar'n't I a Woman?*, 149–150, 154–155.

84. *1855 Territorial Kansas Census*.

85. Hoole, "A Southerner's Viewpoint," 46.

86. John Armstrong, "Reminiscences of Slave Days in Kansas," in Slaves and Slavery Collection, KHS.

87. John Sedgwick Freeland, "The Slaves of Judge Rush Elmore," undated, in Slaves and Slavery Collection, KHS. This account notes that there were two other enslaved men, Nero (an elderly man) and John, who was hired out.

88. John Sedgwick Freeland, "The Slaves of Judge Rush Elmore," undated, in Slaves and Slavery Collection, KHS.

89. John Sedgwick Freeland, "The Slaves of Judge Rush Elmore," undated, in Slaves and Slavery Collection, KHS.

90. W. H. Mackey to George, March 26, 1902, in Slaves and Slavery Collection, KHS.

91. John Armstrong, "Reminiscences of Slave Days in Kansas," in Slaves and Slavery Collection, KHS. John Armstrong was Sarah Armstrong's brother and an active participant in Underground Railroad activities.

92. Bellamy, "The Education of Blacks in Missouri," 154.

93. According to "An Act Respecting Slaves, Free Negroes, and Mulattoes," which the Missouri General Assembly passed in 1847, "no person shall keep or teach any school for the instruction of negroes or mulattoes" (*Laws of the State of Missouri* [1847], in Blacks in Missouri History [pre-1866] Vertical File, SHSM).

94. William Wilson Elwang, *The Negroes of Columbia, Missouri: A Concrete Study of the Race Problem* (Columbia, 1904), 38, quoted in Bellamy, "The Education of Blacks in Missouri," 145.

95. "Execution of Negroes," *Western Journal of Commerce*, January 8, 1859.

96. Miscellaneous manuscript, undated, in Joseph Robidoux Papers, WHMC—C.

97. Most white Missourians preferred colonization to abolitionism. See Bellamy, "The Persistency of Colonization in Missouri," 2–4.

98. Neely, *The Border Between Them*, 33.

99. Shortridge, "People of the New Frontier," in Dean, *Kansas Territorial Reader*, 106-107; Cheatham, "'Slavery All the Time,'" 171; Stampp, *America in 1857*, 148.

100. Neely, *The Border Between Them*, 64.

101. Potter, *Impending Crisis*, 217.

102. Eleanor Turk, "The Germans of Atchison, 1854–1859: Development of an Ethnic Community," in Napier, *Kansas and the West*, 110.

103. Watts, "How Bloody Was Bleeding Kansas?" 123–124.

104. "Kansas Affairs—Peace and Quietude," *Kansas City Enterprise*, January 24, 1857.

105. Wilder, *Annals of Kansas*, 183. Wilder included the full text of the constitution. See also "Constitution of the State of Kansas—Slavery," *Western Journal of Commerce*, November 28, 1857.

106. "Constitution of the State of Kansas—Slavery," *Western Journal of Commerce*, November 28, 1857.

107. Childers, *The Failure of Popular Sovereignty*, 263.

108. Etcheson, *Bleeding Kansas*, 161.

109. Etcheson, *Bleeding Kansas*, 163–164. According to a contemporary newspaper, the vote was 1,788 for Lecompton and 11,300 to reject the Lecompton Constitution. See "Lecompton Election—Official," *Western Journal of Commerce*, August 28, 1858.

110. "The Territory and the Niggers," *Western Journal of Commerce*, May 21, 1859.

111. Cory, "Slavery in Kansas," 232. The president's annual message to Congress was the precursor to today's State of the Union address.

112. "The Territory and the Niggers," *Western Journal of Commerce*, May 21, 1859.

113. Wood, Wisely, and Sharp, *Proceedings of the Pro-Slavery Convention*, 23.

4 / The Tide Turns

1. James Montgomery to George Luther Stearns, October 6, 1860, in George Luther and Mary E. Stearns Collection, KHS.

2. United States Bureau of the Census, *Eighth Census of the United States*, 1860, Slave Schedules.

3. Pred, "Place as Historically Contingent Process," 279.

4. SenGupta, *For God and Mammon*, 120. According to the 1860 Missouri census, which was the first to record the number of slaveholders, there were 3,165 slaveholders and 14,311 enslaved individuals in the seven Missouri counties included in this study (United States Bureau of the Census, *Eighth Census of the United States*, 1860, Slave Schedules and Population Schedules).

5. Camp, *Closer to Freedom*, 7.

6. Isaac Maris, "Early Reminiscences of North-Eastern Kansas in 1857," undated, in Atchison County Manuscripts, KHS.

7. Benjamin Harding to Zu Adams, September 9, 1895, in Slaves and Slavery Collection, KHS.

8. Rush Elmore to Albert S. Elmore, January 13, 1859, in Rush Elmore Miscellaneous Collection, KHS.

9. Rush Elmore to Albert S. Elmore, January 13, 1859, in Rush Elmore Miscellaneous Collection, KHS.

10. Ralph Richards, "The Forts of Fort Scott and the Fateful Borderland," Scrapbook vol. 1, bk. 2, KHS.

11. Cory, "Slavery in Kansas," 239.

12. Allan E. Paris, "Life of 100-Year-Old Lizzie Allen Reflects History of Leavenworth," *Leavenworth Times*, July 2, 1939, in Negroes Clippings, vol. 7, KHS.

13. Fannie E. Cole to Zu Adams, October 20, 1895, in Slaves and Slavery Collection, KHS.

14. "Negro Cook for Sale," *Western Journal of Commerce*, October 31, 1857.

15. "Slavery in Missouri," *Weekly Free Democrat*, August 27, 1859. This was an "organ of the Free Labor Party," according to its slogan.

16. "Slaves," *Weekly Free Democrat*, September 24, 1859.

17. According to Fergus Bordewich, one possible genesis of this term was with two Pennsylvania abolitionists, Emmor Kimber and Elijah Pennypacker, who were also supportive of the development of early railroads in the Philadelphia area. Legend, however, states that the term came about after "an irate slave master who after failing to catch a runaway in Ripley, Ohio, is alleged to have exclaimed, 'He must have gone off on an underground road!'" (Bordewich, *Bound for Canaan*, 237).

18. Richard B. Sheridan, "Editor's Commentary," in Sheridan, *Freedom's Crucible*, 160.

19. Richard B. Sheridan, "Introduction," in Sheridan, *Freedom's Crucible*, xvi, 30.

20. LaRoche, *Free Black Communities*, x; Griffler, *Front Line of Freedom*, 101; Foner, *Gateway to Freedom*, 15.

21. Frazier, *Runaway and Freed Missouri Slaves*, 102; Richard B. Sheridan, "Introduction," in Sheridan, *Freedom's Crucible*, xvii; Lubet, *Fugitive Justice*, 42–45.

22. Mary Abbott, "Reminiscences of Mrs. J. B. Abbott, De Soto," September 1, 1895, in Slaves and Slavery Collection, KHS.

23. Frazier, *Runaway and Freed Missouri Slaves*, 88.

24. Hurt, *Agriculture and Slavery*, 255.

25. Frazier, *Runaway and Freed Missouri Slaves*, 89. Slaveholders were expected to reimburse the cost of the advertisement.

26. Napton et al., *Address to the People*, 8.

27. Trexler, *Slavery in Missouri*, 203.

28. "Negroes and Mulattoes," *Kansas City Enterprise*, November 24, 1855.

29. Kansas Territorial Legislature, "An Act to Punish Offences Against Slave Property, Passed by the Legislative Assembly of the Territory of Kansas, August 14, 1855," in General Pamphlets Collection, KHS.

30. Theodore W. Morse, "The 'Underground Railroad' in Kansas," in Theodore Morse Miscellaneous Collection, KHS.

31. Jabez Smith to Ann Eliza Smith, December 19, 1852, in Jabez Smith Family Papers, JCHS.

32. Frazier, *Runaway and Freed Missouri Slaves*, 93.

33. Stephanie Camp, in writing about women's resistance, noted that men generally had increased mobility that was denied to enslaved women, as "gender altered women's locations in some southern spaces." Camp, *Closer to Freedom*, 28, 32.

34. Kiene, "The Battle of the Spurs," 444. Accounts disagree on which woman was pregnant.

35. Abbott, "Rescue of Dr. John W. Doy," 312.

36. Lewis Bodwell, "A Home Missionary Journey Never Before Reported," *The Kansas Telephone*, August 1893. It is unclear whether this entire article comes from Bodwell's journal or if he added elaborations before publishing it in the newspaper. Although Bodwell never explicitly states that they had lived in Leavenworth, the fact that George's owner was a military officer, coupled with a reference to George working at "The Planters" (a hotel in Leavenworth), makes their presence in that town very likely.

37. Frederick Starr Jr. to Frederick Starr Sr., September 19, 1854, in Frederick Starr Jr. Papers, WHMC—C.

38. *History of Vernon County, Missouri*, 225. According to this history, they were going to be hired out in Jackson and Lafayette counties to the north, by request of the administrator of James Lawrence's estate.

39. Theodore Gardner, "The Last Battle of the Border War," in Sheridan, *Freedom's Crucible*, 65.

40. Scott, "Fleeing Missouri Bloodhounds," 71.

41. Franklin G. Adams, "Early History of the Atchison Church: Part I," *Church Calendar*, April 1897, in Atchison County Clippings, KHS; Franklin G. Adams, "Early History of the Atchison Church: Part II," *Church Calendar*, May 1897, in Atchison County Clippings, KHS.

42. Scott, "Fleeing Missouri Bloodhounds," 71; Ephraim Nute to unidentified recipient, February 24, 1859, in John Brown Collection, KHS. I also base this conclusion on the fact that the majority of runaway advertisements in Missouri newspapers make no mention of the runaway stealing a horse or wagon; since slaveowners valued this other property one might assume that, had fugitives taken horses, slaveholders would include that detail in their description.

43. Richard B. Sheridan, "Introduction," in Sheridan, *Freedom's Crucible*, xv–xvi.

44. Annie Soule Prentiss, "Recollections of the Underground Railroad," in Sheridan, *Freedom's Crucible*, 42.

45. Nancy Smith, "The 'Liberty Line' in Lawrence, Kansas Territory," in Sheridan, *Freedom's Crucible*, 3-4.

46. "The First Railroad in Kansas," *Topeka Daily Capital*, October 14, 1906. Jackson County, Kansas, which lies immediately to the north of Shawnee County, is not to be confused with Jackson County, Missouri.

47. George Allen Root, "Underground Railroad," undated, in George Allen Root Papers, KHS. Root was an amateur historian at the turn of the twentieth century.

48. Richard B. Sheridan, "Introduction," in Sheridan, *Freedom's Crucible*, xvi-xvii.

49. Richard A. Swallow, "Fleeing Slaves Were Hidden in Topeka Building," *Topeka Capital*, April 21, 1929, in Shawnee County Clippings, vol. 1, KHS.

50. George Allen Root, miscellaneous notations, in George Allen Root Papers, KHS.

51. Harrison Hannahs to Harvey D. Rice, July 27, 1896, in Harrison Hannahs Miscellaneous Collection, KHS.

52. Lewis Bodwell, "A Home Missionary Journey Never Before Reported," *The Kansas Telephone*, August 1893.

53. Ephraim Nute to unidentified recipient, February 24, 1859, in John Brown Collection, KHS; Ephraim Nute to Franklin Sanborn, March 22, 1859, in John Brown Collection, KHS. Unfortunately, Nute did not record Mrs. Riley's first name.

54. Scott, "Fleeing Missouri Bloodhounds," 71-75, 77.

55. Patrick Brophy Jr., "Bushwhacker Musings," 1980, in Underground Railroad Vertical File, SHSM. Accounts of the raid vary greatly, so it is difficult to pin down details.

56. Richard J. Hinton and George B. Gill, "John Brown and the Rescue of Missouri Slaves," in Sheridan, *Freedom's Crucible*, 79; *History of Vernon County, Missouri*, 230.

57. Richard J. Hinton and George B. Gill, "John Brown and the Rescue of Missouri Slaves," in Sheridan, *Freedom's Crucible*, 80.

58. According to Llewellyn Kiene's account, these fugitives did not have proper clothing or shoes until abolitionists found some spare items to share, which supports the conclusion that some of these individuals left home in a hurry. See Kiene, "The Battle of the Spurs," 444-445.

59. Richard J. Hinton and George B. Gill, "John Brown and the Rescue of Missouri Slaves," in Sheridan, *Freedom's Crucible*, 80.

60. John Brown to Gents, January 1859, in John Brown Collection, KHS. This letter is known as "Old Brown's Parallels." *History of Vernon County, Missouri*, 227, 230. Some accounts call him John LaRue, not Isaac LaRue.

61. Siebert, *The Underground Railroad*, 163. It appears that Siebert took this quotation from some other account; it is unclear whether Siebert ever interviewed Jane Harper personally.

62. Violette, *A History of Missouri*, 320.

63. Olive Owen, "Some Remembrances of the Underground Railroad," 1908, in Shawnee County History Collection, KHS.

64. Richard J. Hinton and George B. Gill, "John Brown and the Rescue of Missouri Slaves," in Sheridan, *Freedom's Crucible*, 82-84.

65. Frazier, *Runaway and Freed Missouri Slaves*, 146. Patrick Brophy states that Jane was pregnant and delivered her child on the journey, while another source notes that the

pregnant woman was Narcissa Daniels. Patrick Brophy Jr., "Bushwhacker Musings," 1980, in Underground Railroad Vertical File, SHSM. See also Kiene, "The Battle of the Spurs," 444.

66. Nancy Smith, "The 'Liberty Line' in Lawrence, Kansas Territory," in Sheridan, *Freedom's Crucible*, 9–10.

67. Oertel, *Bleeding Borders*, 49–50.

68. Richard A. Swallow, "Fleeing Slaves Were Hidden in Topeka Building," *Topeka Capital*, April 21, 1929, in Shawnee County Clippings, vol. 1, KHS.

69. "Mrs. C.I.H. Nichol's Letter: Recollections," *Wyandotte Gazette*, December 29, 1888.

70. Mrs. H. C. Root, "A Few Incidents in the Life of General John Ritchie," April 27, 1903, in John Ritchie Miscellaneous Collection, KHS. This creek ran underneath what is now Interstate 70 near the 10th Street exit. At the time, apparently, the house stood on the corner of Monroe Street and 12th Street, although today the building's address is 1116 E. Madison.

71. A. Ellis, "Editor, Chautauqua Journal," in Negroes Clippings, vols. 1–2, KHS.

72. There are a number of related cases, but as one example see *Rain Hutchison v. Champion Vaughan*, Case 409, U.S. Territorial Court of Kansas Case Files, Records of District Courts of the United States, Record Group 21, NARA—KC. Some of these abolitionists were also charged with violating the Fugitive Slave Law (by aiding Fisher's escape), although none of these cases went to trial. For an example of these criminal charges, see *United States v. Champion Vaughan*, Case 61, U.S. Territorial Court of Kansas Case Files, Records of District Courts of the United States, Record Group 21, NARA—KC.

73. Mary Abbott, "Reminiscences of Mrs. J. B. Abbott, De Soto," September 1, 1895, in Slaves and Slavery Collection, KHS.

74. Ephraim Nute to Franklin Sanborn, March 22, 1859, in John Brown Collection, KHS.

75. Undated manuscript, in James Hanway Collection, KHS.

76. Richard B. Sheridan, "Editor's Commentary," in Sheridan, *Freedom's Crucible*, 131–132.

77. Shawnee County Historical Society, "Underground Railroad in Topeka," 15.

78. Benjamin Van Horn to George W. Martin, undated, in Benjamin Van Horn Miscellaneous Collection, KHS.

79. "Slave Hunting," *Kansas Herald of Freedom*, November 21, 1857.

80. Benjamin Van Horn to George W. Martin, undated, in Benjamin Van Horn Miscellaneous Collection, KHS. This might have been the Scales' boardinghouse.

81. Benjamin Van Horn to George W. Martin, undated, in Benjamin Van Horn Miscellaneous Collection, KHS. Other reminiscences stated that the Scales and John Armstrong lived in the same house, which was located one block east of the building that Van Horn describes.

82. John E. Stewart to Thaddeus Hyatt, December 20, 1859, in Thaddeus Hyatt Papers, KHS.

83. Richard J. Hinton and George B. Gill, "John Brown and the Rescue of Missouri Slaves," in Sheridan, *Freedom's Crucible*, 85.

84. Doster, "Kansas: Early Judicial History," 59.

85. *Territory of Kansas v. F. Harrison et al.*, in H. Miles Moore Collection, KHS.

86. *Territory of Kansas v. F. Harrison et al.*, in H. Miles Moore Collection, KHS; "Letter from Leavenworth," *Kansas Herald of Freedom*, January 22, 1859. Moore was a lawyer in Leavenworth who worked for the defense.

87. "History Made There; The Planters' House at Leavenworth Sold at Auction," *Topeka Capital*, June 7, 1903, in Leavenworth County Clippings, vol. 1, KHS.

88. Fisher, *The Gun and the Gospel*, 158–159.

89. *Territory of Kansas v. F. Harrison et al.*, in H. Miles Moore Collection, KHS. This skill was corroborated by other testimonies before the court that were less prone to bias.

90. McNeal, *When Kansas Was Young*, 8. *United States v. Lewis L. Weld* was thrown out in 1860, although Territorial Chief Justice John Pettit wrote a short brief explaining his reasons for suppressing the indictments against Weld. See Dassler, *Reports of Cases*, 591–599.

91. Sidney S. Herd and William E. Connelley, "Quantrill and the U.G.R.R. in Lawrence, Kansas Territory," in Sheridan, *Freedom's Crucible*, 17.

92. Charles Leonhardt, "The Last Train that Passed Over the Underground Railroad from Kansas Territory," 1870, in Charles Leonhardt Papers, KHS.

93. Theodore Gardner, "The Last Battle of the Border War," in Sheridan, *Freedom's Crucible*, 62.

94. Frederick Starr Jr. to Frederick Starr Sr., September 19, 1854, in Frederick Starr Jr. Papers, WHMC—C.

95. "An Abolitionist in Our City," *Leavenworth Journal*, October 29, 1856. This newspaper reprinted the original warning from the Weston *Platte Argus*.

96. Untitled, *Westport Border Star*, August 5, 1859.

97. Sidney S. Herd and William E. Connelley, "Quantrill and the U.G.R.R. in Lawrence, Kansas Territory," in Sheridan, *Freedom's Crucible*, 14.

98. Doy, *Narrative*, 24–26, 44–45, 50–51. Doy stated that all the participants in his capture were "Northern men by birth" (26).

99. Lutz, "Quantrill and the Morgan Walker Tragedy," 326. Of course, since this narrative comes from the free-state perspective, and it was written well after Quantrill's raid on Lawrence in 1863, these descriptions of Quantrill's brutality may be exaggerated. The portion of the account dealing with this unidentified slave is not corroborated in other sources, and indeed later in the article Lutz quotes a free stater who heard Walker's own story about the night's occurrences. According to that account, Walker and his companions found Ball and Lipsey's hiding place by tracking a blood trail, not with the aid of this enslaved man. There is no way to be sure which description is more accurate.

100. John Bowles, "The Lawrence Depot of the Underground Railroad," in Sheridan, *Freedom's Crucible*, 52.

101. Theodore Gardner, "The Last Battle of the Border War," in Sheridan, *Freedom's Crucible*, 60.

102. Sheridan, "From Slavery in Missouri to Freedom in Kansas," 31.

103. "Kansas Town's Ruins Hold Tales of Time Slaves Fled to Freedom," in Miscellaneous Quindaro Publications, Kansas Collection, SRL.

104. Frazier, *Runaway and Freed Missouri Slaves*, 176. Quindaro only existed from 1856 to 1862. See Bremer, "'A Species of Town-Building Madness,'" 156–171.

105. "Kansas Town's Ruins Hold Tales of Time Slaves Fled to Freedom," in Miscellaneous Quindaro Publications, SRL.

106. United States Bureau of the Census, *Eighth Census of the United States*, 1860, Population Schedules. The next closest county was Bourbon, which only had sixty-five. Free black communities primarily formed in urban areas, making it likely that Fort Scott contained many of those sixty-five individuals.

107. R. R. Boone to Dear Father, September 12, 1858, in Boone Family Papers, MHML.

108. "Watch the Abolitionists," Atchison *Squatter Sovereign*, August 7, 1855.

109. Hoole, "A Southerner's Viewpoint," 67.

110. Leonhardt, "The Last Train that Passed Over the Underground Railroad from Kansas Territory," in Charles Leonhardt Papers, KHS.

111. John Bowles, "The Lawrence Depot of the Underground Railroad," in Sheridan, *Freedom's Crucible*, 52.

112. "It Is Offensive and Uncalled For," *Western Journal of Commerce*, August 25, 1859.

113. Allan E. Paris, "Life of 100-Year-Old Lizzie Allen Reflects History of Leavenworth," *Leavenworth Times*, July 2, 1939, in Negroes Clippings, vol. 7, KHS.

114. Allan E. Paris, "Life of 100-Year-Old Lizzie Allen Reflects History of Leavenworth," *Leavenworth Times*, July 2, 1939, in Negroes Clippings, vol. 7, KHS.

115. John E. Stewart, "The Fighting Preacher and the Runaway Slaves," in Sheridan, *Freedom's Crucible*, 47.

116. Gray, "Ex Slave Story," in *Slave Narratives*, vol. 6, *Kansas Narratives*, 9.

117. "The Underground Railroad in Kansas," *Kansas City Star*, July 2, 1905, in Negroes Clippings, vol. 7, KHS.

118. Theodore Morse, "The 'Underground Railroad' in Kansas," in Theodore Morse Miscellaneous Collection, KHS.

119. George E. Flanders, "Early Kansas Reminiscences," undated, in Shawnee County History Collection, KHS.

120. John Bowles, "The Lawrence Depot of the Underground Railroad," in Sheridan, *Freedom's Crucible*, 52.

121. "Nigger Stealing," *Western Journal of Commerce*, October 25, 1860.

122. LaRoche, *Free Black Communities*, x.

123. Frederick Starr Jr. to Frederick Starr Sr., February 26, 1855, in Frederick Starr Jr. Papers, WHMC—C.

124. Frederick Starr Jr. to Family, October 18, 1854, in Frederick Starr Jr. Papers, WHMC—C.

125. "Free Negroes," *Western Journal of Commerce*, June 12, 1858.

126. Bierbaum, "Frederick Starr, a Missouri Border Abolitionist," 312–313.

127. Paxton, *Annals of Platte County*, 215; Frederick Starr to Frederick Starr, Sr. & All the Others, November 29, 1854, Frederick Starr Jr. Papers, WHMC—C.

128. "Two Pro-Slavery Families Driven Away," *Kansas City Enterprise*, May 31, 1856.

129. "Two Pro-Slavery Families Driven Away," *Kansas City Enterprise*, May 31, 1856.

130. Magers, "The Raid on the Parkville Industrial Luminary," 40.

131. Frazier, *Runaway and Freed Missouri Slaves*, 144; "Destruction of the Parkville Luminary—Spirit of the State Press," *Jefferson Examiner*, May 3, 1855.

132. "Kansas Meeting," *Liberty Tribune*, April 27, 1855.

133. John R. Kelso's Complete Works in Manuscript, 1873–1882, HL.

5 / Entering the Promised Land

1. Maria Seals (Mother) Pension Application (A#335550), Service of Sam Denny, Sixty-Seventh USCI, Record Group 15, NARA.

2. Entry for Sam Denny, Liberty Recruiting Station, *Descriptive Recruitment Lists*, Record Group 94, NARA. This is also available as Microfilm Publication M1894.

3. Maria Seals (Mother) Pension Application (A#335550), Service of Sam Denny, Sixty-Seventh USCI, Record Group 15, NARA.

4. See Daniel Crofts, *Reluctant Confederates: Upper South Unionists in the Secession Crisis* (Chapel Hill: University of North Carolina Press, 1989).

5. Ponce, *Kansas's War*, 72–73. Also of note is that Kansas enlisted almost thirty-five hundred men above the required quota. See Ponce, 74–75.

6. Harrold, *Border War*, 121, 198. Despite his title, Harrold does not devote significant attention to the Kansas-Missouri line.

7. A. L. Gilstrap to William Rosecrans, February 27, 1864, in *OR*, ser. I, vol. 34, pt. II, 440. *OR* is short for the United States War Department's publication titled *The War of the Rebellion: A Compilation of the Official Records of the Union and Confederate Armies*.

8. Phillips, *Civil War in the Border South*, 5–6. There is some historiographical debate about Missourians' competing identities in the prewar period. No doubt recent German immigration had given those Missourians a dual heritage, but of those who were native born, that identity was complicated. Aaron Astor argues that "the vast majority of whites in the region would have considered themselves 'southern'" (Astor, *Rebels on the Border*, 18), while Christopher Phillips emphasizes the region's Westernness, admittedly though, a Westernness infused with Southern principles (Phillips, *Missouri's Confederate*, 185–186).

9. Siddali, *Missouri's War*, 60–61.

10. Hamilton Gamble to David K. Pittman, December 14, 1861, in Hamilton Gamble Papers, MHML. This letter was unsigned but was written in Gamble's hand.

11. The term "contraband" originated from Union general Benjamin Butler, commander of the Department of Virginia, who developed the concept that slaves could be legally confiscated from Confederates as "contraband of war."

12. Berlin, *Long Emancipation*, 8.

13. Ira Berlin, "Who Freed the Slaves? Emancipation and Its Meaning," in Blight and Simpson, *Union and Emancipation*, 120.

14. Gregory P. Downs, "Force, Freedom, and the Making of Emancipation," in Link and Broomhall, *Rethinking American Emancipation*, 46.

15. Jones, "History and Commemoration," 454.

16. Fields, *Slavery and Freedom on the Middle Ground*, 100. In addition to Berlin and Fields, another historian who argues for what has (sometimes derisively) been called a "self-emancipation thesis" is Vincent Harding, *There Is a River*, 221–222, 226.

17. Richard Cordley, "The Contrabands from the History of Lawrence," undated, in Douglas County Historical Society Manuscripts, Kansas Collection, SRL.

18. In this chapter the term "contraband," though used sparingly, will reference those individuals who entered Union lines directly, as a transitional status. "Refugee" will be used more broadly in reference to any former slaves or free blacks seeking assistance. The terms "former slave," "freedmen," "freedwomen," and "freedpeople" will refer to any person who was formerly enslaved, regardless of how they became legally free. Consequently, there are sections where all three have overlapping definitions. I have chosen to use these disparate terms to reflect both the terminology in use during the Civil War and modern scholarship.

19. Hamilton R. Gamble to Abraham Lincoln, May 19, 1862, in Hamilton Gamble Papers, MHML.

20. John Brown Jr. to Parker Pillsbury, July 18, 1862, in Military History Collection, KHS.

21. "Important from Missouri," *New York Times*, September 1, 1861.

22. Siddali, *Missouri's War*, 102–103.

23. Historian James McPherson considers Delaware a "free state," even though slavery existed within its boundaries, because 90 percent of its black population was legally free. See McPherson, *Battle Cry*, 297.

24. Geiger, "Indebtedness and Guerrilla Violence," 61.

25. "The Contraband Exodus," *Fort Scott Bulletin*, September 13, 1862.

26. Larry Lapsley, "History of Larry Lapsley," undated, in Cecil Howe Papers, KHS.

27. Margaret J. Hays to Elizabeth Watts, June 6, 1861. These letters are available online at http://www.wattshaysletters.com/ (accessed February 8, 2016). They are reportedly being accessioned by the Jackson County Historical Society in Independence, Missouri.

28. Margaret Hays to Elizabeth Watts, November 12, 1861, and Margaret Hays to Elizabeth Watts, November 7, 1863. Available online at http://www.wattshaysletters.com/.

29. B. W. Lewis to Thomas Carney, August 24, 1863, in Slaves and Slavery Collection, KHS.

30. Entry for Spotswood Rice, Glasgow Recruiting Station, *Descriptive Recruitment Lists*, Record Group 94, NARA.

31. Mary Hall to Jacob Hall, May 6, 1863, in Jacob Hall Family Papers, JCHS.

32. S. M. Barrett, "A Brave Mother's Story of Terror in War Days on Missouri Border," *Kansas City Times*, January 21, 1941, in Kansas History Clippings, vol. 10, KHS.

33. Fields, *Slavery and Freedom on the Middle Ground*, 100.

34. John Brown Jr. to Parker Pillsbury, July 18, 1862, in Military History Collection, KHS.

35. Two examples include "Contrabands," *Leavenworth Daily Conservative*, September 19, 1861, and Margaret Hays to Elizabeth Watts, September 26, 1861. Available online at http://www.wattshaysletters.com/.

36. One unidentified author wrote that "the essence of Jayhawking is Democracy. . . . It worked well and every loyal man thanks God it was done" (Web Wilder, "All About Jayhawking," *Leavenworth Daily Conservative*, September 20, 1861).

37. Thomas Ewing Jr. to C. W. Marsh, August 3, 1863, in Berlin et al., *Freedom: A Documentary History*, 229.

38. "An Interesting Negro Character," *The Atchison Daily Globe*, July 12, 1907, in George Remsburg, *Historical and Other Sketches*, vol. 1, KHS. It is unclear whether this was indeed Quantrill's gang, since this story is undated.

39. Harold Coats, "Topeka Woman Recalls Her Early Life Spent as a Slave in Missouri," *Topeka Capital*, May 6, 1941, in Negroes Clippings, vol. 7, KHS.

40. Younger, *The Story of Cole Younger*, 7.

41. "Another Negro Kidnapped," *Freedom's Champion*, April 4, 1863.

42. George Allen Root, "George Ellis Reminiscence," c. 1943, in George Allen Root Papers, KHS.

43. Nelson, "Missouri Slavery," 268–269. Nelson listed thirty-four counties in this chart.

44. United States Bureau of the Census, *Eighth Census of the United States*, 1860, Slave Schedules; United States Bureau of the Census, *Ninth Census of the United States*, 1870, Population Schedules.

45. Yael Sternhell, "Bodies in Motion and the Making of Emancipation," in Link and Broomhall, *Rethinking American Emancipation*, 21.

46. Langsdorf, "The Letters of Joseph H. Trego, Part Two," 297.

47. Henry H. Moore, "A Kansas Chaplain on the War," February 19, 1862, in Military History Collection, KHS.

48. George Titcomb Diary, December 30, 1862, HL. See also Henry Ankeny to Horatia Ankeny, July 15, 1862, in Henry Ankeny Papers, HL. Ankeny served in the Fourth Iowa.

49. Samuel R. Curtis to B. M. Prentiss, March 9, 1863, in *OR*, ser. I, vol. 22, pt. II, 147.

50. Masur, "A Rare Phenomenon of Philological Vegetation," 1051; Glatthaar, *Forged in Battle*, 3–5.

51. Simon Cameron to Benjamin F. Butler, August 8, 1861, in *OR*, ser. II, vol. 1, pt. IV, 762.

52. House of Representatives Resolution, December 20, 1861, in *OR*, ser. II, vol. 1, pt. IV, 790. Apparently some military commanders had misunderstood or disregarded the law's relevance, since Attorney General Edward Bates had to remind the U.S. Marshal in Kansas in July 1861. See Edward Bates to J. L. McDowell, July 23, 1861, in *OR*, ser. II, vol. 1, pt. IV, 761.

53. H. W. Halleck to General Asboth, December 26, 1861, in *OR*, ser. II, vol. 1, pt. IV, 796.

54. The Western Division was renamed the Department of Missouri at that same time. Grimsley, *The Hard Hand of War*, 49. From the very beginning Halleck disagreed with Butler's approach toward fugitives. See Marszalek, *Commander of All Lincoln's Armies*, 111.

55. H. W. Halleck to Colonel Carlin, January 9, 1862, in *OR*, ser. II, vol. 1, pt. IV, 799.

56. Arthur T. Reeve to John Brown Jr., June 26, 1862, in Military History Collection, KHS. Daniel Anthony was from Leavenworth and was a brother to Susan B. Anthony.

57. Arthur T. Reeve to John Brown Jr., July 9, 1862, in Military History Collection, KHS.

58. Fellman, "Emancipation in Missouri," 39–40.

59. White, *Emancipation*, 9.

60. George E. Waring to General Asboth, December 19, 1861, in *OR*, ser. II, vol. 1, pt. IV, 789-790.

61. Unknown author to the editors of the *Democrat*, May 11, 1862, in Samuel Newitt Wood Papers, KHS; George E. Waring to Henry Halleck, December 19, 1861, in *OR*, ser. II, vol. 1, pt. IV, 790.

62. Henry H. Moore, "A Kansas Chaplain on the War," February 19, 1862, in Military History Collection, KHS.

63. John S. Phelps to Grenville M. Dodge, December 2, 1861, in *OR*, ser. II, vol. 1, pt. IV, 781.

64. Charles Chase to the Editor of the Republican, August 19, 1863, in Charles Chase Miscellaneous Collection, KHS.

65. Henry H. Moore, "A Kansas Chaplain on the War," February 19, 1862, in Military History Collection, KHS.

66. John Brown Jr. to Parker Pillsbury, July 18, 1862, in Military History Collection, KHS. John Brown Jr. and his men had joined the Jayhawkers in November 1861.

67. Perl W. Morgan, "Reminiscent of Wyandotte," *Kansas City Star*, August 18, 1905, in Wyandotte County Clippings, vol. 1, KHS.

68. Henry H. Moore, "A Kansas Chaplain on the War," February 19, 1862, in Military History Collection, KHS.

69. Andrew Huntoon to Elizabeth and Prentiss Huntoon, November 20, 1861, in Andrew Jackson Huntoon Papers, KHS.

70. Horace Ladd Moore, "The Second Kansas Infantry and The Second Kansas Cavalry," in Military History Collection, KHS.

71. Langsdorf, "The Letters of Joseph H. Trego: Part Two," 290.

72. Downs, *Sick from Freedom*, 7.

73. Union General Thomas Ewing issued Order No. 11 after Quantrill's raid on Lawrence. It forced those living in rural areas of Jackson, Cass, Bates, and northern Vernon counties to evacuate, hoping that this would flush out Confederate guerrillas who relied on friends and family for support. It attempted to distinguish between loyal and disloyal citizens by stating that those who could prove their loyalty could remain on the border, as long as they settled in Kansas or near a Union installation at Independence, Harrisonville, Hickman Mills, or Pleasant Hill. The order did not ease tensions on the border. See Neely, *The Border Between Them*, 120–122.

74. F. R. Newell to H. D. Fisher, August 13, 1863, in Hugh Dunn Fisher Papers, KHS.

75. Henry Halleck, General Order No. 3, November 20, 1861, in *OR*, ser. II, vol. 1, pt. IV, 778.

76. Henry H. Moore, "A Kansas Chaplain on the War," February 19, 1862, in Military History Collection, KHS.

77. Henry H. Moore, "A Kansas Chaplain on the War," February 19, 1862, in Military History Collection, KHS; H. H. Moore, "The Black Brigade," *Lawrence Republican*, November 21, 1861. In his role as assistant superintendent of contrabands, he made at least three additional trips, including one to Fort Scott and one to Lawrence.

78. Henry H. Moore, "A Kansas Chaplain on the War," February 19, 1862, in Military History Collection, KHS.

79. Perl W. Morgan, "Reminiscent of Wyandotte," *Kansas City Star*, August 18, 1905, in Wyandotte County Clippings, vol. 1, KHS.

80. Armitage, "'Seeking a Home,'" 156; Lowery and Sweets, *African-Americans in the 1865 Kansas State Census*, iii.

81. Richard Cordley, "The Contrabands from the History of Lawrence," undated, in Douglas County Historical Society Manuscripts, Kansas Collection, SRL.

82. George Allen Root, "George Ellis Reminiscence," c. 1943, in George Allen Root Papers, KHS.

83. Edward S. Harvey, "Rebecca Brooks Harvey," 1946, in Edward S. Harvey Papers, Kansas Collection, SRL; Armitage, "'Seeking a Home,'" 155.

84. Ruth E. Love, "Ed Harvey's Parents, Born in Slavery, Sent Sons Thru K.U.," *Lawrence Journal World*, October 13, 1953, in Harvey Family Papers, Kansas Collection, SRL.

85. John B. Wood to George L. Stearns, November 19, 1861, in George Luther and Mary E. Stearns Collection, KHS.

86. Castel, *Civil War Kansas*, 8; United States Bureau of the Census, "Population of the 100 Largest Urban Places, 1870" http://www.census.gov/population/www/documentation/twpso027/tab10.txt (accessed May 31, 2015).

87. Sheridan, "From Slavery in Missouri to Freedom in Kansas," 38, 41.

88. *Leavenworth Daily Conservative*, February 12, 1862, quoted in Sheridan, "From Slavery in Missouri to Freedom in Kansas," 42.

89. "The Mother of Port William," *The Atchison Daily Globe*, April 23, 1909, in George Remsburg, *Historical and Other Sketches*, vol. 1, KHS.

90. Oliva, *Fort Scott*, 67.

91. John B. Wood to George L. Stearns, November 19, 1861, in George Luther and Mary E. Stearns Collection, KHS.

92. "Kansas Towns," *Leavenworth Daily Conservative*, August 6, 1863.

93. John B. Wood to George L. Stearns, November 19, 1861, in George Luther and Mary E. Stearns Collection, KHS.

94. Charles Chase to Editor of the Republican, August 19, 1863, in Charles Chase Miscellaneous Collection, KHS.

95. James E. Yeatman to Hugh D. Fisher, November 10, 1863, in Hugh Dunn Fisher Papers, KHS.

96. James E. Yeatman, George Partridge, John B. Johnson, Carlos S. Greeley and William G. Eliot to Abraham Lincoln, November 6, 1863, in Hugh Dunn Fisher Papers, KHS.

97. Samuel Curtis to Henry Barnes Curtis, November 21, 1862, in Samuel R. Curtis Papers, HL.

98. Perl W. Morgan, "Reminiscent of Wyandotte," *Kansas City Star*, August 18, 1905, in Wyandotte County Clippings, vol. 1, KHS.

99. Henry H. Moore, "A Kansas Chaplain on the War," February 19, 1862, in Military History Collection, KHS.

100. Richard Cordley, "The Contrabands from the History of Lawrence," undated, in Douglas County Historical Society Manuscripts, Kansas Collection, SRL.

101. Glaathaar, *Forged in Battle*, 121; Spurgeon, *Soldiers in the Army of Freedom*, 7.

102. Cornish, *Kansas Negro Regiments*, 4. See also Williams, *A History of the Negro Troops*, 69. Missouri and Kansas black troops make only a brief appearance in this otherwise comprehensive treatment.

103. James Lane to S. D. Sturgis, October 3, 1861, in *OR*, ser. II, vol. 1, pt. IV, 771. However, in typical Lane style, he spoke from both sides of his mouth. In this same letter, he assured the general that his men were "not here for the purpose of interfering in anywise with the institution of slavery. They shall not become negro thieves nor shall they be prostituted into negro-catchers."

104. Captain Ethan Earle, who served under Lane in Company F of the First Kansas Colored, wrote in his memoir that "General Lane's ideas about the negro were that they ought to be enfranchised at some future time when it could be done with safety but the two races could never live in harmony and equality together, one or the other must rule; he would therefore have the negroes used as servants to the white men, during the war, and then colonize the entire colored population in a state or country. This in his opinion was the only way which the negro could ever enjoy freedom and equality" (Earle, Journal of Captain Ethan Earle, KHS). The Kansas Historical Society owns a microfilm copy of the original, which is housed at the New England Historic Genealogical Society in Boston, Massachusetts, in a collection on the First Kansas Colored Infantry.

105. It was not until Lincoln began contemplating emancipation's significance to the war effort, which culminated in the Emancipation Proclamation on January 1, 1863, that black enlistment became a tool for waging war. Because this proclamation only freed slaves living in areas under rebellion, it did not apply to slaves in Missouri. See Foner, *Forever Free*, 50.

106. Spurgeon, *Soldiers in the Army of Freedom*, 53, 74.

107. Siddali, *From Property to Person*, 81, 92, 228–229; Dobak, *Freedom by the Sword*, 164. As a government publication, this is available at http://www.history.army. mil/html/books/030/30-24/CMH_pub_30-24.pdf (accessed February 8, 2016).

108. Senate Report No. 1214, 51st Congress, 1st session, in James Monroe Williams Papers, KHS.

109. James Monroe Williams to T. J. Anderson, undated, in James Monroe Williams Papers, KHS.

110. Lucy Crowbarger (Widow) Pension Application (A#506419), Service of Henderson (alias Crowbarger) Davenport, Eighty-Third USCI, Record Group 15, NARA.

111. Bird, *Civil War in Kansas*, 65; "The Negro Regiment," *Atchison Freedom's Champion*, January 24, 1863; Cornish, *Kansas Negro Regiments*, 7–8. This was also true for Douglas's Battery at Leavenworth. See Gabriel Grays, et al., to Capt. H. Ford Douglas, June 19, 1865, in Berlin et al., *Freedom: A Documentary History*, 421.

112. Spurgeon, *Soldiers in the Army of Freedom*, 69.

113. Cornish, *The Sable Arm*, 78; Dobak, *Freedom by the Sword*, 240.

114. Cornish, *Kansas Negro Regiments*, 12.

115. Cunningham, "Douglas's Battery," 204.

116. "To Arms! To Arms!" *Leavenworth Daily Conservative*, July 30, 1864. Interestingly, this advertisement stated "Avenge Fort Pillow!" in large type. The massacre of surrendered black troops at Fort Pillow, Tennessee, occurred on April 12, 1864.

117. Michael T. Meier, "Lorenzo Thomas and the Recruitment of Blacks in the Mississippi Valley, 1863–1865" in John David Smith, *Black Soldiers in Blue*, 249, 259.

118. Dobak, *Freedom by the Sword*, 167–168, 179, 191.

119. Blassingame, "The Recruitment of Negro Troops in Missouri," 329–330; Dyer, *Compendium*, 1000.

120. Nelson, "Missouri Slavery," 264. This order had originally stated that the provost marshals should attempt to "circulate the provisions of this order among slaveholders and slaves," but that had been deleted from the first draft, a fact that Pile called "an office secret." See Testimony of William A. Pile before the American Freedmen's Inquiry Commission, November 29, 1863, in Berlin et al., *Freedom: A Documentary History*, 235.

121. Margaret Hays to Elizabeth Watts, January 25, 1864. Available online at http://www.wattshaysletters.com/.

122. Lucy Crowbarger (Widow) Pension Application (A#506419), Service of Henderson (alias Crowbarger) Davenport, Eighty-Third USCI, Record Group 15, NARA.

123. See *Descriptive Recruitment Lists*, Record Group 94, NARA, which is grouped according to location.

124. Michael T. Meier, "Lorenzo Thomas and the Recruitment of Blacks in the Mississippi Valley, 1863–1865," in John David Smith, *Black Soldiers in Blue*, 263.

125. Diane Mutti Burke, "'Slavery Dies Hard': Enslaved Missourians' Struggle for Freedom," in Earle and Burke, *Bleeding Kansas, Bleeding Missouri*, 160–162; Testimony of William A. Pile before the American Freedmen's Inquiry Commission, November 29, 1863, in Berlin et al., *Freedom: A Documentary History*, 233.

126. Margaret Hays to Elizabeth Watts, December 28, 1863. Available online at http://www.wattshaysletters.com/.

127. Margaret Hays to Elizabeth Watts, January 25, 1864. Available online at http://www.wattshaysletters.com/.

128. Michael T. Meier, "Lorenzo Thomas and the Recruitment of Blacks in the Mississippi Valley, 1863–1865," in John David Smith, *Black Soldiers in Blue*, 263.

129. James Monroe Williams to T. J. Anderson, undated, in James Monroe Williams Papers, KHS; Dobak, *Freedom by the Sword*, 165–166. Other secondary sources cite different casualty numbers. See Miesner, "The First Kansas Colored," 15.

130. Spurgeon, *Soldiers in the Army of Freedom*, 106–108.

131. Hamilton R. Gamble to Abraham Lincoln, September 8, 1862, in Hamilton Gamble Papers, MHML.

132. James Monroe Williams to T. J. Anderson, undated, in James Monroe Williams Papers, KHS; Cornish, *The Sable Arm*, 145–146.

133. Urwin, "We Cannot Treat Negroes," 193–194; Fisher, "The First Kansas Colored," 121.

134. Committee on Military Affairs, House Report No. 2971, 51st Congress, 1st session, in James Monroe Williams Papers, KHS.

135. James M. Williams, Report on Poison Springs, April 24, 1864, in James Monroe Williams Papers, KHS.

136. Urwin, "We Cannot Treat Negroes," 197–199.

137. Cornish, *Kansas Negro Regiments*, 14.

138. Urwin, "We Cannot Treat Negroes," 207.

139. General Samuel Curtis, General Order No. 1, October 11, 1864, in Military History Collection, KHS.

140. Cunningham, "Welcoming 'Pa' on the Kaw," 89–90, 93.

141. Forman, *The Western Sanitary Commission*, 74.

142. Hunt, *The Last Battle of the Civil War*, 65–66.

143. For an excellent discussion of white officers' attitudes toward black soldiers, see chapter 5 of Glatthaar, *Forged in Battle*. He argues that white officers' perceptions of African Americans were shaped by caricatures from literature and the media, not by personal interactions; "what developed among the white officers was a peculiarly contradictory portrait of blacks as a whole" (Glatthaar, *Forged in Battle*, 82).

144. James Monroe Williams to T. J. Anderson, undated, in James Monroe Williams Papers, KHS.

145. Cunningham, "Douglas's Battery," 202.

146. Cunningham, "Douglas's Battery," 206.

147. Cunningham, "Douglas's Battery," 205.

148. N. P. Chipman to Samuel R. Curtis, October 16, 1862, in Berlin et al., *Freedom: A Documentary History*, 71.

149. James G. Blunt, Report on the Battle of Honey Springs, July 17, 1863, in James Monroe Williams Papers, KHS.

150. N. P. Chipman to Samuel R. Curtis, October 16, 1862, in Berlin et al., *Freedom: A Documentary History*, 71.

151. John M. Williams to H. Q. Loring, April 21, 1863, in Berlin et al., *Freedom: A Documentary History*, 72.

152. John M. Williams to H. Q. Loring, April 21, 1863, in Berlin et al., *Freedom: A Documentary History*, 72.

153. Testimony of William A. Pile before the American Freedmen's Inquiry Commission, November 29, 1863, in Berlin et al., *Freedom: A Documentary History*, 376.

154. Armstead Bradford Invalid Pension Application (C#545702), Eighty-Third USCI, Record Group 15, NARA.

155. Allen Claybrook Invalid Pension Application (A#908197, C#975363), Sixty-Eighth USCI, Record Group 15, NARA.

156. Joseph Carras Invalid Pension Application (A#419714, C#230304), Seventy-Ninth USCI, Record Group 15, NARA. This file also includes a widow and minor application.

157. Henry Phillips (alias Frank Biggs) Invalid Pension Application (A#439928, C#1006513), Sixty-Seventh USCI, Record Group 15, NARA; Shelby Bannon Invalid Pension Application (A#122564, C#95473), Seventy-Ninth USCI, Record Group 15, NARA.

158. Martha Glover to Richard Glover, December 30, 1863, in Berlin et al., *Freedom: A Documentary History*, 244.

159. William Pile to General William Rosecrans, February 23, 1864, in Berlin et al., *Freedom: A Documentary History*, 245.

160. Fellman, "Emancipation," 40.

161. Lee, "Missouri's Fight over Emancipation," 258.

162. Hamilton Gamble, "Gentlemen of the Convention," June 15, 1863, in Hamilton Gamble Papers, MHML.

163. Astor, *Rebels on the Border*, 176.

Epilogue

1. "The Colored Emigrants," *The Colored Citizen*, March 29, 1879.

2. Leiker, "Race Relations in the Sunflower State," 236.

3. Williams, "Negro Public School System," 142. See United States Bureau of the Census, *Ninth Census of the United States*, 1870, Population Schedules. Jackson County ranked second in the size of its African American population.

4. Astor, *Rebels on the Border*, 171.

5. Goodlander, *Memoirs and Recollections*, 107.

6. Bates County, as one example, had been completely depopulated. When new emigrants and original settlers returned in the postwar period, the demographics of the county changed radically. Consult Neely, *The Border Between Them*, 147.

7. There are many letters in the Kansas Historical Society that Southern freedpeople wrote to the governor, John P. St. John, stating they had heard about Kansas and wanted to make a new life for themselves in a free state. See John P. St. John Received Correspondence, in Governor's Papers, KHS. Also, for discussion of white reactions, see Schwendemann, "The 'Exodusters' on the Missouri," 32–35.

8. John W. McKerley, "'We Promise to Use the Ballot as We Did the Bayonet': Black Suffrage Activism and the Limits of Loyalty in Reconstruction Missouri," in Earle and Burke, *Bleeding Kansas, Bleeding Missouri*, 210.

9. Astor, *Rebels on the Border*, 211. The 1870 census stated that there were 1,192 African Americans in Platte County; even assuming that out-migration occurred between 1865 and 1870, it seems likely that this high number would reflect signatures from multiple adjacent counties. See United States Bureau of the Census, *Ninth Census of the United States*, 1870, Population Schedules.

10. One reference to the weakness of Radical Republicanism in western Missouri is "What Will They Do," *Platte City Reveille*, June 10, 1870.

11. White newspapers on the border tended to reprint suffrage articles from Saint Louis newspapers with limited commentary, and there were no black newspapers in western Missouri until the twentieth century.

12. "An Address by the Colored People of Missouri to the Friends of Equal Rights," in Langston, *A Speech on Equality before the Law, Delivered by J. Mercer Langston*, 24.

13. Astor, *Rebels on the Border*, 217. See also "The Radical Schism," *Platte City Reveille*, June 10, 1870.

14. Astor, *Rebels on the Border*, 227-228.

15. United States Bureau of the Census, *Ninth Census of the United States*, 1870, Population Schedules; United States Bureau of the Census, *Tenth Census of the United States*, 1880, Population Schedules.

16. Cox, *Blacks in Topeka*, 21.

17. R. W. Massey to S. N. Wood, May 16, 1867, in Women Suffrage History Collection, KHS.

18. Campney, "'Light Is Bursting Upon the World!'" 181.

19. While many complaints were rooted in racist or sexist rhetoric, depending on the perspective, there were also practical considerations, including a fear that pushing for women's suffrage and black suffrage simultaneously would ensure both platforms' defeat. Women in Kansas gained equal voting rights with an amendment to the state constitution in 1912.

20. Sheridan, "Charles Henry Langston," 279.

21. This term referenced the Biblical story of Hebrew slaves in Egypt who fled to the promised land of Canaan. See Earle, *The Routledge Atlas*, 68.

22. Neely, *The Border Between Them*, 151.

23. Painter, *Exodusters*, 184–185.

24. "The Refugees," *The Colored Citizen*, May 31, 1879.

25. Coulter, *Black Man's Burden*, 24–26.

26. "A Lesson of the Exodus," *Topeka Daily Capital*, April 23, 1879.

27. Ledger Book, in Freedmen History Collection, KHS.

28. Wilmer Walton to Governor John P. St. John, February 7, 1881, in Governor John P. St. John Received Correspondence, Governor's Papers, KHS. Governor St. John was on the board of the KFRA.

29. Minutes of the Board of Directors of the Kansas Freedmen's Relief Association, in Freedmen History Collection, KHS; Schwendemann, "'Exodusters' on the Missouri," 36–40.

30. "Kansas State Colored Emigration Bureau," *Topeka Daily Capital*, April 30, 1879. Other black churches aided these efforts too. See Schwendemann, "Nicodemus," 21.

31. Schwendemann, "Nicodemus," 11–12.

32. Interview with Columbus Johnson, 1879, in Exodus History Collection, KHS.

33. Constitution of the United Transatlantic Society, in Exodus History Collection, KHS.

34. Gary Entz has argued that the Singleton Colony's significance has been greatly exaggerated (Entz, "Image and Reality," 139).

35. Campney, "'Light Is Bursting Upon the World!'" 177.

36. Painter, *Exodusters*, 257.

37. Painter, *Exodusters*, 260.

Bibliography

Newspapers

(Westport) *Border Star*
(Topeka) *Colored Citizen*
The First Kansas
Fort Scott Bulletin
Fort Scott Colored Citizen
Fort Scott Democrat
(Atchison) *Freedom's Champion*
(Lawrence) *Herald of Freedom*
Kansas City Daily Journal of Commerce
Kansas City Enterprise
(Topeka) *Kansas Daily Tribune*
(Lawrence) *Kansas Tribune*
Leavenworth Daily Conservative
Leavenworth Daily Times
Leavenworth Herald
Leavenworth Journal
Liberty Tribune
Platte City Reveille
(Paola) *Southern Kansas Herald*
(Atchison) *Squatter Sovereign*
St. Joseph Gazette
Topeka Capital
(Saint Joseph) *Weekly Free Democrat*
(Weston) *Weekly Platte Argus*
Western Journal of Commerce
Weston Reporter

Archival Materials

Combined Arms Research Library, Fort Leavenworth, Kansas

Fort Leavenworth—Topical—Buildings—Sutler's House Vertical File

Huntington Research Library, San Marino, California

Henry Ankeny Papers
Obadiah Baker Papers
Newton Bateman Correspondence
Charles Carman Papers
Samuel Curtis Papers and Addenda
R. Curtis Edgerton Papers
William Fairholme, "Journal of an Expedition to the Grand Prairies of the Missouri"
John Kelso Manuscript
Orville Nixon Papers
Israel Prince Letters
Thomas Reynolds Letter Books
Charles Rowe Diaries
William Steel Letter Books
Thomas Sweeny Papers
George Titcomb Diary

Jackson County Historical Society, Independence, Missouri

Burdette Cogswell Papers
Joanne Chiles Eakin Papers
Jacob Hall Family Papers
John Hambright Family Papers
Thomas Hudspeth Papers
Monograph Collection
Nathan W. Perry Letters
Jabez Smith Family Papers

Kansas Historical Society, Topeka, Kansas

Miscellaneous Collections

Peter T. Abell Miscellaneous Collection
John Armstrong Miscellaneous Collection
Nora Bayne Miscellaneous Collection
W. R. Bernard Miscellaneous Collection
George Washington Clarke Miscellaneous Collection
Charles E. Cory Miscellaneous Collection
Rush Elmore Miscellaneous Collection
John Hamilton Miscellaneous Collection

William Alexander Hammond Miscellaneous Collection
Benjamin Harding Miscellaneous Collection
E. F. Heisler Miscellaneous Collection
Cecil Howes Miscellaneous Collection
Alexander and Thomas Johnson Miscellaneous Collection
Thomas Johnson Miscellaneous Collection
Samuel McAfee Miscellaneous Collection
Miscellaneous Pamphlet Collection
Theodore Morse Miscellaneous Collection
E. H. Paramore Miscellaneous Collection
John Speer Miscellaneous Collection
Mrs. E. E. Winchell Miscellaneous Collection

Clippings Volumes

Atchison County Clippings
Bourbon County Clippings
Doniphan County Clippings
Douglas County Clippings
Geary County Clippings
History of Fort Leavenworth Clippings
Indian Mission Clippings
Jefferson County Clippings
Johnson County Clippings
Kansas History Clippings
Kansas Territorial Clippings
Leavenworth County Clippings
Linn County Clippings
Miami County Clippings
Negroes Clippings
George Remsburg, *Historical and Other Sketches*
Shawnee County Clippings
Wyandotte County Clippings

Other Manuscripts

Zu Adams Papers (#254)
Atchison County History Collection (#665)
John Brown Collection (#299)
Journal of Captain Ethan Earle (MS 1319)
Hugh Dunn Fisher Papers (#343)
Franklin County History Collection (#687)
Freedmen History Collection (#586)
James Hanway Collection (#372)
Andrew Jackson Huntoon Papers (#398)
Thaddeus Hyatt Papers (#401)

Indians History Collection (#590)
John James Ingalls Papers (#177)
Charles Leonhardt Papers (#416)
Military History Collection (#617)
William A. Phillips Papers (#470)
George Allen Root Papers (#490)
Shawnee County History Collection (#729)
Slaves and Slavery Collection (#640)
John Speer Papers (#506)
George Luther and Mary E. Stearns Collection (#507)
Thomas Nesbit Stinson Papers (#511)
Trails History Collection (#648)
William Walker Papers (#527)
James Monroe Williams Papers (#545)
Hiero Tennant Wilson Daybooks (MS 1295)
Women Suffrage History Collection (#656)
Samuel Newitt Wood Papers (#548)

Government and Legal Documents

Atchison County Probate Court Case Files, 1857–1917
Governor Thomas Carney Correspondence
Governor Samuel Crawford Correspondence
Governor Charles Robinson Correspondence
Governor John P. St. John Correspondence
Leavenworth County Probate Court Inventory of Estates, 1857–1858
1855 Territorial Kansas Census
U.S. District Court Journals, 1858–1860

Kenneth Spencer Research Library, Lawrence, Kansas

Thomas Carney Papers
Douglas County Historical Society Manuscripts
Joel Grover Diary
Joel Grover Miscellaneous Items
Edward S. Harvey Papers
(Rebecca) Harvey Family Papers
Miscellaneous Quindaro Publications
William Patton Papers
William Walker Clippings

Midwest Genealogy Center, Independence, Missouri

Bates County Will Book A
Bates County Wills, 1845–1898
Buchanan County Wills and Administrations, 1839–1857
Civil War Records, Office of the Adjutant General

Clay County Circuit Court, 1836–1852
Clay County Negro Marriages, 1865–1891
Independence Wills, 1831–1863
Jackson County Wills and Administrations, 1828–1834
Vernon County Wills and Administrations Book A

Missouri History Museum Library and Research Center, Saint Louis, Missouri

Boone Family Papers
Peter Boyd Narrative
Civil War Collection
Civil War Manuscripts
Peter Clark Papers
George Cruzen Reminiscence
Willard Frissell Family Papers
Hamilton Gamble Papers
Herbert Hadley Papers
James Hyder Papers
Ellen Waddle McCoy Papers
George Sibley Papers
Slaves and Slavery Collection
William L. Sublette Collection
David Waldo Papers

Missouri Valley Special Collections, Kansas City Public Library, Kansas City, Missouri

Mildred Cox, "James Hyatt McGee"
Mildred Cox, "Town of Kansas"

National Archives and Records Administration, Central Plains Branch, Kansas City, Missouri

Records of District Courts of the United States (Record Group 21)
Records of the Mississippi Freedmen's Department ("Pre-Bureau Records"), Office of the Assistant Commissioner, Bureau of Refugees, Freedmen, and Abandoned Lands, 1863–1865 (Record Group 105)

National Archives and Records Administration, Main Branch, Washington, D.C.

Adjutant General's Office, Descriptive Recruitment Lists of Volunteers for the United States Colored Troops for the State of Missouri, 1863–1865 (Record Group 94)

Records of the Department of Veterans Affairs (Record Group 15)
  Eighty-Third USCI (Second Kansas Colored) Pension Files
  Independent (Douglas's) Colored Battery Pension Files
  Seventy-Ninth USCI (First Kansas Colored) Pension Files
  Sixty-Eighth USCI (Fourth Missouri Colored) Pension Files
  Sixty-Fifth USCI (Second Missouri Colored) Pension Files
  Sixty-Seventh USCI (Third Missouri Colored) Pension Files

State Historical Society of Missouri, Columbia, Missouri

Blacks in Missouri History (pre-1866) Vertical File
Choteau Family Vertical File
Chrisman Family Vertical File
Dean(e) Family Vertical File
Estes Family Vertical File
Robidoux Family Vertical File
Slaughter Family Vertical File
Snyder Family Vertical File
Story Family Vertical File
Tapp Family Vertical File
Underground Railroad Vertical File
Vanbibber Family Vertical File
Withers Family Vertical File

Western Historical Manuscript Collection, Columbia Branch, Columbia, Missouri

John Corby Family Papers
Joseph Robidoux Family Papers
Frederick Starr, Jr. Papers

Western Historical Manuscript Collection, Kansas City Branch, Kansas City, Missouri

Ellen Waddle McCoy Papers
Elijah Milton McGee Papers
(Thomas) Mockbee and (Eliza) Chiles Papers
Robert M. Snyder, Jr. Papers
(Abner) Staples Family Papers
Matthew Rankin Walker Papers

Published Primary Sources

Abbott, James B. "The Rescue of Dr. John W. Doy." *Transactions of the Kansas State Historical Society, 1889–1890* 4 (1890): 312–323.

Berlin, Ira, Joseph P. Reidy, and Leslie S. Rowland, eds. *Freedom: A Documentary History of Emancipation, 1861–1867.* Vol. II, *The Black Military Experience.* New York: Cambridge University Press, 1982.

Blassingame, John W., ed. *Slave Testimony: Two Centuries of Letters, Speeches, Interviews, and Autobiographies.* Baton Rouge: Louisiana State University Press, 1977.

Brown, William Wells. *The Narrative of William W. Brown, A Fugitive Slave.* Mineola, NY: Dover Publications, 1969.

Bruce, Henry Clay. *The New Man: Twenty-nine Years a Slave, Twenty-nine Years a Free Man.* York, PA: P. Anstadt and Sons, 1895.

Butler, Pardee. *Personal Recollections of Pardee Butler.* Cincinnati: Standard Publishing, 1889.

Caldwell, Martha B. *Annals of the Shawnee Methodist Mission and Indian Manual Labor School.* 2nd ed. Topeka: Kansas State Historical Society, 1977.

Chick, Washington Henry. "A Journey to Missouri in 1822." *State Centennial Souvenir Number and Program 1821–1921* 1, no. 1 (October 1921): 97–103.

Curtis, Annette W. *Jackson County, Missouri, in Black and White.* Vol. 2, *Jabez Smith: His Slaves, Plantations, Estate, and Heirs.* Independence, MO: Self-published, 1992.

Dassler, C. F. *Reports of Cases Argued and Determined in the Supreme Court of the State and Territory of Kansas.* Vol. 1. Saint Paul: West Publishing Co., 1889.

Doy, John. *Narrative of John Doy.* New York: Thomas Holman, 1860.

Eakin, Joanne C. "Richard Fristoe: Administration of His Estate in 1848." *Kansas City Genealogist* 39, no. 1 (Summer 1998): 22–29.

Everett, John, and Sarah Everett. "Letters of John and Sarah Everett, 1854–1864, Miami County Pioneers (Introduction)." *Kansas Historical Quarterly* 8, no. 1 (February 1939): 3–34.

Federal Writers' Project, eds. *Slave Narratives: A Folk History of Slavery in the United States From Interviews with Former Slaves.* Vol. 6, Kansas Narratives. Washington, D.C.: Library of Congress, 1941.

Fisher, Hugh Dunn. *The Gun and the Gospel: Early Kansas and Chaplain Fisher.* 2nd ed. Chicago: Medical Century Co., 1899.

Flint, Timothy. *Recollections of the Last Ten Years, Passed in Occasional Residences and Journeyings in the Valley of the Mississippi.* New York: De Capo Press, 1968.

Forman, Jacob Gilbert. *The Western Sanitary Commission; A Sketch of Its Origin, History, Labors for the Sick and Wounded of the Western Armies, and Aid Given to Freedmen and Union Refugees, with Incidents of Hospital Life.* Saint Louis: R. P. Studley, 1864.

Goodlander, Charles W. *Memoirs and Recollections of Charles W. Goodlander of the Early Days of Fort Scott.* Fort Scott, KS: Monitor Printing, 1899.

Goodloe, Daniel R. *Is It Expedient to Introduce Slavery into Kansas? A Tract for the Times.* Cincinnati, 1854.

Greene, Belle. "Life at Shawnee Mission." *The Annals of Kansas City* 1, no. 4 (October 1924): 457–458.

Greene, Thomas Johnson. "Recollections of Shawnee Mission." *The Annals of Kansas City* 1, no. 4 (October 1924): 454–456.

An Illustrated Historical Atlas Map, Jackson County, Mo., 1877. Philadelphia: Brink, McDonough, and Co., 1877.

Harris, Nellie McCoy. "Memories of Old Westport." *The Annals of Kansas City* 1, no. 4 (October 1924): 465–475.

Harris, William H. "A Brief History of Old Westport." *Kansas City Genealogist* 44, no. 3 (Spring 2004): 115–119.

Hewitt, J. N. B., ed., and Myrtis Jarrell, trans. *Journal of Rudolph Friederich Kurz, An Account of His Experiences Among Fur Traders and American Indians on the Mississippi and the Upper Missouri Rivers during the Years 1846 to 1852.* Washington, D.C.: United States Government Printing Office, 1937.

Hoole, William Stanley, ed. "A Southerner's Viewpoint of the Kansas Situation, 1856–1857: The Letters of Lieut. Col. A. J. Hoole, C. S. A." *Kansas Historical Quarterly* 3 (February 1934): 43–68.

Hutchings, James Mason. *Seeking the Elephant, 1849: James Mason Hutchings' Journal of His Overland Trek to California, Including His Voyage to America, in 1848 and Letters from the Mother Lode.* Glendale, CA: A. H. Clark, 1980.

Kansas Adjutant General's Office. *Report of the Adjutant General of the State of Kansas 1861–1865.* Vol. I. Topeka: Kansas State Printer, 1896.

Langsdorf, Edgar, ed. "The Letters of Joseph H. Trego, 1857–1864, Linn County Pioneer, Part One, 1857, 1858." *Kansas Historical Quarterly* 19, no. 2 (May 1951): 113–132.

———. "The Letters of Joseph H. Trego, 1857–1864, Linn County Pioneer, Part Two, 1861, 1862." *Kansas Historical Quarterly* 19, no. 3 (August 1951): 287–309.

Langston, J. Mercer. *A Speech on Equality before the Law, Delivered by J. Mercer Langston, in the Hall of Representatives, in the Capitol of Missouri, on the Evening of the 9th Day of January 1866.* Saint Louis: Democrat Book and Job Printing House, 1866.

Lowery, Debby, and Judy Sweets, eds. and comps. *African-Americans in the 1865 Kansas State Census (Douglas County).* Lawrence: Self-published, 2006.

Mallory, Rudena Kramer. *Claims by Missourians for Compensation of Enlisted Slaves: Records of the U.S. District Court of Kansas, Slave Compensation Records, November 3, 1866 to February 21, 1867, Record Group 21.* Kansas City: Self-published, 1992.

Marra, Dorothy Brandt. *Cher Oncle, Cher Papa: The Letters of Francois and Berenice Chouteau.* Edited by David Boutros. Translated by Marie-Laure Dionne Pal. Kansas City, MO: Western Historical Manuscript Collection—Kansas City, 2001.

Missouri General Assembly. *Laws of the State of Missouri, Passed at the First Session of the Fourteenth General Assembly.* Jefferson City: James Lusk, 1847.

Moore, Frank, ed. *The Rebellion Record: A Diary of American Events, with Documents, Narratives, Illustrative Incidents, Poetry, etc.* Vol. 8. New York: G. P. Putnam, 1865.

Napton, William B., Sterling Price, M. Oliver, and S. H. Woodson. *Address to the People of the United States Together with the Proceedings and Resolutions of the Pro-Slavery Convention of Missouri, Held at Lexington, July 1855.* Saint Louis: Republican Office, 1855.

Overdyke, W. Darrell. "A Southern Family on the Missouri Frontier: Letters from Independence, 1843–1855." *The Journal of Southern History* 17, no. 2 (May 1951): 216–237.

Pantle, Alberta, ed. "The Story of a Kansas Freedman." *Kansas Historical Quarterly* 11, no. 4 (November 1942): 341–369.

Peck, John Mason. *Forty Years of Pioneer Life: Memoir of John Mason Peck, D.D.* Edited by Rufus Babcock. Carbondale: Southern Illinois University Press, 1965.

Platte County Self-Defensive Association. *Negro-Slavery No Evil; Or The North and the South; The Effects of Negro-Slavery, As Exhibited in the Census, By a Comparison of the Condition of the Slaveholding and Non-Slaveholding States.* Saint Louis: M. Niedner and Co., 1854.

Ponce, Pearl T., ed. *Kansas's War: The Civil War in Documents.* Athens: Ohio University Press, 2011.

Purdue, Theda, and Michael Green, eds. *The Cherokee Removal: A Brief History with Documents.* Boston: Bedford St. Martins, 2005.

Rawick, George P., ed. *The American Slave: A Composite Autobiography.* 19 vols. Westport, CT: Greenwood Press, 1972.

Robards, William A. *Reports of Cases Argued and Determined in the Supreme Court of the State of Missouri.* Vol. XIII. Jefferson City, MO: James Lusk, 1850.

Scarritt, Nathan. "Reminiscences of the Methodist Shawnee Mission and Religious Work Among That Tribe." *The Annals of Kansas City* 1, no. 4 (October 1924): 434–445.

Scholl, Daniel B., Septimus Scholl, D. B. Shull, et al. *A Collection of Letters Written by the Scholl Family and Their Kin, 1836–1897.* Saint Louis, 1959.

Scott, Mark Chapin, ed. "Fleeing Missouri Bloodhounds: Pappy Carr's Escape to Free Kansas." *Kansas History* 37, no. 2 (Summer 2014): 66–77.

Sheridan, Richard B. *Freedom's Crucible: The Underground Railroad in Lawrence and Douglas County, Kansas, 1854–1865: A Reader.* Lawrence: University of Kansas Division of Continuing Education, 1998.

Siddali, Silvana R., ed. *Missouri's War: The Civil War in Documents.* Athens: Ohio University Press, 2009.

Spencer, Joab. "A Short History of the Shawnee Methodist Mission." *The Annals of Kansas City* 1, no. 4 (October 1924): 446–453.

United States Bureau of the Census. *Eighth Census of the United States.* Washington, D.C.: Government Printing Office, 1864.

———. *Fifth Census of the United States.* Washington, D.C.: Government Printing Office, 1831.

———. *Fourth Census of the United States.* Washington, D.C.: Government Printing Office, 1821.

———. *Ninth Census of the United States.* Washington, D.C.: Government Printing Office, 1871.

———. *Seventh Census of the United States.* Washington, D.C.: Government Printing Office, 1853.

———. *Sixth Census of the United States.* Washington, D.C.: Government Printing Office, 1841.

———. *Tenth Census of the United States.* Washington, D.C.: Government Printing Office, 1881.

United States House of Representatives. 34th Congress. 1st Session. *Report 200: Report of the Special Committee Appointed to Investigate the Troubles in Kansas; with the Views of the Minority of Said Committee.* Washington, D.C.: Cornelius Wendell, Printer, 1856.

———. 36th Congress. 2nd Session. *Reports of Committees of the House of Representatives Made during the Second Session of the Thirty-Sixth Congress, 1860–1861.* Washington, D.C.: Government Printing Office, 1861.

United States Senate. 46th Congress. 2nd Session. *Report and Testimony of the Select Committee of the United States Senate to Investigate the Causes of the Removal of the Negroes from the Southern States to the Northern States, in Three Parts, 46th Congress, 2nd Session, Senate Report 693.* Washington, D.C.: Government Printing Office, 1880.

United States War Department. *The War of the Rebellion: A Compilation of the Official Records of the Union and Confederate Armies.* Series I–IV. Washington, D.C.: Government Printing Office, 1880–1901.

Wetmore, Alphonso, comp. *Gazetteer of the State of Missouri: With a Map of the State.* Saint Louis: C. Kemmle, 1837.

Wood, William T., L. A. Wisely, and L. J. Sharp. *Proceedings of the Pro-Slavery Convention, Held at Lexington, Mo.* Saint Louis: Republican Office, 1855.

Younger, Cole. *The Story of Cole Younger, by Himself.* Chicago: The Henneberry Co., 1903.

Secondary Sources

Abel, Annie Heloise. *The American Indian as Slaveholder and Secessionist.* Vol. 1, *The Slaveholding Indians.* Lincoln: University of Nebraska Press, 1992.

Abing, Kevin. "Before Bleeding Kansas: Christian Missionaries, Slavery, and the Shawnee Indians in Pre-Territorial Kansas, 1844–1854." *Kansas History* 24, no. 1 (Spring 2001): 54–71.

———. "A Fall from Grace: Thomas Johnson and the Shawnee Indian Manual Labor School, 1839–1862." PhD diss., University of Wisconsin—Milwaukee, 1995.

———. "A Holy Battleground: Methodist, Baptist, and Quaker Missionaries Among the Shawnee Indians, 1830–1844." *Kansas History* 21, no. 2 (Summer 1998): 188–237.

Adelman, Jeremy, and Stephen Aron. "From Borderlands to Borders: Empires, Nation-States, and the Peoples in Between in North American History." *American Historical Review* 104, no. 3 (June 1999): 814–841.

Allen County Historical Society. *Tales of Early Allen County.* Iola, KS: Allen County Historical Society, 1966.

Anderson, Hattie M. "Missouri, 1804–1828: Peopling a Frontier State." *Missouri Historical Review* 31, no. 2 (January 1937): 150–180.

Anderson, James. "The Methodist Shawnee Mission in Johnson County, Kansas, 1830–1862." *The Trail Guide* 1, no. 2 (January 1956): 7–20.

Armitage, Katie R. "'Seeking a Home Where He Himself Is Free': African Americans Build a Community in Douglas County, Kansas." *Kansas History* 31, no. 3 (Autumn 2008): 154–175.

Armstrong, Warren B. "Union Chaplains and the Education of the Freedmen." *The Journal of Negro History* 52, no. 2 (April 1967): 104–115.

Arnold, Brie Swenson. "'To Inflame the Mind of the North': Slavery Politics and the Sexualized Violence of Bleeding Kansas." *Kansas History* 28, no. 1 (Spring 2015): 22–39.

Aron, Stephen. *American Confluence: The Missouri Frontier from Borderland to Border State.* Bloomington: Indiana University Press, 2006.

Astor, Aaron. *Rebels on the Border: Civil War, Emancipation, and the Reconstruction of Kentucky and Missouri.* Baton Rouge: Louisiana State University Press, 2012.

Athearn, Robert G. *In Search of Canaan: Black Migration to Kansas, 1879–1880.* Lawrence: Regents Press of Kansas, 1978.

Baltimore, Lester B. "Benjamin F. Stringfellow: The Fight for Slavery on the Missouri Border." *Missouri Historical Review* 62, no. 1 (October 1967): 14–29.

Baptist, Edward E. *The Half Has Never Been Told: Slavery and the Making of American Capitalism.* New York: Basic Books, 2014.

Barry, Louise. "The New England Emigrant Aid Company Parties of 1854." *Kansas Historical Quarterly* 12 (May 1943): 115–155.

———. "The New England Emigrant Aid Company Parties of 1855." *Kansas Historical Quarterly* 12 (August 1943): 227–268.

Barton, Keith C. "'Good Cooks and Washers': Slave Hiring, Domestic Labor, and the Market in Bourbon County, Kentucky." *The Journal of American History* 84, no. 2 (September 1997): 436–460.

Baud, Michiel, and Willem Van Schendel. "Toward a Comparative History of Borderlands." *Journal of World History* 8, no. 2 (Fall 1997): 211–242.

Beilein, Joseph, Jr. "The Guerrilla Shirt: A Labor of Love and the Style of Rebellion in Civil War Missouri." *Civil War History* 58, no. 2 (June 2012): 151–179.

Bellamy, Donnie D. "The Education of Blacks in Missouri Prior to 1861." *The Journal of Negro History* 59, no. 2 (April 1974): 143–157.

———. "The Persistency of Colonization in Missouri." *Missouri Historical Review* 72, no. 1 (October 1977): 1–24.

———. "Slavery, Emancipation, and Racism in Missouri, 1850–1865." PhD diss., University of Missouri—Columbia, 1971.

Benedict, Bryce D. *Jayhawkers: The Civil War Brigade of James Henry Lane*. Norman: University of Oklahoma Press, 2009.

Berlin, Ira. *Generations of Captivity: A History of African-American Slaves*. Cambridge, MA: Belknap Press, 2003.

———. *The Long Emancipation: The Demise of Slavery in the United States*. Cambridge, MA: Harvard University Press, 2015.

———. *Many Thousands Gone: The First Two Centuries of Slavery in North America*. New ed. Cambridge, MA: Belknap Press, 2000.

Berry, Daina Ramey. *"Swing the Sickle for the Harvest Is Ripe": Gender and Slavery in Antebellum Georgia*. Urbana: University of Illinois Press, 2007.

Berwanger, Eugene. "Western Prejudice and the Extension of Slavery." *Civil War History* 12, no. 3 (September 1966): 197–212.

Bierbaum, Milton E. "Frederick Starr, a Missouri Border Abolitionist: The Making of a Martyr." *Missouri Historical Review* 58, no. 3 (April 1964): 309–325.

Bigham, Darrel E. *On Jordan's Banks: Emancipation and Its Aftermath in the Ohio River Valley*. Lexington: University Press of Kentucky, 2006.

Billington, Monroe Lee, and Roger D. Hardaway, eds. *African Americans on the Western Frontier*. Boulder: University Press of Colorado, 1998.

Bird, Roy. *Civil War in Kansas*. Gretna, LA: Pelican Publishing, 2004.

Blackett, R. J. M. *Making Freedom: The Underground Railroad and the Politics of Slavery*. Chapel Hill: University of North Carolina Press, 2013.

Blackmar, Frank Wilson. *Kansas: A Cyclopedia of State History, Embracing Events, Institutions, Industries, Counties, Cities, Towns, Prominent Persons, Etc*. Vol. 1. Chicago: Standard Publishing, 1912.

Blassingame, John. "The Recruitment of Negro Troops in Missouri During the Civil War." *Missouri Historical Review* 58, no. 3 (April 1964): 326–338.

———. *The Slave Community: Plantation Life in the Antebellum South*. 2nd ed. New York: Oxford University Press, 1979.

———. "Using the Testimony of Ex-Slaves: Approaches and Problems." *The Journal of Southern History* 41, no. 4 (November 1975): 473–492.

Blight, David, and Brooks D. Simpson, eds. *Union and Emancipation: Essays on Politics and Race in the Civil War Era*. Kent, OH: Kent State University Press, 1997.

Boman, Dennis K. "The Dred Scott Case Reconsidered: The Legal and Political Context in Missouri." *American Journal of Legal History* 44, no. 4 (October 2000): 405–428.

Bontrager, Shannon. "'From a Nation of Drunkards, We Have Become a Sober People': The Wyandot Experience in the Ohio Valley during the Early Republic." *Journal of the Early Republic* 32, no. 4 (Winter 2012): 603–632.

Bordewich, Fergus M. *Bound for Canaan: The Underground Railroad and the War for the Soul of America*. New York: HarperCollins, 2005.

Boutros, David. "Confluence of People and Place: The Chouteau Posts on the Missouri and Kansas Rivers." In *Cher Oncle, Cher Papa: The Letters of Fran-*

cois and Berenice Chouteau, 191–204. Kansas City: Western Historical Manuscript Collection—Kansas City, 2001.

Bowen, Don R. "Guerrilla War in Western Missouri, 1862–1865: Historical Extensions of the Relative Deprivation Hypothesis." *Comparative Studies in Society and History* 19, no. 1 (January 1977): 30–51.

Bowes, John P. *Exiles and Pioneers: Eastern Indians in the Trans-Mississippi West.* New York: Cambridge University Press, 2007.

Brant, Marley. *The Outlaw Youngers: A Confederate Brotherhood.* Lanham, MD: Madison Books, 1992.

Bremer, Jeff R. "Frontier Capitalism: The Market Revolution in the Antebellum Lower Missouri River Valley, 1803–1860." PhD diss., University of Kansas, 2006.

——. "'A Species of Town-Building Madness': Quindaro and Kansas Territory, 1856–1862." *Kansas History* 25, no. 3 (Autumn 2003): 156–171.

Brooks, James. *Captives and Cousins: Slavery, Kinship, and Community in the Southwest Borderlands.* Chapel Hill: University of North Carolina Press for the Omohundro Institute of Early American History and Culture, 2002.

——, ed. *Confounding the Color Line: The Indian-Black Experience in North America.* Lincoln: University of Nebraska Press, 2002.

Buckmaster, Henrietta. *Let My People Go: The Story of the Underground Railroad and the Growth of the Abolition Movement.* Boston: Harper and Brothers, 1941.

Burke, Diane Mutti. *On Slavery's Border: Missouri's Small-Slaveholding Households, 1815–1865.* Athens: University of Georgia Press, 2010.

Calloway, Colin G. "'We Have Always Been the Frontier': The American Revolution in Shawnee Country." *American Indian Quarterly* 16, no. 1 (Winter 1992): 39–52.

Camp, Stephanie M. H. *Closer to Freedom: Enslaved Women and Everyday Resistance in the Plantation South.* Chapel Hill: University of North Carolina Press, 2004.

Campbell, Randolph B. "Research Note: Slave Hiring in Texas." *American Historical Review* 93, no. 1 (February 1988): 107–114.

Campbell, Stanley W. *The Slave Catchers: Enforcement of the Fugitive Slave Law, 1850–1860.* Chapel Hill: University of North Carolina Press, 1968.

Campney, Brent M. S. "'Light Is Bursting Upon the World!': White Supremacy and Racist Violence against Blacks in Reconstruction Kansas." *The Western Historical Quarterly* 41, no. 2 (Summer 2010): 171–194.

——. "W. B. Townsend and the Struggle Against Racist Violence in Leavenworth." *Kansas History* 31, no. 4 (Winter 2008–2009): 260–273.

Carlson, Becky. "'Manumitted and Forever Set Free': The Children of Charles Lee Younger and Elizabeth, A Woman of Color." *Missouri Historical Review* 96, no. 1 (October 2001): 16–31.

Carruth, William H. "The New England Emigrant Aid Company as an Investment Society." *Transactions of the Kansas State Historical Society, 1897–1900* 6 (1900): 90–96.

Carter, Michael E. "First Kansas Colored Volunteers: Contributions of Black Union Soldiers in the Trans-Mississippi West." MA thesis, U.S. Army Command and General Staff College, 2004.

Castel, Albert. *Civil War Kansas: Reaping the Whirlwind.* 2nd ed. Lawrence: University Press of Kansas, 1997.

———. "Kansas Jayhawking Raids into Western Missouri in 1861." *Missouri Historical Review* 54, no. 1 (October 1959): 1–11.

———. "Order No. 11 and the Civil War on the Border." *Missouri Historical Review* 57 (July 1963): 357–368.

Cecil-Fronsman, Bill. "'Advocate the Freedom of White Men, As Well As That of Negroes': The *Kansas Free State* and Antislavery Westerners in Territorial Kansas." *Kansas History* 20, no. 2 (Summer 1997): 102–115.

———. "'Death to All Yankees and Traitors in Kansas': The *Squatter Sovereign* and the Defense of Slavery in Kansas." *Kansas History* 16, no. 1 (Spring 1993): 22–33.

Cheatham, Gary L. "'If the Union Wins, We Won't Have Anything Left': The Rise and Fall of the Southern Cherokees in Kansas." *Kansas History* 30, no. 3 (Autumn 2007): 154–177.

———. "'Kansas Shall Not Have the Right to Legislate Slavery Out': Slavery and the 1860 Antislavery Law." *Kansas History* 23, no. 3 (Autumn 2000); 154–171.

———. "'Slavery All the Time, Or Not At All': The Wyandotte Constitution Debate, 1859–1861." *Kansas History* 21, no. 3 (Autumn 1998): 168–187.

———. "'Within the Limits of the Southern Confederacy': The C.S.A.'s Interest in the Quapaw, Osage, and Cherokee Tribal Lands of Kansas." *Kansas History* 26, no. 3 (Autumn 2003): 172–185.

Chiarelli, Anne. "A Look at Slavery in Missouri." *Jackson County Historical Society Journal* 28 (Winter 1986): 12–22.

Childers, Chris. *The Failure of Popular Sovereignty: Slavery, Manifest Destiny, and the Radicalization of Southern Politics.* Lawrence: University Press of Kansas, 2012.

Christopher, Adrienne. "Captain Joseph Parks: Chief of the Shawnee Indians." *Westport Historical Quarterly* 50, no. 1 (June 1969): 13–17.

Clark, Jerry E. *The Shawnee.* Louisville: University Press of Kentucky, 1993.

Clinton, Catherine. *The Plantation Mistress: Woman's World in the Old South.* New York: Pantheon, 1982.

Cohen, William. *At Freedom's Edge: Black Mobility and the Southern White Quest for Racial Control, 1861–1915.* Baton Rouge: Louisiana State University Press, 1991.

Collins, Steve, and Dorothy Collins. "Quindaro Underground Railroad: A Unique Ethnic Unity in America's Past." *KCKCC e-Journal* 1, no. 1 (October 2007): 1–27.

Combs, H. Jason. "The Platte Purchase and Native American Removal." *Plains Anthropologist* 47, no. 182 (August 2002): 265–274.

———. "The South's Slave Culture Transplanted to the Western Frontier." *The Professional Geographer* 56, no. 3 (2004): 361–371.

Connelley, William E. *The Emigrant Indian Tribes of Wyandotte County.* Topeka: Crane and Co., 1901.

———. *History of Kansas Newspapers; A History of the Newspapers and Magazines Published in Kansas from the Organization of Kansas Territory, 1854, to January 1, 1916.* Topeka: Kansas State Printing Plant, 1916.

Cornish, Dudley Taylor. *Kansas Negro Regiments in the Civil War.* Topeka: Kansas Commission on Civil Rights, 1969.

———. *The Sable Arm: Black Troops in the Union Army, 1861–1865.* Rev. ed. Lawrence: University Press of Kansas, 1987.

Cory, Charles E. "Slavery in Kansas." *Transactions of the Kansas State Historical Society, 1901–1902* 7 (1902): 229–242.

Coulter, Charles E. *Take Up the Black Man's Burden: Kansas City's African American Communities, 1865–1939.* Columbia: University of Missouri Press, 2006.

Cox, Thomas C. *Blacks in Topeka, Kansas, 1865–1915: A Social History.* Baton Rouge: Louisiana State University Press, 1982.

Craik, Elmer LeRoy. "Southern Interest in Territorial Kansas, 1854–1858." *Collections of the Kansas State Historical Society, 1919–1922* 15 (1923): 334–450.

Craven, Avery O. *Soil Exhaustion in the Agricultural History of Virginia and Maryland, 1606–1860.* New ed. Columbia: University of South Carolina Press, 2006.

Crisler, Robert M. "Missouri's 'Little Dixie.'" *Missouri Historical Review* 42, no. 2 (January 1948): 130–139.

Cunningham, Roger D. "Douglas's Battery at Fort Leavenworth: The Issue of Black Officers During the Civil War." *Kansas History* 23, no. 4 (Winter 2000–2001): 200–217.

———. "Welcoming 'Pa' on the Kaw: Kansas's 'Colored' Militia and the 1864 Price Raid." *Kansas History* 25, no. 2 (Summer 2002): 86–101.

Curtin, Philip D. *The Rise and Fall of the Plantation Complex.* 2nd ed. New York: Cambridge University Press, 1998.

Dean, Virgil W., ed. *John Brown to Bob Dole: Movers and Shakers in Kansas History.* Lawrence: University Press of Kansas, 2006.

———. *Kansas Territorial Reader.* Topeka: Kansas State Historical Society and the Kansas Territorial Sesquicentennial Commission, 2005.

Delo, David Michael. *Peddlers and Post Traders: The Army Sutler on the Frontier.* Salt Lake City: University of Utah Press, 1992.

Deyle, Steven. *Carry Me Back: The Domestic Slave Trade in American Life.* New York: Oxford University Press, 2005.

Dobak, William A. *Freedom by the Sword: The U.S. Colored Troops, 1862–1867.* Washington, D.C.: United States Army Center of Military History, 2011.

Dorsett, Lyle Wesley. "Slaveholding in Jackson County, Missouri." In *Plantation, Town, and Country: Essays on the Local History of American Slave Society*, edited by Elinor Miller and Eugene D. Genovese, 146–160. Urbana-Champaign: University of Illinois Press, 1974.

Doster, Frank. "Kansas: Early Judicial History." *The Medico-Legal Journal* 18, no. 1 (1900): 54–77.

Downs, Jim. *Sick from Freedom: African-American Illness and Suffering during the Civil War and Reconstruction*. New York: Oxford University Press, 2012.

Duffner, Robert W. "Slavery in Missouri River Counties, 1820–1865." PhD diss., University of Missouri–Columbia, 1974.

Durant, Thomas J., Jr., and Nicole Moliere. "Plantation Slavery among Native Americans: The Creation of a Red, White, and Black America." In *Plantation Society and Race Relations: The Origins of Inequality*, edited by Thomas J. Durant Jr. and J. David Knottnerus, 113–124. Westport, CT: Praeger, 1999.

Dyer, Frederick H. *A Compendium of the War of the Rebellion, Compiled and Arranged from Official Records of the Federal and Confederate Armies, Reports of the Adjutant Generals of the Several States, the Army Registers, and Other Reliable Documents and Sources*. Des Moines, IA: The Dyer Publishing Co., 1908.

Eakin, Joanne C. *Tears and Turmoil: Order #11*. Independence, MO: Two Trails Publishers, 1996.

Earle, Carville. "Regional Economic Development West of the Appalachians, 1815–1860." In *North America: The Historical Geography of a Changing Continent*, edited by Thomas F. McIlwraith and Edward K. Muller, 172–197. Totowa, NJ: Rowman and Littlefield, 1987.

Earle, Jonathan H. *Jacksonian Antislavery and the Politics of Free Soil, 1824–1854*. Chapel Hill: University of North Carolina Press, 2004.

———. *The Routledge Atlas of African American History*. New York: Routledge, 2000.

Earle, Jonathan, and Diane Mutti Burke, eds. *Bleeding Kansas, Bleeding Missouri: The Long Civil War on the Border*. Lawrence: University Press of Kansas, 2013.

Eaton, Clement. "Slave-Hiring in the Upper South: A Step Toward Freedom." *Mississippi Valley Historical Review* 46, no. 4 (March 1960): 663–678.

Eaton, Miles W. "The Development and Later Decline of the Hemp Industry in Missouri." *Missouri Historical Review* 43, no. 4 (July 1949): 344–359.

Edwards, Tai S. "Disruption and Disease: The Osage Struggle to Survive in the Nineteenth-Century Trans-Missouri West." *Kansas History* 36, no. 4 (Winter 2013–2014): 218–233.

Eldridge, William E. "Major John Dougherty, Pioneer." *The Trail Guide* 7, no. 4 (December 1962): 1–15.

Ellis, Tom. "Uniontown and Plowboy—Potawatomi Ghost Towns: Enigmas of the Oregon-California Trail." *Kansas History* 37, no. 4 (Winter 2014–2015): 210–225.

Emberton, Carole. "Unwriting the Freedom Narrative: A Review Essay." *The Journal of Southern History* 82, no. 2 (May 2016): 377–294.

Entz, Gary R. "Image and Reality on the Kansas Prairie." *Kansas History* 19, no. 2 (Summer 1996): 124–139.

Etcheson, Nicole. *Bleeding Kansas: Contested Liberty in the Civil War Era.* Lawrence: University Press of Kansas, 2004.

———. "Microhistory and Movement: African American Mobility in the Nineteenth Century: A Review Essay." *The Journal of the Civil War Era* 3, no. 3 (September 2013): 392–404.

Etulain, Richard W., ed. *Lincoln Looks West: From the Mississippi to the Pacific.* Carbondale: Southern Illinois University Press, 2010.

Everett, Derek R. *Creating the American West: Boundaries and Borderlands.* Norman: University of Oklahoma Press, 2014.

Fausz, J. Frederick. "Becoming a 'Nation of Quakers': The Removal of the Osage Indians from Missouri." *Gateway Heritage* 21, no. 1 (Summer 2000): 28–39.

Fehrenbacher, Don E. *The Dred Scott Case: Its Significance in American Law and Politics.* New York: Oxford University Press, 1978.

Fellman, Michael. "Emancipation in Missouri." *Missouri Historical Review* 83, no. 1 (October 1988): 36–56.

———. *Inside War: The Guerrilla Conflict in Missouri during the American Civil War.* New York: Oxford University Press, 1989.

Fields, Barbara Jeanne. *Slavery and Freedom on the Middle Ground: Maryland During the Nineteenth Century.* New Haven, CT: Yale University Press, 1985.

Finnie, Gordon E. "The Antislavery Movement in the Upper South before 1840." *The Journal of Southern History* 35, no. 3 (August 1969): 319–342.

Fischer, David Hackett, and James C. Kelly. *Bound Away: Virginia and the Westward Movement.* Charlottesville: University of Virginia Press, 2000.

Fisher, Mike. "The First Kansas Colored—Massacre at Poison Springs." *Kansas History* 2, no. 2 (Summer 1979): 121–128.

Fogel, Robert William, and Stanley L. Engerman. *Time on the Cross: The Economics of American Negro Slavery.* Reissue. New York: W. W. Norton, 1995.

Foley, William E. *The Genesis of Missouri: From Wilderness Outpost to Statehood.* Columbia: University of Missouri Press, 1989.

———. *A History of Missouri.* Vol. I, 1673 to 1820. Columbia: University of Missouri Press, 1999.

Foner, Eric. *Forever Free: The Story of Emancipation and Reconstruction.* New York: Vintage Books, 2005.

———. *Free Soil, Free Labor, Free Men: The Ideology of the Republican Party Before the Civil War.* New York: Oxford University Press, 1995.

———. *Gateway to Freedom: The Hidden History of the Underground Railroad.* New York: W. W. Norton, 2015.

———. *Reconstruction: America's Unfinished Revolution, 1863–1877.* New York: Harper and Row, 1988.

Fox-Genovese, Elizabeth. *Within the Plantation Household: Black and White Women of the Old South*. Chapel Hill: University of North Carolina Press, 1988.

Franklin, John Hope, and Loren Schweninger. *Runaway Slaves: Rebels on the Plantation*. New York: Oxford University Press, 1999.

Frazier, Harriet C. *Runaway and Freed Missouri Slaves and Those Who Helped Them, 1763-1865*. Jefferson, NC: McFarland, 2004.

——. *Slavery and Crime in Missouri, 1773-1865*. Jefferson, NC: McFarland, 2001.

Gara, Larry. *The Liberty Line: The Legend of the Underground Railroad*. Lexington: University Press of Kentucky, 1961.

Geiger, Mark W. "Indebtedness and the Origins of Guerrilla Violence in Civil War Missouri." *The Journal of Southern History* 75, no. 1 (February 2009): 49–82.

Genovese, Eugene D. *The Political Economy of Slavery: Studies in the Economy and Society of the Slave South*. London: MacGibbon and Kee, 1966.

——. *Roll, Jordan, Roll: The World the Slaves Made*. New York: Vintage Books, 1976.

Gerteis, Louis S. *From Contraband to Freedman: Federal Policy Toward Southern Blacks, 1861–1865*. Westport, CT: Greenwood Press, 1973.

Gitlin, Jay. *The Bourgeois Frontier: French Towns, French Traders, and American Expansion*. New Haven, CT: Yale University Press, 2010.

Glatthaar, Joseph T. *Forged in Battle: The Civil War Alliance of Black Soldiers and White Officers*. Baton Rouge: Louisiana State University Press, 1990.

Glenn, Allen. *History of Cass County, Missouri*. Topeka, KS: Historical Publishing Co., 1917.

Glymph, Thavolia. *Out of the House of Bondage: The Transformation of the Plantation Household*. New York: Cambridge University Press, 2008.

——. "Rose's War and the Gendered Politics of a Slave Insurgency in the Civil War." *The Journal of the Civil War Era* 3, no. 4 (December 2013): 501–532.

Gordon-Reed, Annette, ed. *Race on Trial: Law and Justice in American History*. New York: Oxford University Press, 2002.

Greenberg, Kenneth S. *Honor and Slavery*. Princeton, NJ: Princeton University Press, 1997.

Greene, Lorenzo Johnston, Gary R. Kremer, and Antonio Frederick Holland. *Missouri's Black Heritage*. Rev. ed. Columbia: University of Missouri Press, 1993.

Griffler, Keith P. *Front Line of Freedom: African Americans and the Forging of the Underground Railroad in the Ohio Valley*. Lexington: University Press of Kentucky, 2004.

Guelzo, Allen C. *Lincoln's Emancipation Proclamation: The End of Slavery in America*. New York: Simon and Schuster, 2004.

Gutman, Herbert G. *The Black Family in Slavery and Freedom, 1750–1925*. New York: Vintage Books, 1976.

Hahn, Steven. *A Nation Under Our Feet: Black Political Struggles in the Rural South from Slavery to the Great Migration.* Cambridge, MA: Belknap Press, 2003.

Hämäläinen, Pekka, and Samuel Truett. "On Borderlands." *The Journal of American History* 98, no. 2 (September 2011): 338–361.

Hammond, John Craig. "Slavery and Freedom in the Early American West: From the Northwest Ordinance to the Missouri Controversy, 1787–1861." PhD diss., University of Kentucky, 2004.

Hancock, Scott. "Crossing Freedom's Fault Line: The Underground Railroad and Recentering African Americans in Civil War Causality." *Civil War History* 59, no. 2 (June 2013): 169–205.

Harding, Vincent. *There Is a River: The Black Struggle for Freedom in America.* New York: Harcourt Brace and Co., 1981.

Harris, Charles F. "Catalyst for Terror: The Collapse of the Women's Prison in Kansas City." *Missouri Historical Review* 89, no. 3 (1995): 290-306.

Harrold, Stanley. *The Abolitionists and the South, 1831–1861.* Lexington: University Press of Kentucky, 1995.

———. *Border War: Fighting Over Slavery before the Civil War.* Chapel Hill: University of North Carolina Press, 2010.

Henderson, Timothy J. *A Glorious Defeat: Mexico and Its War with the United States.* New York: Hill and Wang, 2007.

Hickman, Russell K. "The Reeder Administration Inaugurated, Part II—The Census of Early 1855." *Kansas Historical Quarterly* 36, no. 4 (Winter 1970): 424–455.

Hickman, W. Z. *History of Jackson County, Missouri.* Topeka, KS: Historical Publishing Co., 1920.

Hilliard, Sam Bowers. *Atlas of Antebellum Southern Agriculture.* Baton Rouge: Louisiana State University Press, 1984.

Hine, Robert V., and John Mack Faragher. *The American West: A New Interpretive History.* New Haven, CT: Yale University Press, 2000.

The History of Buchanan County, Missouri, Containing A History of the County, Its Cities, Towns, etc., Biographical Sketches of Its Citizens, Buchanan County in the Late War, General and Local Statistics, Portraits of Early Settlers and Prominent Men, History of Missouri, Map of Buchanan County, etc. Saint Joseph, MO: Union Historical Co., 1881.

History of Clay and Platte Counties, Missouri. Saint Louis: National Historical Co., 1885.

The History of Jackson County, Missouri, Containing a History of the County, Its Cities, Towns, etc. Kansas City: Union Historical Co., 1881.

History of Vernon County, Missouri, Written and Compiled from the Most Authentic Official and Private Sources . . . . Saint Louis: Brown and Co., 1887.

Hoig, Stan. *The Chouteaus: First Family of the Fur Trade.* Albuquerque: University of New Mexico Press, 2008.

Holt, Michael. *The Fate of Their Country: Politicians, Slavery Extension, and the Coming of the Civil War.* New York: Hill and Wang, 2004.

———. *The Political Crisis of the 1850s.* New York: W. W. Norton, 1978.

Howard, Michelle J. "Slaves, Contrabands, and Freedmen Union Policy in the Civil War." PhD diss., U.S. Army Command and General Staff College, 1998.

Hughes, J. Patrick. *Fort Leavenworth: Gateway to the West.* Topeka: Kansas State Historical Society, 2000.

Hughes, Sarah S. "Slaves for Hire: The Allocation of Black Labor in Elizabeth City County, VA, 1782–1810." *William and Mary Quarterly* 3rd Ser., 5, no. 2 (April 1978): 260–286.

Hunt, Jeffrey William. *The Last Battle of the Civil War: Palmetto Ranch.* Austin: University of Texas Press, 2002.

Hurt, R. Douglas. *Agriculture and Slavery in Missouri's Little Dixie.* Columbia: University of Missouri Press, 1992.

Hyde, Anne F. *Empires, Nations, and Families: A New History of the North American West, 1800–1860.* New York: HarperCollins, 2012.

Jewett, Clayton E., and John O. Allen. *Slavery in the South: A State-by-State History.* Westport, CT: Greenwood Press, 2004.

Johnson, James. "The Life and Times of George Washington (1840–1931)." *Platte County Missouri Historical and Genealogical Society Bulletin* 47, no. 3 (July, August, September 1994): 10–16.

Johnson, Samuel A. *The Battle Cry of Freedom: The New England Emigrant Aid Company in the Kansas Crusade.* Lawrence: University Press of Kansas, 1954.

Johnson, Walter, ed. *The Chattel Principle: Internal Slave Trades in the Americas.* New Haven, CT: Yale University Press, 2004.

———. "On Agency." *Journal of Social History* 37, no. 1 (Autumn 2003): 113–124.

———. *Soul by Soul: Life Inside the Antebellum Slave Market.* Cambridge, MA: Harvard University Press, 1999.

Jones, Jacqueline. *Labor of Love, Labor of Sorrow: Black Women, Work, and the Family, from Slavery to the Present.* New ed. New York: Vintage Books, 1995.

Jones, Martha S. "History and Commemoration: The Emancipation Proclamation at 150." *The Journal of the Civil War Era* 3, no. 4 (December 2013): 452–457.

Kantrowitz, Stephen. *More Than Freedom: Fighting for Black Citizenship in a White Republic, 1829–1889.* New York: Penguin Press, 2012.

Katz, William. *The Black West: A Documentary and Pictorial History of the African American Role in the Westward Expansion of the United States.* Rev. ed. New York: Broadway Books, 2005.

Kaye, Anthony. *Joining Places: Slave Neighborhoods in the Old South.* Chapel Hill: University of North Carolina Press, 2007.

Kiene, Llewellyn L. "The Battle of the Spurs and John Brown's Exit from Kansas." *Transactions of the Kansas State Historical Society* 8 (1904): 443–449.

King, Wilma. *Stolen Childhood: Slave Youth in Nineteenth-Century America.* Bloomington: Indiana University Press, 1995.

Kinney, Brandon G. *The Mormon War: Zion and the Missouri Extermination Order of 1838.* Yardley, PA: Westholme Publishing, 2011.

Kirkpatrick, Arthur R. "Missouri in the Early Months of the Civil War." *Missouri Historical Review* 55 (April 1961): 235–266.

Kolchin, Peter. *American Slavery: 1619–1877.* 10th ed. New York: Hill and Wang, 2003.

Lamb, Martha J. ed. *Magazine of American History with Notes and Queries, Volume XXVI, July-December 1891.* New York: Historical Publication Co., 1891.

LaRoche, Cheryl Janifer. *Free Black Communities and the Underground Railroad: The Geography of Resistance.* Urbana: University of Illinois Press, 2014.

Lechner, Zachary J. "'Are We Ready for the Conflict?': Black Abolitionist Response to the Kansas Crisis, 1854–1856." *Kansas History* 31, no. 1 (Spring 2008): 14–31.

Lee, Bill R. "Missouri's Fight over Emancipation in 1863." *Missouri Historical Review* 45, no. 3 (April 1951): 256–274.

Lee, Fred L. "Kansas City Had Its Beginnings in 'An Unpretending Edifice of John Barleycorn.'" *Kansas City Genealogist* 36, no. 4 (1995): 177–181.

Lehman, Christopher P. *Slavery in the Upper Mississippi Valley, 1787–1865.* Jefferson, NC: McFarland, 2011.

Leiker, James M. "Race Relations in the Sunflower State." *Kansas History* 25, no. 3 (Autumn 2002): 214–236.

Lepore, Jill. "Historians Who Love Too Much: Reflections on Microhistory and Biography." *The Journal of American History* 88, no. 1 (June 2001): 129–144.

LeSueur, Stephen C. *The 1838 Mormon War in Missouri.* Columbia: University of Missouri Press, 1987.

Lewis, Hugh M. *Robidoux Chronicles: French-Indian Ethnoculture in the Trans-Mississippi West.* Victoria, BC: Trafford Publishing, 2004.

Link, William A., and James J. Broomhall, eds. *Rethinking American Emancipation: Legacies of Slavery and the Quest for Black Freedom.* New York: Cambridge University Press, 2016.

Lubet, Steven. *Fugitive Justice: Runaways, Rescuers, and Slavery on Trial.* Cambridge, MA: Harvard University Press, 2010.

Lutz, John J. "Quantrill and the Morgan Walker Tragedy." *Transactions of the Kansas State Historical Society* 8 (1904): 324–331.

Lyman, Clifford H. *Aaahh Bourbon, 1842–1865.* Self-published, 1984.

Mack, John N. "A Second Revolution: The Struggle to Define the Meaning of the Civil War in Southeast Kansas, 1867–1876." *Kansas History* 32, no. 1 (Spring 2009): 2–17.

Magers, Roy V. "The Raid on the Parkville *Industrial Luminary.*" *Missouri Historical Review* 30 (October 1935): 39–46.

Malin, James C. "The Proslavery Background of the Kansas Struggle." *Mississippi Valley Historical Review* 10, no. 3 (December 1923): 285–305.

Maltz, Earl M. *Dred Scott and the Politics of Slavery.* Lawrence: University Press of Kansas, 2007.

Marshall, Howard Wight. *Folk Architecture in Little Dixie: A Regional Culture in Missouri.* Columbia: University of Missouri Press, 1981.

Marszalek, John F. *Commander of All Lincoln's Armies: A Life of General Henry W. Halleck.* Cambridge, MA: Harvard University Press, 2004.

Martin, Jonathan D. *Divided Mastery: Slave Hiring in the American South.* Cambridge, MA: Harvard University Press, 2004.

Masur, Kate. "'A Rare Phenomenon of Philological Vegetation': The Word 'Contraband' and the Meanings of Emancipation in the United States." *The Journal of American History* 93, no. 4 (March 2007): 1050–1084.

Mattox, Joelouis. "Taking Steps to Record Steptoe, Westport's Vanishing African American Neighborhood." *Jackson County Historical Society Journal* 49, no. 1–2 (Spring and Autumn 2008): 22–25.

McCandless, Perry. *A History of Missouri.* Vol. 2, 1820 to 1860. Columbia: University of Missouri Press, 2000.

McCurry, Stephanie. *Masters of Small Worlds: Yeoman Households, Gender Relations, and the Political Culture of the Antebellum South Carolina Low Country.* New York: Oxford University Press, 1995.

McGettigan, James William, Jr. "Boone County Slaves: Sales, Estate Divisions, and Families, 1820-1865, Part II." *Missouri Historical Review* 72, no. 3 (April 1978): 271-295.

McLaurin, Melton A. *Celia, a Slave: A True Story.* New York: Avon, 1999.

McMillen, Sally G. *Motherhood in the Old South: Pregnancy, Childbirth, and Infant Rearing.* Baton Rouge: Louisiana State University Press, 1990.

McNeal, T. A. *When Kansas Was Young.* New York: Macmillan Co., 1922.

McPherson, James M. *Battle Cry of Freedom: The Civil War Era.* New York: Oxford University Press, 1988.

———. *The Negro's Civil War: How American Blacks Felt and Acted During the War for the Union.* New York: Vintage Books, 1991.

———. *The Struggle for Equality: Abolitionists and the Negro in the Civil War and Reconstruction.* Princeton, NJ: Princeton University Press, 1964.

Merchant, Carolyn. *The Columbia Guide to American Environmental History.* New York: Columbia University Press, 2005.

Merkel, Benjamin G. "The Abolition Aspects of Missouri's Antislavery Controversy, 1819–1865." *Missouri Historical Review* 44, no. 3 (April 1950): 232–253.

———. "The Underground Railroad and the Missouri Borders, 1840–1860." *Missouri Historical Review* 37, no. 3 (April 1943): 271–285.

Miesner, William J. "The First Kansas Colored Volunteer Infantry Regiment in the Civil War." *Oklahoma State Historical Review* 2 (Spring 1981): 13-26.

Miller, Irma Robinson. "Chanteau—Chatillon—Chouteau: Genealogical Chaos." *St. Louis Genealogical Society Quarterly* 14, no. 1 (Spring 1981): 1-4.

Miller, James David. *South by Southwest: Planter Emigration and Identity in the Slave South.* Charlottesville: University of Virginia Press, 2002.

Miner, Craig. *Kansas: The History of the Sunflower State, 1854-2000.* Lawrence: University Press of Kansas, 2002.

Miner, Craig, and William E. Unrau. *The End of Indian Kansas: A Study of Cultural Revolution, 1854-1871.* New ed. Lawrence: University Press of Kansas, 1990.

Missouri Mormon Frontier Foundation. "Jones H. Flournoy House." *Missouri Mormon Frontier Foundation Newsletter* no. 21/22 (August 1999): 1-3.

Missouri River Heritage Association. *The Heritage of Buchanan County.* Vol. 1. Saint Joseph: Missouri River Heritage Association, 1984.

Monaghan, Jay. *Civil War on the Western Border, 1854-1865.* Omaha: University of Nebraska Press, 1984.

Morgans, James Patrick. *The Underground Railroad on the Western Frontier: Escapes from Missouri, Arkansas, Iowa, and the Territories of Kansas, Nebraska, and the Indian Nations, 1840-1865.* Jefferson, NC: McFarland, 2010.

Morton, Patricia, ed. *Discovering the Women in Slavery: Emancipating Perspectives on the American Past.* Athens: University of Georgia Press, 1996.

Mullis, Tony R. *Peacekeeping on the Plains: Army Operations in Bleeding Kansas.* Columbia: University of Missouri Press, 2004.

Napier, Rita, ed. *Kansas and the West: New Perspectives.* Lawrence: University Press of Kansas, 2003.

Neely, Jeremy. *The Border Between Them: Violence and Reconciliation on the Kansas-Missouri Line.* Columbia: University of Missouri Press, 2007.

Nelson, Earl J. "Missouri Slavery, 1861-1865." *Missouri Historical Review* 28, no. 4 (July 1934): 260-274.

Newton, James E., and Ronald L. Lewis, eds. *The Other Slaves: Mechanics, Artisans, and Craftsmen.* Boston: G. K. Hall, 1978.

Nichols, Roy F. "Kansas Historiography: The Technique of Cultural Analysis." *American Quarterly* 9, no. 1 (Spring 1957): 85-91.

O'Brien, William Patrick. "Hiram Young: Pioneering Black Wagonmaker for the Santa Fe Trade." *Gateway Heritage* 14 (Summer 1993): 56-67.

Oakes, James. *Freedom National: The Destruction of Slavery in the United States, 1861-1865.* New York: W. W. Norton, 2013.

———. "Reluctant to Emancipate? Another Look at the First Confiscation Act." *The Journal of the Civil War Era* 3, no. 4 (December 2013): 458-466.

———. *The Ruling Race: A History of American Slaveholders.* New York: Vintage Books, 1982.

———. *Slavery and Freedom: An Interpretation of the Old South.* New York: Alfred A. Knopf, 1990.

Oates, Stephen B. *To Purge This Land with Blood: A Biography of John Brown.* Amherst: University of Massachusetts Press, 1984.

Oertel, Kristen Tegtmeier. *Bleeding Borders: Race, Gender, and Violence in Pre-Civil War Kansas.* Baton Rouge: Louisiana State University Press, 2009.

Oliva, Leo E. *Fort Scott: Courage and Conflict on the Border.* Topeka: Kansas State Historical Society, 1996.

Omi, Michael, and Howard Winant. *Racial Formation in the United States: From the 1960s to the 1990s.* 2nd ed. New York: Routledge, 1994.

Painter, Nell Irvin. *Exodusters: Black Migration to Kansas after Reconstruction.* New York: Alfred Knopf, 1977.

Parrish, William E. *A History of Missouri.* Vol. III, 1860 to 1875. Columbia: University of Missouri Press, 2001.

Partin, John W., ed. *A Brief History of Fort Leavenworth.* Leavenworth: U.S. Army Command and General Staff College, Combat Studies Institute, 1983.

Paxton, Matthew. "Jackson County's First Courthouse Built in 1827." *State Centennial Souvenir Number and Program, 1821–1921* 1, no. 1 (October 1921): 122–123.

Paxton, William M. *The Annals of Platte County, Missouri.* Kansas City: Hudson Kimberly Publications, 1897.

Penningroth, Dylan C. *The Claims of Kinfolk: African American Property and Community in the Nineteenth-Century South.* Chapel Hill: University of North Carolina Press, 2003.

Perry, Lewis, and Michael Fellman, eds. *Antislavery Reconsidered: New Perspectives on the Abolitionists.* Baton Rouge: Louisiana State University Press, 1979.

Phillips, Christopher. *The Civil War in the Border South.* Santa Barbara: Praeger, 2013.

———. "'The Crime Against Missouri': Slavery, Kansas, and the Cant of Southernness in the Border West." *Civil War History* 48, no. 1 (March 2002): 60–81.

———. *Missouri's Confederate: Claiborne Fox Jackson and the Creation of Southern Identity in the Border West.* Columbia: University of Missouri Press, 2000.

Ponce, Pearl T. *To Govern the Devil in Hell: The Political Crisis in Territorial Kansas.* DeKalb: Northern Illinois University Press, 2014.

Porter, Kenneth. "Negroes and the Fur Trade." *Minnesota History* 15 (1934): 421–433.

Potter, David M. *The Impending Crisis, 1848–1861.* New York: Harper and Row, 1976.

Pred, Allan. "Place as Historically Contingent Process: Structuration and the Time-Geography of Becoming Places." *Annals of the Association of American Geographers* 74, no. 2 (June 1984): 279–297.

Rawley, James A. *Race and Politics: "Bleeding Kansas" and the Coming of the Civil War.* 2nd ed. Lincoln: University of Nebraska Press, 1980.

Redd, Emmett, and Nicole Etcheson. "'Sound on the Goose': A Search for the Answer to an Age Old 'Question.'" *Kansas History* 32, no. 3 (August 2009): 204–217.

Regosin, Elizabeth A., and Donald R. Shaffer. *Voices of Emancipation: Understanding Slavery, the Civil War, and Reconstruction through the U.S. Pension Bureau Files.* New York: New York University Press, 2008.

Renehan, Edward J., Jr. *The Secret Six: The True Tale of the Men Who Conspired with John Brown.* New York: Crown Publishers, 1995.

Richardson, Heather Cox. *West from Appomattox: The Reconstruction of America after the Civil War.* New Haven, CT: Yale University Press, 2007.

Robley, T. F. *History of Bourbon County, Kansas, to the Close of 1865.* Fort Scott, 1894.

Roe, Catherine, and Bill Roe. *Atchison Centennial, June 20–26, 1854–1954.* Atchison, KS: Lockwood Co., 1954.

Romeo, Sharon. "'The First Morning of Their Freedom': African American Women, Black Testimony, and Military Justice in Civil War Missouri." *Missouri Historical Review* 110, no. 3 (April 2016): 196-216.

Rossbach, Jeffery S. *Ambivalent Conspirators: John Brown, the Secret Six, and a Theory of Slave Violence.* Philadelphia: University of Pennsylvania Press, 1983.

Rothman, Adam. *Slave Country: American Expansion and the Origins of the Deep South.* Cambridge, MA: Harvard University Press, 2005.

Salafia, Matthew. *Slavery's Borderland: Freedom and Bondage along the Ohio River.* Philadelphia: University of Pennsylvania Press, 2013.

Sampson, F. A., and W. C. Breckenridge. "Bibliography of Slavery and the Civil War in Missouri." *Missouri Historical Review* 2 (April 1908): 233–248.

Schirmer, Sherry Lamb, and Richard D. McKinzie. *At the River's Bend: An Illustrated History of Kansas City.* Woodland Hill, CA: Windsor Publications, 1982.

Schwendemann, Glen. "The 'Exodusters' on the Missouri." *Kansas Historical Quarterly* 29, no. 1 (Spring 1963): 25–40.

———. "Nicodemus: Negro Haven on the Solomon." *Kansas Historical Quarterly* 34, no. 1 (Spring 1968): 10–31.

SenGupta, Gunja. "Bleeding Kansas: A Review Essay." *Kansas History* 24, no. 4 (Winter 2001–2002): 318–341.

———. *For God and Mammon: Evangelicals and Entrepreneurs, Masters and Slaves in Territorial Kansas, 1854–1860.* Athens: University of Georgia Press, 1996.

Shaffer, Donald R. *After the Glory: The Struggles of Black Civil War Veterans.* Lawrence: University Press of Kansas, 2004.

Shannon, Fred A. "The Federal Government and the Negro Soldier, 1861–1865." *The Journal of Negro History* 11, no. 4 (October 1926): 563–583.

Sharp, Teron Delivia. "The Social Apathies of Violence Toward Slaves in Missouri." MA thesis, Southern Illinois University at Carbondale, 2006.

Shawnee County Historical Society. "Underground Railroad in Topeka." *Bulletin of the Shawnee County Historical Society*, no. 15 (December 1951): 9, 15.

Shearer, Gary W. *The Civil War, Slavery, and Reconstruction in Missouri: A Bibliographic Guide to Secondary Sources and Selected Primary Sources*. Angwin, CA: G. Shearer, 1997.

Sheridan, Richard B. "Charles Henry Langston and the African American Struggle in Kansas." *Kansas History* 22, no. 4 (Winter 1999–2000): 268–283.

———. *Freedom's Crucible: The Underground Railroad in Lawrence and Douglas County, Kansas, 1854–1865: A Reader*. Lawrence: University of Kansas Division of Continuing Education, 1998.

———. "From Slavery in Missouri to Freedom in Kansas: The Influx of Black Fugitives and Contraband into Kansas, 1854–1865." *Kansas History* 12, no. 1 (Spring 1989): 28–47.

Siebert, Wilber Henry. *The Underground Railroad from Slavery to Freedom*. New York: Macmillan Co., 1898.

Smith, John David, ed. *Black Soldiers in Blue: African American Troops in the Civil War Era*. Chapel Hill: University of North Carolina Press, 2002.

Smith, Robert E. *Keepers of the Council Fire: A Brief History of the Wyandot Indians*. Joplin, MO: Missouri Southern State College, 1974.

Smith, W. Wayne. "An Experiment in Counterinsurgency: The Assessment of Confederate Sympathizers in Missouri." *The Journal of Southern History* 35, no. 3 (August 1969): 361–380.

Spurgeon, Ian Michael. *Soldiers in the Army of Freedom: The 1st Kansas Colored, The Civil War's First African American Combat Unit*. Norman: University of Oklahoma Press, 2014.

Stampp, Kenneth. *America in 1857: A Nation on the Brink*. New York: Oxford University Press, 1990.

Stauf, Margaret. "John Dougherty, Indian Agent." *Mid-America: An Historical Review* 16, no. 3 (January 1934): 135–146.

Stone, Jeffrey C. *Slavery, Southern Culture, and Education in Little Dixie, Missouri, 1820–1860*. New York: Routledge, 2006.

Strickland, Arvarh E. "Aspects of Slavery in Missouri, 1821." *Missouri Historical Review* 65, no. 4 (July 1971): 505–526.

Syrett, John. *The Civil War Confiscation Acts: Failing to Reconstruct the South*. New York: Fordham University Press, 2005.

Tadman, Michael. *Speculators and Slaves: Masters, Traders, and Slaves in the Old South*. Madison: University of Wisconsin Press, 1989.

Tathwell, S. L. *The Old Settlers' History of Bates County, Missouri*. Amsterdam, MO: Tathwell and Maxey, 1897.

Taylor, Quintard. *In Search of the Racial Frontier: African Americans in the American West, 1528–1990*. New York: W. W. Norton, 1998.

————, and Shirley Ann Wilson Moore, eds. *African American Women Confront the West, 1600–2000*. Norman: University of Oklahoma Press, 2003.

Thorne, Tanis C. *The Many Hands of My Relations: French and Indians on the Lower Missouri*. Columbia: University of Missouri Press, 1996.

Thrapp, Dan L. *Encyclopedia of Frontier Biography*, Vol. III, P–Z. Lincoln: University of Nebraska Press, 1988.

Trexler, Harrison Anthony. *Slavery in Missouri, 1804–1865*. Baltimore: Johns Hopkins University Press, 1914.

————. "The Value and the Sale of the Missouri Slave." *Missouri Historical Review* 8, no. 2 (January 1914): 69–85.

Tri-Tabula Inc. *Pictorial Atlas of Doniphan County, Kansas*. Minneapolis: Tri-Tabula, 1972.

Tuttle, William M., Jr., and Surendra Bhana. "New Resources in American Studies: Black Newspapers in Kansas." *American Studies* 13, no. 2 (October 1972): 119–124.

"The Underground Railroad in Kansas." *Kansas City Genealogist* 34, no. 1 (Summer 1993): 29–31.

Unrau, William E. *Indians of Kansas: The Euro-American Invasion and Conquest of Indian Kansas*. Topeka: Kansas State Historical Society, 1991.

Unruh, John D., Jr. *The Plains Across: The Overland Emigrants and the Trans-Mississippi West, 1840–60*. Urbana: University of Illinois Press, 1993.

Urwin, Gregory J. W. "'We Cannot Treat Negroes . . . as Prisoners of War': Racial Atrocities and Reprisals in Civil War Arkansas." *Civil War History* 42, no. 3 (September 1996): 193–210.

VanderVelde, Lea. *Mrs. Dred Scott: A Life on Slavery's Frontier*. New York: Oxford University Press, 2009.

Violette, Eugene Morrow. *A History of Missouri*. Boston: D.C. Heath and Co., 1918.

Wagnon, William O. "Wrecking Slavery from the Kansas Territory: The 'Topeka Boys' as Saboteurs, 1855–1861." Unpublished paper presented at the 48th Annual Missouri Valley History Conference, Omaha, Nebraska, March 4, 2005.

Walsh, Martin W. "The 'Heathen Party': Methodist Observation of the Ohio Wyandot." *American Indian Quarterly* 16, no. 2 (Spring 1992): 189–211.

Warren, Stephen. *The Shawnees and Their Neighbors, 1795–1870*. Urbana-Champaign: University of Illinois Press, 2005.

Watson, James L., ed. *Asian and African Systems of Slavery*. Berkeley: University of California Press, 1980.

Watts, Dale E. "How Bloody Was Bleeding Kansas?: Political Killings in Kansas Territory, 1854–1861." *Kansas History* 18, no. 2 (Summer 1995): 116–129.

White, Deborah Gray. *Ar'n't I a Woman?: Female Slaves in the Plantation South*. Rev. ed. New York: W. W. Norton, 1999.

White, Jonathan W. *Emancipation, the Union Army, and the Reelection of Abraham Lincoln*. Baton Rouge: Louisiana State University Press, 2014.

White, Richard. "Race Relations in the American West." *American Quarterly* 38, no. 3 (1986): 396–416.

Whites, LeeAnn. "Forty Shirts and a Wagonload of Wheat: Women, the Domestic Supply Line, and the Civil War on the Western Border." *The Journal of the Civil War Era* 1, no. 1 (March 2011): 56–78.

Whitney, Carrie Westlake. *Kansas City, Missouri: Its History and Its People, 1808–1908*. Chicago: S. J. Clarke Publishing, 1908.

Wilcox, Pearl. *Jackson County Pioneers*. Independence, MO: Jackson County Historical Society, 1975.

Wilder, Daniel. *The Annals of Kansas*. Topeka: Kansas Publishing House, 1875.

Williams, George. *A History of the Negro Troops in the War of the Rebellion, 1861–1865*. New ed. New York: Fordham University Press, 2012.

Williams, Henry Sullivan. "The Development of the Negro Public School System in Missouri." *The Journal of Negro History* 5, no. 2 (April 1920): 137–165.

Williams, William H. *Slavery and Freedom in Delaware, 1639–1865*. Wilmington, DE: Scholarly Resources, 1996.

Willoughby, Robert J. *The Brothers Robidoux and the Opening of the American West*. Columbia: University of Missouri Press, 2012.

Woodson, W. H. *History of Clay County, Missouri*. Topeka: Historical Publishing Co., 1920.

Woodward, C. Vann. "History from Slave Sources." *American Historical Review* 79, no. 2 (April 1974): 470–481.

Wyatt-Brown, Bertram. *Southern Honor: Ethics and Behavior in the Old South*. New York: Oxford University Press, 1982.

Index

EARLY AMERICAN PLACES

On Slavery's Border: Missouri's Small Slaveholding Households, 1815–1865
by Diane Mutti Burke

Sounds American: National Identity and the Music Cultures of the Lower Mississippi River Valley, 1800–1860
by Ann Ostendorf

The Year of the Lash: Free People of Color in Cuba and the Nineteenth-Century Atlantic World
by Michele Reid-Vazquez

Ordinary Lives in the Early Caribbean: Religion, Colonial Competition, and the Politics of Profit
by Kirsten Block

Creolization and Contraband: Curaçao in the Early Modern Atlantic World
by Linda M. Rupert

An Empire of Small Places: Mapping the Southeastern Anglo-Indian Trade, 1732–1795
by Robert Paulett

Everyday Life and the Construction of Difference in the Early English Caribbean
by Jenny Shaw

Natchez Country: Indians, Colonists, and the Landscapes of Race in French Louisiana
by George Edward Milne

Slavery, Childhood, and Abolition in Jamaica, 1788–1838
by Colleen A. Vasconcellos

Privateers of the Americas: Spanish American Privateering from the United States in the Early Republic
by David Head

Charleston and the Emergence of Middle-Class Culture in the Revolutionary Era
by Jennifer L. Goloboy

Anglo-Native Virginia: Trade, Conversion, and Indian Slavery in the Old Dominion, 1646–1722
by Kristalyn Marie Shefveland

CPSIA information can be obtained
at www.ICGtesting.com
Printed in the USA
LVOW10s1144250518
578391LV00006B/118/P